Convergences

SUNY series in Gender Theory

Tina Chanter, editor

Convergences

Black Feminism and Continental Philosophy

Edited by

Maria del Guadalupe Davidson
Kathryn T. Gines
and
Donna-Dale L. Marcano

Cover sculpture by Sohail H. Shehada

Published by State University of New York Press, Albany

Printed in the United States of America

For information, contact State University of New York Press, Albany, NY
www.sunypress.edu

Production by Eileen Meehan
Marketing by Michael Campochiaro

Library of Congress Cataloging-in-Publication Data

Convergences : Black feminism and Continental philosophy / edited by
Maria del Guadalupe Davidson, Kathryn T. Gines, and Donna-Dale L. Marcano.
p. cm. — (SUNY series in gender theory)
Includes bibliographical references and index.
ISBN 978-1-4384-3267-0 (hardcover : alk. paper)
ISBN 978-1-4384-3266-3 (pbk. : alk. paper)
1. Womanism. 2. Women, Black. 3. Feminism. 4. Continental philosophy.
I. Davidson, Maria del Guadalupe. II. Gines, Kathryn T., 1978– III. Marcano, Donna-Dale L., 1962–

HQ1197.C66 2010
305.48'896073—dc2 2010005369

10 9 8 7 6 5 4 3 2 1

I dedicate this book to my husband, Scott Davidson.
Thank you for your foundational love and abundant patience.

—Maria del Guadalupe Davidson

For the first black feminist influences in my life:
Kathleen Smallwood-Johnson, Kathryn Harris,
and Serena Smallwood.

—Kathryn T. Gines

For my grandmother, Clarissa Cupid, who provided
comfort in these difficult times.

—Donna-Dale L. Marcano

Contents

Foreword

Beverly Guy-Sheftall

> [W]e are actively committed to struggling against racial, sexual, heterosexual, and class oppression and see as our particular task the development of integrated analysis and practice based upon the fact that the major systems of oppression are interlocking. The synthesis of these oppressions creates the conditions of our lives. As black women we see black feminism as the logical political movement to combat the manifold and simultaneous oppressions that all women of color face.
>
> —The Combahee River Collective, 1982

I have been preoccupied with documenting and analyzing the rich intellectual and activist tradition of African American women whose struggles around black feminist politics have been in recent years both celebrated and demonized. This painstaking work involved probing and making more visible the divergent philosophies embedded in black feminist theorizing among women and men since the midnineteenth century. *Words of Fire: An Anthology of African-American Feminist Thought* (New Press, 1995) and *Traps: African American Men on Gender and Sexuality* (coedited with Rudolph Byrd, Indiana University Press, 2001) are the two anthologies that have been most responsive to the erasures and silences surrounding the intellectual work among African American women and men that falls under the rubric of feminist thought/theory. In the preface to *Words of Fire,* I articulated what I meant by "feminist": "I use the term 'feminist' to capture the emancipatory vision and acts of resistance among a diverse group of African American women who attempt in their writings to articulate their understanding of the complex nature of black womanhood, the interlocking nature of the oppressions black women suffer, and the necessity of sustained struggle in their quest for self-definition, the liberation of black people, and gender equality."

Despite our long history as producers of knowledge, the idea of black women as intellectuals, thinking women, has been elusive if not impossible to imagine. The American Negro Academy (ANA), the first learned society for persons of African descent in the United States and globally, was founded in Washington, DC, in March 1897 by Rev. Alexander Crummell, then seventy-eight years old. Born in New York City and educated at London's Queens College, Cambridge University, he was an Episcopalian minister, educator, writer, missionary, and one of the most prominent and visionary nineteenth-century black intellectuals. Though women were not barred from membership (whose numbers were limited to fifty), it remained an all-male organization during its thirty-one year existence (1897–1924). Its Constitution announces itself as "an organization of authors, scholars, artists, and those distinguished in other walks of life, men of African descent, for the promotion of Letters, Science, and Art." Their overall goal was to "lead and protect their people" and be a mighty "weapon to secure equality and destroy racism." Its specific objectives were to defend blacks against racist attacks; publish scholarship about the black experience by black authors; foster higher education and intellectual projects; promote literature, science, and art in the black community; and create a black intellectual elite, whom William E. B. Du Bois would later conceptualize as "the Talented Tenth."

Since the ANA was conceptualized as an elite research institute, its major goal was the production of scholarly works that would assist in the overall struggle for racial equality. Eventually, they would publish twenty-two occasional papers. They met annually in DC, usually in late December, to hear research papers generated by their members. The wider public was also invited. Kelly Miller, a young Howard University professor, produced the first paper, "A Review of Hoffman's Race Traits and Tendencies of the American Negro." The second paper was produced by Crummell, "Civilization, the Primal Need of the Race," followed by Du Bois' "Conservation of the Races." Alexander Grimke, who followed Du Bois as the third president, produced seven publications, including "Right on the Scaffold, or the Martyrs of 1922," "The Ballotless Victims of One-Party Government," and "The Shame of America or the Negro's Case against the Republic."

Despite its commitment to eradicating racial inequalities, the American Negro Academy reflected prevailing gender attitudes, as would subsequent black male-dominated organizations. At its first organizing meeting, a male member argued that women should be admitted and was assured by the other founding members that women could join, but no efforts were made to recruit black women. In 1898, Alexander Crummell invited prominent Anna Julia Cooper, clubwoman, intellectual, and author of *A Voice from the South* (1892), to present a paper at the second annual meeting, which was the only occasion during which a female presented. Contemporary black feminist scholars credit *A Voice from the South* with being the first book-length black feminist text produced in the United States. This collection of essays provides a global perspective on racism, imperialism, and colonialism; praises black achievements, especially those of women; promotes black women's education; and critiques black male sexism and the racism of white women. Despite the outstanding contributions of many black women during this era, among them Mary Church Terrell, Frances E. W. Harper, Fannie Barrier Williams, and Josephine St. Pierre Ruffin, none was ever invited to join the ANA. Though these and other black women intellectuals and activists assumed there existed a natural alliance between them and black men, they were rejected, ironically, on the basis of their gender.

Among the many contemporary black women intellectuals committed to feminist theorizing, bell hooks, who wrote her first book while a college student at age nineteen, *Ain't I a Black Woman,* has been the most vocal and adamant about the importance of seeing herself as a "thinker." Without question, "intellectual" has been an identity marker that few African American women wear with the same ease they are likely to embrace other identities: mother, worker, activist, lover, teacher, academic, even comrade. bell hooks is certainly atypical in this regard, for she claims the identities—intellectual and writer—with a level of comfort that our mothers and grandmothers proudly wore the labels *cook, gardener, mama, sister*–identities that did not alienate or announce up front that you thought you were intelligent, or worse, a *thinking* woman. It was appropriate to be hard-working, selfless, nurturing, spiritual, religious, even a "take charge" sister, but not brilliant, not too analytical.

Growing up, I knew I was surrounded by smart black women, but few seemed to notice, and if they did, these women were often distrusted or considered troublemakers, especially if they were outspoken. My own mother, Ernestine Varnado Guy, was one of the smartest women I have known (I discovered after she died that her college transcript from Lane College had only A's), but what got noticed about her more often was her beauty, her caring, her common sense, but not her intellect! Reflecting upon my childhood, the experiences of black women with the ANA, and the absence of black women in contemporary discussions about "public intellectuals," I am compelled to ask: Why have black women not been as validated for our intellects, our scholarship, our theorizing? Why has "intellectual" been such a contested descriptor for black women? Why have black women not been seen as smart, publicly acknowledged in the ways men are for our brilliance? Perhaps more perplexing, why have black women been uncomfortable asserting their "thinking" selves as opposed to their "nurturing" selves?

Convergences: Black Feminism and Continental Philosophy, which includes the brilliant thinking of women of color and white women, interrupts a largely male intellectual tradition. The courageous work of these sister-scholars, many of whom are trained philosophers, reminds us of the significant impact of black

Acknowledgments

Davidson: I would like to thank my coeditors. I would also like to thank the contributors for their willingness to participate in this project. I would like to thank Jane Bunker, Dr. Tina Chanter, and the State University of New York Press for providing us with the opportunity to publish this important volume. Finally I would like to acknowledge my friends and colleagues in the African and African American Studies Program at the University of Oklahoma, especially Dr. Jeanette R. Davidson, Dr. Melanie Bratcher, Dr. Sharri Coleman, Dr. Roosevelt Wright, Dr. Meta Carstarphen, Lt. Col. (Ret.) Randy Garibay, and Ruth Gomez. I deeply appreciate your support.

Gines: I would like to thank the coeditors of and contributors to this project, without whom this collection would not have been possible. I would also like to acknowledge the philosophy department at the University of Memphis for providing me with a space and place where race, feminism, and philosophy were not treated as mutually exclusive categories and each was deemed worthy of critical philosophical inquiry. Last but not least, I acknowledge and thank the philosophy department and the Africana Research Center at the Pennsylvania State University for supporting my research in the form of a fellowship during the 2008–2009 academic year.

Marcano: I am grateful to the coeditors for their patience and hard work in making this volume possible. My thanks to the contributors of this volume who so willingly offered their brilliance to this project. I would also like to acknowledge the generous support and kindness of the philosophy department at Trinity College. Most important, I am deeply grateful to the women in philosophy whose presence in conversation have been the foundation for my intellectual enthusiasm as well as friendship, especially Anika Mann, Janine Jones, Kristie Dotson, Emily Lee, and Linda Martin-Alcoff.

Introduction

Black Feminism and Continental Philosophy

Convergences: Black Feminism and Continental Philosophy explores the connections between the traditions of black feminism and continental philosophy. Several of the chapters collected here use resources in continental philosophy to engage in discussions about gender and race and/or use black feminism to shed new light on themes within continental philosophy. Others draw from both traditions in a call for the further development of black feminist philosophy and black feminist ethics. Contributors include both women of color and white women as well as both established and emerging scholars. Overall, the project has been conceived as a discourse between black feminism and continental philosophy that encourages the reader to consider what these traditions offer one another or can learn from one another. The purpose of this book is *not* to argue that continental philosophy should provide the justification or conceptual framework for black feminism, as if black feminism had not yet established itself as an autonomous theoretical discourse, and as if it would stand in need of a conceptual grounding. Rather, this volume seeks to engage in a critical and constructive dialogue over how black feminism, as both a discourse and a practice, has thus far been treated/untreated in the space of continental philosophy and over the resources that it may offer to the continental tradition, in turn.

By addressing black feminist issues specifically within the context of the continental tradition, this book clearly opens up a space for a new and important set of questions to be addressed, including the dialogical tension between race and gender, the negative inscription of the black female body and sexuality, the black female as other, the denial of agency, voice, and language to black women, the exclusion of black women from the definition of woman, along with issues of performativity, sisterhood, and community within the black feminist tradition. Such a project is pertinent, even crucial, at this historical juncture, not only because the face of philosophy in general is slowly changing to include more women and people of color, but also because there is a small but critical mass of black women philosophers emerging on the philosophy scene.

These changes increasingly pose new questions for the identity of philosophy, including continental philosophy and feminist philosophy.[1]

The history of black women in philosophy in the United States is short but significant. Joyce Mitchell Cook made her mark by becoming the first African American woman to earn a Ph.D. in philosophy just over forty years ago in 1965. She earned her degree from Yale University and specialized in value theory. The first African American woman to be tenured in philosophy is Adrian Piper who earned her Ph.D. from Harvard in 1981. In addition to having John Rawls as a supervisor, Piper also studied Kant and Hegel with Dieter Heinrich. Her specializations and publications in philosophy have been on Kant, ethics, and metaethics. Anita Allen-Castellitto is the first African American woman to hold both a Ph.D. in philosophy (University of Michigan) and a J.D. (Harvard University). The growing number of black women in philosophy led to the establishment of the Collegium of Black Women Philosophers by Kathryn T. Gines in 2007. But as this is being written, there are still fewer than thirty black women (including black women who are not African American) holding a Ph.D. in philosophy and working in a philosophy department in academia. These women have various philosophical interests in both the continental and the analytic traditions. Of course, there are also several black women holding doctorates in other disciplines who are still actively engaged in philosophical scholarship and inquiry.

Today, there is a small but steady increase of women of color who insist on inserting their voices, collectively and individually, into the discipline of philosophy. This, at a time when philosophy has wielded the discourse of the social construction of race and gender, often with a heavy hand, which poses real challenges to acknowledging the concrete existence of these raced, sexed, and gendered women who have raced, sexed, and gendered identities. These women are insisting on inserting their voices at a time when the mantra that race and gender do not exist could again attempt to displace the presence of those long made absent from philosophical life and thought. Even as these mantras aim to address past deficiencies in thought regarding the nature and place of many displaced groups, women of color are seeking to make themselves known. We must, for we cannot go another hundred years without acknowledging the ever-present relationship between philosophy, even continental philosophy, and its outcasts.

The lengthy history of black feminism in the United States has taken up how race, gender, class, religion, education, labor/work, and sexuality are interrelated aspects of black women's identities. This black feminist intellectual and activist tradition, going back at least to the early 1830s, has long exposed and confronted the racism of white men *and* women alongside the sexism of black *and* white men while simultaneously making efforts to build coalitions both within and across concrete and imagined boundaries. Early manifestations of black feminism emerged with black women abolitionists and suffragists. This tradition would persist with the Black Women's Club movement and continue to gain momentum during the civil and women's rights movements. The black feminist literature and scholarship, thought by many to have commenced with the publication of Anna Julia Cooper's *Voice of the South* (1892), would find myriad more voices and gain recognition in the many decades that followed.

In *Words of Fire: An Anthology of African American Feminist Thought*, Beverly Guy-Sheftall notes, "While black feminism is not a monolithic, static ideology, and there is considerable diversity among African American feminists, certain premises are constant."[2] Guy-Sheftall identifies the following five premises of black feminism:

> 1. Black Women experience a special kind of oppression and suffering in this country which is racist, sexist, and classist because of their dual racial and gender identity and their limited access to economic resources;
> 2. This "triple jeopardy" has meant that the problems, concerns, and needs of black women are different in many ways from those of both white women and black men;
> 3. Black women must struggle for black liberation and gender equality simultaneously;
> 4. There is no inherent contradiction in the struggle to eradicate sexism and racism as well as the other "isms" which plague the human community, such as classism and heterosexism;
> 5. Black women's commitment to the liberation of blacks and women is profoundly rooted in their lived experience.[3]

When black feminism is accurately and historically situated, it becomes clear that it has its own origins, commitments, and trajectories. Still, black women intellectuals have always engaged the important philosophical ideas of their time, utilizing, developing, and critiquing these ideas as they saw fit in order to address concerns of race, gender, and more specifically their place in social systems in which their race, gender, and sexuality designated them as absences from intellectual life. More often than not, their works have been taken to be merely political with little or no basis in philosophical content because of the political goals they hoped to achieve or illuminate.

That black women's intellectual work is absent from the broader philosophical canons is a sign of the long history of philosophy's exclusionist tendencies. Indeed even today Beauvoir's *Second Sex* is not included in anthologies of classical philosophical texts despite its foundational use of existential thought and principles to describe and critique the role of "woman" in philosophy and the particularized situation of women. *The Second Sex* was a groundbreaking work that not only could temper the inclination to see existentialism as an extreme form of apolitical individualism but also was an important foundation for a whole school of thought known now in the American context as French feminism. Even as Europe's well-known female intellectuals are still on the fringes of the canons, so too are black women's intellectual work cast out beyond the fringes.

If all the women are white and all the blacks are men,[4] black women's voices are lost to philosophy's pretensions to universality, even in what we understand to be the continental tradition. Caught in a nexus of scholarship dominated by white men in the broader continental tradition, by white women in continental feminism, and by black men in philosophy of race, black women's scholarship, which has not only been informed by these areas but also has informed these areas of their limitations, is cast out of philosophy's light. And yet we find that philosophy, and in this case the continental tradition, has much to offer.

Like black feminism, what has come to be called "continental philosophy" is neither static nor monolithic. The term is often used to describe philosophy on the rise in post–World War II Europe—particularly existentialism and phenomenology in Germany and France—that eventually spread to Britain, the United States, and elsewhere. As black feminism is habitually thought in contradistinction (or even in contradiction) with white feminism, continental philosophy is frequently juxtaposed with analytic philosophy. In "What Is Continental Philosophy," Simon Critchley points out, "Continental philosophy is a highly eclectic and disparate series of intellectual currents that could hardly be said to amount to a unified tradition."[5] According to Critchley, "there exists and has existed, at least since the Second World War, a de facto distinction between analytic and Continental philosophy. What must be emphasized here is that this distinction is essentially a *professional self-description*."[6] Of interest for this volume are some of the central threads, questions, figures, and texts that are prominent in continental philosophy.

Charting the Terrain of Black Feminism and Continental Philosophy

The chapters in this volume on black feminism and continental thought have taken what some may see as the incommensurability between philosophy and black women hoping to find similarities where others only see difference. We have sought to be bold and to defy the established conventions and themes of most philosophical thought. Here the reader will find new convergences between Ann duCille and Gilles Deleuze, Patricia Hill Collins and Foucault, Patricia Williams and Merleau-Ponty, to name a few. In what follows, it is suggested that this convergence of black feminism and continental philosophy resembles the creative activity described above as a bending together—a merger—of disparate elements.

Continental philosophy, in spite of its concern with a number of issues relevant to black feminism, has rarely, if ever, engaged black feminism. Continental philosophy, to be sure, offers valuable contributions to understanding issues of agency, subjectivity, the feminine, marginalization, and difference, all of which are relevant to black feminist thought. Yet its approach to these issues does not thematize the black woman *as such* or give voice to the philosophical concerns of black feminists. Since black women remain external or other to the continental tradition, this leads us to ask what resources continental philosophy might offer to black feminism, and conversely, what challenges black feminism might pose to the established patterns of continental philosophy. In taking up these key questions, the essays collected in *Convergences: Black Feminism and Continental Philosophy* explore the possible convergences and incommensurable divergences between black feminism and continental philosophy. This convergence is not random or forced but, in some way, natural and necessary. Black feminist and womanist thinkers inevitably address the very same issues of agency, identity, alienation, power, and so on that are raised in much recent continental philosophy. Likewise, from Immanuel Kant to the feminist thinkers of the present, continental philosophy has been engaged, to some extent, with issues of race and gender.

Each of the chapters, in its own unique way, seeks to chart the terrain of continental philosophy and black feminism today. In the design of the book, we did not want the contributors to be constrained by a preestablished set of themes or issues. So, rather than imposing rubrics onto this text, each of the contributions is presented as a freestanding chapter. While remaining independent, the chapters cohere to constitute a collective discourse on both black feminism and continental philosophy. As authors' chapters place race and gender at the forefront of their philosophical engagement, the reader will notice similar themes, questions, and considerations in the authors' attempts to bring the insights of black feminism to bear upon those of continental philosophy. For instance, chapters by Davidson, James, Lee, and Russell place black feminist thinkers in conversation with prominent continental philosophical thinkers and concepts in order to show how continental philosophy can expand and help to further articulate the concerns of black feminism. Specifically, these chapters are important examples of how one can use the conceptual resources of particular continental philosophers and thus illuminate the promise of convergent analyses of continental thought and black feminism to further explore race and gender.

In other chapters, the reader will notice the approach as articulating more of a critique or problematic within continental philosophy which poses limitations for diversity as well as for inclusivity across that diversity. This approach, exemplified in the works of Chanter, West, and Glass, further radicalizes continental philosophy in a way that enables the reader to reenvision or newly vision a radical politics that rethinks humanity, common struggle, and/ or sisterhood once those limitations are addressed.

Last, some authors are more concerned with how canonical philosophical resources within and outside feminism may inhibit or simply cannot address the possibility for creating black feminist philosophy. Chapters by Gines, Mann, Marcano, and Rowe address the critiques and problematics leveled against black feminists in order to consider the conditions for theoretical work that holds race and gender to be important poles of new philosophical work to be done. These chapters highlight the challenges to black feminist philosophical thought either through the philosophy's inability to appropriately address race *and* gender or through contemporary philosophy's eschewing of the concepts of race and gender.

Diane Perpich, in "Black Feminism, Poststructuralism, and the Contested Character of Experience," is keenly aware of the challenges to "unmediated personal experience" posed by continental thinkers such as Beauvoir, Foucault, and Butler. Yet Perpich also notes that nonwhite women (specifically Chicana and black women) have used calls to experience for the purpose of "establishing the authority of the marginalized between these two diametrically opposed positions." Perpich identifies what she calls the "sticking points" and then seeks to "disentangl[e] the question of experience from a broader distrust of postmodernism" while also "considering the epistemological and political dimensions of appeals to experience."

In "Sartre, Beauvoir, and the Race/Gender Analogy: A Case for Black Feminist Philosophy," Kathryn T. Gines examines the issue of intersectionality as it relates to the race/gender analogy and the shortcomings of using racial oppression as an analogy of gender oppression. After outlining the use of the race/gender analogy in Jean-Paul Sartre's *Respectful Prostitute* and Simone de Beauvoir's *Second Sex*, Gines points to influences on their analyses from black intellectual Richard Wright. While these influences offer insights into racial oppression, still ignored is the problem of intersecting racial and gender oppression. To address this void Gines highlights two staple themes of black feminism while emphasizing the scholarship of Anna Julia Cooper. The chapter concludes by making the case for the expansion of the philosophy canon to include more black feminist philosophical thinkers and a call for the further development of black feminist philosophy.

"The Difference That Difference Makes: Black Feminism and Philosophy" explores the problems and possibilities of thinking through what it might mean to pursue black feminism within the context and confines of the discipline of philosophy. Donna-Dale L. Marcano frames these problems from two separate vantage points, from within and without the discipline of philosophy. First, she addresses the complications for writing through a subtopic, black feminism, that is challenged by contemporary articulations of both feminism and race theory, which both hold that race and sex are socially constructed. Second, Marcano tackles the problems and critiques of philosophy and black feminism in general by black female authors who worry that theory always forecloses the articulation of difference among black women themselves. Marcano underscores that philosophy's grip on assuming its universality begs the question of whether the particularity of a black female identity can ever be seen within the domain of philosophy, and as another viewpoint, from which the fundamental questions of philosophy are confronted. Ultimately, she insists that the question of what is philosophy continues to be rethought and developed.

Sophocles' *Antigone* can be said to be one of the founding texts of continental philosophical tradition. Interpreted by Hegel and Freud, and thus scholars of the psychoanalytic and continental feminist traditions, *Antigone* has provided an analysis for the founding moments of Law, patriarchy, familial bonds, and incest taboos. Yet, in "Antigone's Other Legacy: Slavery and Colonialism in *Tègònni*: An African Antigone," Tina Chanter points out that the history of scholarly work, including Hegel's reading, has failed to attend to the dynamic of slavery present in the text. She asks, "What would the tradition have looked like had it been capable of attending to the character Antigone's apparently unproblematic endorsement of slavery?" Chanter explores the Nigerian playwright Femi Òsafisan's *Tègònni*, a version of Antigone set in apartheid Africa, to show that the marker of race that qualifies some as human and others as not quite human illustrates the possibility that incest prohibitions are intimately tied to racial prohibitions. In doing so, Chanter forces us to consider how attending to race and slavery, to who is considered human or not, may have altered the philosophical tradition that celebrates *Antigone* as a founding text.

In "L Is for . . . : Longing and Becoming in *The L Word's* Racialized Erotic," Aimee Carrillo Rowe begins with a discussion of the dubious position of the "post"—that is, "postracism, postfeminism, postidentity, postmodernism"—in current U.S. "cultural politics." Rowe argues, "The organizing principle through which these post-'s cohere is marked by the loosening of boundaries of difference, a slide into a potentially productive, and potentially dangerous, uncertainty about the politics of looking." To this end, Rowe analyzes the effects on racial difference—especially in the form of interracial relationships and bodies that are "ambiguously racialized"—in the era of the "post."

"Race and Feminist Standpoint Theory" by Anika Maaza Mann revisits the debates surrounding black feminism and feminist standpoint theory. Using examples ranging from nineteenth-century black feminism to the more contemporary 2008 Democratic primary elections, Mann contributes new insights into the significance of intersectionality and group formation in relation to standpoint epistemology. Using resources from black feminism in the work of Patricia Hill Collins and from existential phenomenology in the work of Jean-Paul Sartre, Mann critiques calls for universal sisterhood and the notion of a single woman's/women's standpoint proposed by white feminist philosophers such as Sandra Harding and Sonia Kruks. Mann argues, against objections raised by Harding and Kruks, that a continued development of black feminist standpoint theory is still needed, and such a project should not be reduced to identity politics.

Maria del Guadalupe Davidson's "Black Feminist Subjectivity: Ann duCille and Gilles Deleuze" evaluates the postmodern identification of black women as other. Starting from the work of black feminist thinker Ann duCille, Davidson suggests that just as the modern project has been shown to harbor violence against the other, "a similar violence is likewise carried over into the postmodern exaltation of otherness, in spite of its best intentions." From the vantage point of duCille and many other black feminists, postmodernism's othering of black women has further "solidified" black women's position as errant and marginalized. Davidson then calls on the work of Gilles Deleuze, specifically his notion of the *fold*, as a possible resource for resisting black women's status as other and developing an account of radical black female subjectivity.

Despite awareness and acknowledgment that "aesthetic agency and pleasure are, in the West, deeply racialized and gendered," Robin James contends that "recent attempts to rethink the politics of aesthetic pleasure have not adequately addressed the intersection of race, gender, *and* the aesthetic." Her essay "From Receptivity to Transformation: On the Intersection of Race, Gender, and the Aesthetic in Contemporary Continental Philosophy" underscores the critical merits of contemporary continental philosophy's attempt at deconstructing the racialized and gendered metaphysics of the aesthetic paradigm. James pays particular attention to the insights of the works of Julia Kristeva, Robert Gooding-Williams, and Angela Davis in order to theorize the intersection of race and gender with the aesthetic. She argues that despite the limitations of these accounts, they can "provide us with a powerful diagnostic tool to apply to contemporary cultural politics."

In "Extending Black Feminist Sisterhood in the Face of Violence: Fanon, White Women, and Veiled Muslim Women" Traci C. West seeks to "conceptualize a notion of sisterhood that extends to women whose social status is distinctly other than that of African American women, such as sexually objectified white women or veiled Muslim women in a foreign nation." Toward this end, West reflects on a black feminist method placed in conversation with Frantz Fanon. She explores both the theoretical tools available in Fanon's scholarship (underscoring, for example, how he is a "resource for crafting a black Diasporic framework [that] destabilizes the Eurocentric continental emphasis that dominates Western religious studies and philosophy, especially in the subfield of Christian studies) as well as the limitations of Fanon (explaining that "some of Fanon's reflections on race, gender, and sexual violence include disturbing depictions of women's culpability that I reject"). Rather than presenting her own project as incompatible with Fanon's, West considers how the projects might productively converge in a way that allows "possibilities to emerge for a more expansive black feminist ethic." She proposes a common freedom struggle that does not ignore the realities of racism and an antiviolence ethic that is "built by embracing the truths of how certain forms of complicity in dehumanizing practices and histories of subjugation divide us and hide the means of supporting one another's self-determining spiritual, bodily, political, and socioeconomic well-being."

In her essay "Madness and Judiciousness: A Phenomenological Reading of a Black Woman's Encounter with a Saleschild" Emily S. Lee employs Maurice Merleau-Ponty's notion of "horizon" as a "conceptual framework to understand the depth of the racial association we make during our perceptions of our own and others' embodiment." Using as her example the well-known encounter between Patricia Williams and a Benetton store employee in which Williams was refused entry into the store, Lee argues that despite the critiques that such a notion naturalizes racist and sexist beliefs and behaviors, the framework of the horizon shows us how meanings and associations attached to embodied subjects are both sedimented and contested. Indeed, as Lee explains, Patricia Williams seems to be "doing" phenomenology in her account of the encounter; and, by utilizing the notion of horizon, we can account not only for the behavior of the "saleschild" but how in a world with given meanings attached to bodies, the saleschild's refusal is taken to be reasonable and judicious even as William's response is taken to be madness.

Camisha Russell's "Black American Sexuality and the Repressive Hypothesis: Reading Patricia Hill Collins with Michel Foucault" puts Hill Collins' *Black Sexual Politics* in conversation with Foucault's *History of Sexuality*. In particular, Russell is interested in the ways in which the repressive hypothesis, the notion of confession, and the emergence of populations as targets of government intervention in Foucault might contribute to Hill Collins' analysis of black sexuality and potentially create new possibilities for developing a genealogy of black sexuality in America. Additionally, Russell examines connections between Foucault's notion of power and Hill Collins' notion of controlling images. She concludes that "while her analysis must necessarily go beyond what Foucault has to say there about racism and resistance, Collins indeed has every reason to follow Foucault in his rejection of the 'repressive hypothesis' and turn instead to a more Foucauldian, productive model of power, exploiting his insights to give her own arguments better explanatory force."

In the final chapter, "Calling All Sisters: Continental Philosophy and Black Feminist Thinkers," Kathy Glass shows how black feminist thinkers and continental feminists have both actively participated in "feminist politics" and "community building strategies." Though they share similar concerns, Glass contends that they remain divided along racial, cultural, and even economic lines. The French feminist tradition, according to Glass, is marked by "racial exclusion" and an adherence to patriarchal patterns that have complicated the relationship between these two groups. Using as a resource the works of Simone de Beauvoir, Hélène Cixous, Audre Lorde, and bell hooks, Glass seeks to establish a "transracial sisterhood," which she suggests is necessary if the "radical social transformation" that both black feminists and French Feminists advocate is to occur.

Convergence is "the action or fact of converging; movement directed toward or terminating in the same point (called the "point of convergence")." It is derived from the Latin prefix *com-*, which means "together," and the Latin noun, *-vergere,* meaning "to bend."[7] Convergences can take place either as matters of fact or as the result of deliberate actions. As matters of fact, convergences occur when two disparate things come together naturally, while deliberate actions produce convergences by bending two disparate things so that they can be joined together. If this volume signifies a convergence between black feminism and continental philosophy, then an obvious question is how this particular convergence has come to take place: has it occurred as a matter of fact or as a deliberate choice? A simple reply to this question is that the convergences between black feminism and continental philosophy explored in this volume have occurred in both ways: as a matter of fact and a calculated, deliberate choice. As a matter of fact, black feminists have frequently used the resources made available through the continental tradition, such as the critique of agency and issues related to embodiment and identity. Due to the value of these connections, the convergences explored in this volume also result from a calculated and deliberate choice on the part of the contributors to take up this connection explicitly and to pursue it further. In either case, the key point is that convergences are essentially generative of new meanings. By bringing together what some might consider two disparate fields of inquiry, something distinct—a *new* space for inquiry and a *new* combination of concepts—can be created. As such, the convergences generated in this text do not seek to end the conversation or to act as the definitive discourse; instead this text strives to open up a neoteric space for critical analysis and to provide a model for further investigation in the convergences between black feminism and continental philosophy.

Notes

1. For detailed information on the lives and philosophies of Cook, Piper, Allen, and other black women in philosophy, see George Yancy's *African American Philosophers, Seventeen Conversations* (New York: Routledge, 1998).

2. Beverly Guy-Sheftall, *Words of Fire: An Anthology of African American Feminist Thought* (New York: New, 1995).

3. Ibid,, 2.

4. A reference to *All of the Women Are White, All Blacks Are Men, but Some of Us Are Brave: Black Women's Studies*, ed. Gloria T. Hull, Patricia Bell Scott, and Barbara Smith (New York: Feminist Press at CUNY, 1982).

5. Simon Critchley, "What Is Continental Philosophy?" *International Journal of Philosophical Studies* 5, no. 3: 350.

6. Ibid., 348; emphasis in original.

7. *Oxford English Dictionary*, online, "Convergence."

1

Black Feminism, Poststructuralism, and the Contested Character of Experience

Diane Perpich

Contemporary continental philosophy, going back at least to Simone de Beauvoir, poses challenges to the idea of direct, unmediated personal experience. For Beauvoir, the idea is rejected the moment she writes, "One is not born but *becomes* a woman."[1] A woman's life and her perspective on it is not a naturally occurring given like eye color or a heartbeat; experience is the product of historical and social forces and is forged in the crucible of hierarchically organized relationships and institutions. For Beauvoir, there is no essence of womanhood and, likewise, no essential female experience; there is only one's situation and then what one freely makes of it. The rejection of unmediated experience is even more powerfully articulated in the work of Michel Foucault. For Foucault, discursive practices and networks of power, working at the level of the macro (social) and micro (individual) body, produce the forms that subjectivity takes. The body is not the locus of experience or that which has experiences; rather, social and political practices and institutions produce the form taken by a body. The soldier body, the delinquent body, the homosexual body are the products of specific disciplinary arts that partition, code, and organize the movements of the body and its distribution in social space.[2] Judith Butler and Anne-Fausto Sterling, working in different disciplines but both indebted in important respects to Foucault, have argued that the gendered and sexed body is likewise the product of discursive practices.[3] Again this suggests that the body is not the original locus of experience, but that forces other than the individual or nature shape or construct our experience of bodies, including our own.

In a series of essays published in the early 1990s, feminist historian Joan Scott marshaled the resources of contemporary continental philosophy, especially the work of Foucault, to develop a sustained critique of appeals to experience. Scott argues that it is not preexisting subjects or selves who come to have certain kinds of experience, but rather experience that constitutes the subjects or selves who then recognize themselves as the bearers of experience.

With this thesis, Scott contests the validity of appeals to experience as the bedrock from which social theory can be elaborated. Appeals to experience, Scott warns, even when they issue from those constructed as a dominant society's "others," do as much to naturalize differences, and thus to support existing social hierarchies that depend on an ontology of natural difference, as they do to uncover and critically expose the processes by which such differences are instituted and maintained.

Scott's critique has met with opposition in various quarters—as have Foucault and poststructuralism generally—but the opposition from within feminism has been strongest among theorists with a continued commitment to some form of identity-based politics. Black and Latina feminists, third-world feminists, lesbian feminists, and others have voiced their resistance to a theoretical stance that seemingly delegitimates personal and group experience as an authoritative source for the production of oppositional knowledge and demands for justice. Paula Moya, author of *Learning from Experience*, has been one of the most pronounced voices in this chorus. In an interview, Moya recalls reading Scott's essay "Experience" as a graduate student and says: "I became really angry while reading it. I had just spent 10 years being a political wife and an activist, raising a family on very little money, going through the upheaval of a divorce and moving my children across the country. All of it taught me to think of myself as a Chicana and a feminist. And here was this essay telling me that, basically, any account I could give of my own experience would be complicit with the dominant order of things. It made me furious."[4] Moya argues in *Learning from Experience* that an account like Scott's delegitimizes "*all* accounts of experience" and undermines "*all* forms of identity politics" and holds this view of postmodernism generally.[5] More sympathetic to postmodernism, Mae Henderson nonetheless gives voice to the reservations of many feminists when she writes: "What is questionable is that [poststructuralism] is a project that dismantles notions of authority . . . notions of tradition . . . and notions of subjectivity . . . during a period when blacks, feminists and other marginalized groups are asserting authorship, tradition, and subjectivity."[6]

Appeals to experience played a fundamental role in establishing the authority of the marginalized voices Henderson speaks of and lent a vital force to the emerging disciplines of women's studies, African American studies, and ethnic studies in the 1970s and 1980s. It is no wonder that many who worked to establish those disciplines are reluctant to relinquish the notion of experience in the face of a poststructuralist challenge. Nonetheless, there is more common ground between the two sides than might appear at first glance. Scott is not interested (as Moya mistakenly suggests) in delegitimating all notions of identity or banishing all appeals to experience; and African American, Latina, and third-world feminists have been equally critical of the usefulness and theoretical cogency of naked claims to experience. Still, there remain important disagreements between the two sides of the debate, and the aim of this chapter is to locate those sticking points more exactly, first, by disentangling the question of experience from a broader distrust of postmodernism, and second by considering the epistemological and political dimensions of appeals to experience.

Questioning Experience

Joan Scott begins her essay on "Experience" with a critical, though appreciative, appraisal of science fiction writer Samuel Delany's memoir *The Motion of Light in Water*. In the memoir, Delany tells the tale of his political awakening in St. Mark's bathhouse in 1963. At the sight of gay male bodies stretching "wall to wall" across a gymnasium-sized room, lit by a dim blue light, Delany reports being forcibly struck by the realization that there was a *collective history* of gay life and of public sexual institutions that had yet to be told and that could be politically galvanizing.[7] Delany attributes the political power of this moment, Scott notes, to the *visibility* of the mass of bodies: they saturate his visual field, and this visibility stands in literally for the possibility of making gay experience and gay political struggles equally visible. Scott writes that for Delany in this moment, "Knowledge is gained through vision," and vision suggests a "direct, unmediated apprehension" of what is seen.[8] In its desire to render gay life visible (and thus intelligible) to a world that seems otherwise out to erase and annihilate it, Delany's project parallels that of other historians of difference whose aim has been to remedy the occlusion of subordinated and marginalized groups within the pages of history. Such projects, Scott maintains, have been effective but also limited. Their success comes from the fact that they remain comfortably within a familiar disciplinary framework that views history as capable of successively correcting its own narrative, filling in gaps through the discovery of fresh evidence and new testimony. The limitation of such projects, however, is more to Scott's point and is not just historical but political: by appealing to experience "as uncontestable evidence and as an originary point of explanation—as a foundation on which analysis is based" such studies fail to raise questions about "the assumptions and practices that excluded considerations of difference in the first place"[9]

The critical potential of histories that rely on first-person appeals to experience is weakened, Scott argues, because they tend to repeat and reinforce the central terms and assumptions that structure dominant accounts. Delany's recounting of his bathhouse experience, for example, assumes the preexistence of gay and straight identities suggesting only that they need to be given equal representation and equal opportunity for self-expression. Not only does this view lend tacit support to the perception of sexual identities as fixed by nature and tethered to an unchanging set of cultural practices and meanings, but it potentially overlooks the ways in which 'homosexual' and 'heterosexual' are interrelated terms whose meanings have varied over time and that together shape and reshape the contested terrain of sexuality. Delany's account likewise appears to adopt a problematically naturalized model of desire. Homosexual desire, his awakening story suggests, has been made to seem abnormal by a dominant society that prefers it to remain invisible (if not nonexistent), but like a stream forced underground it nonetheless finds practices and institutions (like the baths) through which it can surface and see the light of day. The historical and cultural forces that shape homosexual (and heterosexual) desire in its current form are potentially obscured by this account, which makes desire simply a natural force that will eventually find an outlet. Thus, though an ostensible aim of Delany's account is to render gay sexual practices visible, it risks rendering *invisible* the role of social and political factors in the construction and institution of gay sexual practices and identities. As Scott makes clear, when experience is invoked as direct evidence, it assumes that "the facts of history speak for themselves."[10] And in claiming simply to make a certain experience *visible*, histories of difference run the risk of neglecting a "critical examination of the workings of the ideological system itself, its categories of representation (homosexual/heterosexual, man/woman, black/white as fixed immutable identities), its premises about what these categories mean and how they operate, and of its notions of subjects, origin, and cause."[11]

Delany, of course, is not Scott's principal target, and at the end of her essay she suggests that the fault may lie less in the memoir itself than in a certain kind of reading of it, exemplified by the first part of her own essay.[12] The trouble arises not because there has been an appeal to experience; rather it is when experience is understood ahistorically, reflecting the assumption that both the individual and the experience arise organically from the way the world is, that political recuperation becomes possible and even likely.

> When experience is taken as the origin of knowledge, the vision of the individual subject . . . becomes the bedrock of evidence on which explanation is built. Questions about the constructed nature of experience, about how subjects are constituted as different in the first place, about how one's vision is structured—about language (or discourse) and history—are left aside. The evidence of experience then becomes evidence for the fact of difference, rather than a way of exploring how difference is established, how it operates, how and in what ways it constitutes subjects who see and act in the world.[13]

Several interrelated points are crucial to Scott's analysis. First, identities or identity groups do not preexist but *follow from* discrimination.[14] This may initially sound counterintuitive since we tend to think of discrimination as action that prejudicially targets a specific group for unwarranted exclusion or unfair treatment. The landlord who refuses to rent to African Americans or gays, for example, picks out and discriminates against the members of a preexisting group. But the group identity itself arose through earlier mechanisms of oppression. Black identity in America, to take an obvious example, has its roots in slavery, though it is not fully determined by that event (which itself has a history and took different forms in different geographical regions and for differently positioned subjects, for example, men and women). The slave trade took Africans with various cultural and ethnic identities (identities themselves forged in specific contexts) and attempted to create a uniform slave identity. The oppressions of slavery became the basis for the later development during the civil rights era of African American identity. Of course, dominant identities no less than subordinate or minoritized ones are, on this view, the product of practices of discrimination. What it means to be white or Southern is just as much a product of social and historical forces as Black, Latino, or Northern identities.

Scott interestingly points out that identities have long been seen as historical and suggests that a failure to see them this way is a more recent phenomenon tied to a return of ideological individualism. "In the 1960s and '70s proponents of affirmative action and identity politics took economic, political, and social structures for granted in their analyses (one could invoke 'experience,' for example, and mean something historically, culturally, and discursively produced, as feminists did in consciousness-raising sessions to great political effect); but in the 1980s and '90s the ideological pendulum has swung back to individualism (and 'experience' now signifies a prediscursive, direct, and unmediated apprehension of social truth)."[15] This mistaken view of experience is symptomatic, on Scott's account, of the equally mistaken view of identities as fixed and readily identifiable categories. The corollary to both is an impoverished view of "diversity" as "a condition of human existence rather than as the effect of an enunciation of difference that constitutes hierarchies and asymmetries of power."[16] Diversity, on the mistaken view, is a given of the human condition and as such must be tolerated (though where the "problem" is seen as natural and the "solution" as social or cultural, the implication is that by nature we find diversity difficult to bear or intolerable). Moreover, tolerance for difference is understood in terms of respect for the equality of individual choices and lifestyles and, once again, the ways in which identity categories are mutually constructed by social forces in specific historical contexts is overlooked or ignored. This oversight prepares the ground for seeing such categories as natural or inevitable, and this is the main political target of Scott's critique.

Scott identifies two further problems of exclusion that arise from the ahistorical view of identity and from taking direct experience, without critical analysis, as the bearer of an original truth. First, those who are deemed group outsiders are thought to be unable fully to understand the experiences of those on the inside. And, second, a dominant class *within* the identity group claims to speak on behalf of the whole, forcing those whose viewpoints or life choices do not conform to the prevailing group model either to drop out or bring their actions and choices into greater conformity with the whole.[17]

Scott's central thesis on experience inverts the assumption that subjects preexist and are the bearers of a given experience. If experience appears to be given it is because it is constructed as the given, as that which is primitive, basic, or natural. Moreover, the subject of an experience is not a naturally occurring individual who then just happens to have this or that experience. Rather, experience *constructs* the subject: "It is not individuals who have experience, but subjects who are constituted through experience. Experience in this definition then becomes not the origin of our explanation, not the authoritative (because seen or felt) evidence that grounds what is known, but rather that which we seek to explain, that about which knowledge is produced. To think about experience in this way is to historicize it as well as to historicize the identities it produces."[18] In its strongest version, Scott's theory claims not only that identities must be viewed as historical products but that they are *discursively* produced. If naive appeals to direct experience mask the work of social forces in the construction of identity, they equally mask, Scott says, "the necessarily discursive character of these experiences" as well.[19] Scott admits that the discursive character of experience is likely to be rejected by historians wedded to the idea of a reality outside of language that serves as the ground or foundation for historical explanation. Experience, for such historians, functions as both the starting point for historical narrative and also as a privileged and conclusive kind of evidence. But this view precludes our asking important questions about "what counts as experience and who gets to make that determination"—questions that are crucial to reflecting critically on the historical production of difference and identity. Scott's aim is to understand the processes by which identities are "ascribed, resisted, or embraced" but also to discover the means by which such processes remain unremarked, achieving their effect precisely because they go unnoticed. To historicize identity and experience means taking them as objects in need of an explanation. It does not necessitate dismissing the effects of identity and experience or even of explaining behavior as the determined result of such processes. "It does mean assuming that the appearance of a new identity is not inevitable or determined, not something that was always there simply waiting to be expressed, not something that will always exist in the form it was given in a particular political movement or at a particular historical moment."[20] Identities and the experiences that shape them are mutable, unstable, constructed rather than found or given by nature; moreover, they have a history that cannot simply be recounted from personal experience but that must be gotten at by other critical tools and means.

Challenging Postmodernism

As already noted, black, Latina, and third-world feminists, among others, have been reticent to embrace postmodernist theories. Postmodernism, poststructuralism, and deconstruction are accused of elitism, of the corrosion of normative discourse, with undermining the notions of identity, agency, and autonomy necessary for resistance, and with failing to offer a progressive politics. More specifically, a challenge to experience like that posed by Scott appears to go directly against a long-standing tradition, evident especially in black feminism, of using autobiography as a source for the production of social theory.[21]

The charge that postmodernism and poststructuralism have been elitist, both in theory and in practice, may well be the hardest to shake. In an essay that is largely sympathetic to poststructuralism and that grapples with its significance for contemporary black experience, bell hooks nonetheless rightly chides postmodernism for enshrining talk of "difference" and "Otherness" in language whose stylistic conventions leave most people "on the outside of the discourse looking in" even when they, their race, or their gender is the topic under discussion.[22] Barbara Christian likewise condemns the ugliness, lack of clarity, and alienating quality of poststructuralist discourse[23] and both remark the irony of postmodernism's claim to break with notions of 'authority' and 'mastery' without attending to its own political commitments as a form of "high" theory. As hooks emphasizes, in order to have a transformative impact, postmodernism's dismantling of authority cannot be reflected only at the level of its rhetoric but must extend more widely to its "habits of being, including styles of writing as well as chosen subject matter"[24] Christian suggests that poststructuralist politics—and in particular the condemnation of appeals to experience—are themselves part of a larger politics of containment. While Christian readily admits that African American literature, her area of concern, can be approached from numerous perspectives and by people of all kinds, she dismisses the claim that race and gender have no influence on the questions that are brought to a text or the approaches that are privileged in its interpretation.[25] Making the racial and gender experience of the interpreter irrelevant is one more way to discount historically marginalized voices. Indeed, Christian points out that the focus on the historical construction of race and gender has had little impact on the politics of publishing and the makeup of academic departments: "[A]lthough everything (in the philosophical discussion about race and gender) has changed, everything (as to whose voices are privileged in institutions, publishing outlets, universities) remains the same."[26] Moreover, Christian laments the fact that as postmodernism absorbs the energies of African American scholars (and returns attention to the classics of the Western canon, whose dominance it thus reestablishes), less energy is devoted to the critical task of reclaiming past and present third-world and African-American literatures.[27]

Rey Chow also takes a pragmatic, political perspective in explaining the rejection of postmodernism by third-world feminists. She explains, "If the First World has rejected modernism, such rejection is not so easy for the world which is still living through it as cultural trauma and devastation."[28] If postmodernism historicizes and consequently relativizes the cultural terrain through which it passes, critiques of first-world imperialism seemingly stand to lose much of their critical normative force by association, as well as having to sacrifice their commitments to a narrative of social progress.[29] Further, though third-world feminists (among others) share postmodernism's antiessentialist project of "dismantling universal claims," they are reluctant, Chow explains, to embrace a theoretical stance that seemingly leaves subject positions too fluid and unstable to serve as the basis for a unified politics based on the harms suffered by an identifiable group, for example, African American or third-world women.[30]

This last criticism has been a flashpoint for feminist critics of poststructuralism. As hooks points out, the African American rejoinder to postmodernism's antiessentialism and its critique of identity politics is likely to be, "Yeah, it's easy to give up identity, when you got one."[31] Linda Alcoff agrees with the poststructuralist antiessentialism and its emphasis on "social explanations of individual practices and experiences," but she sees poststructuralism as too ready "to erase any room for maneuver by the individual within a social discourse or set of institutions."[32] In effect, Alcoff worries that poststructuralism eliminates the individual agent capable of autonomous action and resistance. Similar concerns animate Patricia Hill Collins's worry that deconstruction of the notion of "woman" appears to leave feminist political praxis without a viable agent of change, and her concern that the simultaneous deconstruction of "reason" and "truth" appears to make all interpretations equally valid: "[B]y rejecting the notion that 'truths' such as Black feminist thought exist, deconstructive methodologies seem to be advocating the impossibility of objectivity and rationality for anyone, including Black women." Collins goes on to say, "From the relativist perspective implicit in extreme versions of postmodernism, no group can claim to have a better interpretation of any 'truth,' *including its own experience with oppression*, than another."[33]

Collins and Alcoff, like hooks and Christian, worry additionally that poststructuralist thought, and Derridean deconstruction in particular, has no viable positive politics to offer. Alcoff speculates that poststructuralist feminism "could only be a wholly negative feminism, deconstructing everything and refusing to construct anything.[34] Collins sounds a note that echoes hooks when she suggests that symbolic inclusion is no substitution for political action and theoretical sophistication is no substitute for change on the ground: "[A] Black mother who may be unable to articulate her political ideology but who on a daily basis contests school policies harmful to her children may be more an 'activist' than the most highly educated Black feminist who, while she can manipulate feminist, nationalist, postmodern, and other ideologies, produces no tangible political changes in anyone's life but her own."[35] Collins brings the critique home for black feminism more specifically in *Fighting Words* by posing the question: "What good is a theory that aims to dismantle the authority that Black women in the United States have managed to gain via group solidarity and shared traditions?" She responds to this question by stating that it is "[b]y removing altogether the notion of a 'center,' that is, a belief in some sort of verifiable, objective knowledge that one can deploy with authority, the rubric of deconstruction disempowers the very same historically marginalized groups who helped create the space for postmodernism to emerge."[36]

Appeals to Experience

Sojourner Truth's bared arm is in many respects emblematic of the role played by appeals to experience in African American women's struggles for liberation. Truth demands: "Look at my arm! I have ploughed, and planted, and gathered into barns, and no man could head me! And a'n't I a woman? I could work as much and eat as much as a man—when I could get it—and bear de lash as well! And a'n't I a woman? I have borne thirteen chilern, and seen 'em mos' all sold off to slavery, and when I cried out with my mother's grief, none but Jesus heard me! And a'n't I a woman?"[37] Truth's muscled arm and powerful form—she stood 5'11"—were direct evidence against the dominant stereotype that viewed women as too fragile and feeble to stand on their own two feet or make their own decision.[38] Her mother's grief brings to light the glaring contradiction between the view of women as in need in special protections and the brutal treatment of female slaves who, after all, were women, too. To see Truth's arm was to see conventional wisdom about women turned on its head and to see the brutality of enslaved women's lives exposed. By appealing to her own experience, Truth made black women newly visible *as women* even as she challenged the prevailing view of what that was supposed to mean and insisted that women should be the bearers of all the rights afforded to men. The Salem, Ohio, *Anti-Slavery Bugle* reported the next day that only those who saw her "whole-souled, earnest gesture" could truly understand the impact she had on her audience.[39]

Appeals to experience have typically shared the vital power of a gesture: they make visible and shed light on what has been otherwise hidden or ignored (often despite its being in plain sight). Writing some forty years after Truth's speech was delivered Anna Julia Cooper diagnosed the cause of black women's continuing invisibility. White women, Cooper noted, had been able to plead for their own emancipation, but "the black women doubly enslaved, could but suffer and struggle and be silent."[40] Cooper's point is not just that the black woman is enslaved once for her race and a second time for her gender; after all, as Cooper remarks, white women were speaking out effectively at the time, as had black men in gaining the vote. The problem is not race or gender or even race *and* gender; it is the way race and gender intersect that conditions the unique invisibility and inaudibility of black women's experiences and voices. When black women speak to the question of race, their voices risk being discounted within their own community because they are the voices of women, notes Cooper; when they speak to the woman question among white feminists, they are likely to be discounted because of their race. Thus, the "colored woman of to-day . . . is confronted by both a woman question and a race problem, and is as yet an unknown or an unacknowledged factor in both."[41] Frances Beale speaks of this as the "double jeopardy" of being both black and female,[42] and Deborah King, who introduces the term *multiple jeopardy*, explains that it is not a matter of additive or incremental injuries (race *plus* sex *plus* class) but of interdependent systems of control that have to be seen as they interact with one another.[43]

Overcoming this double or multiple jeopardy has meant that black women had to begin to speak *for themselves*. As Barbara Christian put it in an essay remembering Audre Lorde: "Audre's courage, her honesty, reminded us that we could not act for ourselves or others if we could not transform our silence into speech."[44] "Breaking the silence" and "coming to voice" became central themes of black feminist writing and first-person narratives—memories, personal reflections, vignettes, or full-fledged autobiography—became a standard and recognizable feature of academic works by African American feminists.[45]

Visibility and authority intertwine in the idea of coming to voice. Although there was a rich tradition of intellectual work by women of African descent in the late 1800s and in the early part of the twentieth century—one has only to think of the writings of Maria Miller Stewart, Anna Julia Cooper, Frances Watkins Harper, Ida B. Wells-Barnett, Mary Church Terrell, and others—this tradition remained virtually invisible both within the academy and without and was just as invisible within feminism as anywhere else.[46] Literary and artistic works by black women (with the exception, perhaps, of their contributions to jazz and blues) were similarly ignored or marginalized within both African American and dominant white cultures. Black women's struggles and the issues they faced in their daily lives were likewise rendered invisible, and if there were few enough books devoted to the experiences of African American women, even fewer of them were written by black women themselves. Commenting on the dearth of materials treating the sexuality of black women, Hortense Spillers comments that "black women are the beached whales of the sexual universe, unvoiced, misseen, not doing, awaiting *their* verb."[47] If Truth's arm is emblematic of the power of experience, Zora Neale Hurston's unmarked grave may well be emblematic of the neglect and invisibility that experience was called upon to overcome.[48]

In her acknowledgments to *Ain't I a Woman*, on a page that academic writers traditionally fill with sincere and heartfelt thanks to friends, colleagues, and mentors who have encouraged the writer and her project, hooks instead tells of a dinner party at which her topic—"the lot of black women in the United States"—became a source of loud laughter and amusement. "I had written in the manuscript," says hooks, "that the existence of black women was often forgotten, that we were often ignored or dismissed, and my lived experience as I shared the ideas in this book demonstrated the truth of this assertion."[49] This sentiment is given a sharper form when the women of the Combahee River Collective write, "We realize that the only people who care enough about us to work consistently for our liberation is us."[50] Black, lesbian, and feminist, the women of the Collective consciously pursued an identity politics based on their experience of the intersecting oppressions of racism, sexism, and homophobia. Appealing to and building on personal experience was crucial for women unrepresented within a larger culture (within *multiple* larger cultures, including heterosexist, patriarchal African American cultures); it was a way in which African American women actualized themselves as full subjects, claimed authority for their voices and perspectives, created solidarity among themselves and with other groups and movements, and became agents of change.

Breaking the silence has thus been an important, even necessary step in the process of black women's self-education and arrival at critical consciousness.[51] Toni Morrison's *Bluest Eye* (1970) and Alice Walker's *Color Purple* (1982), for example, broke the silence around damaging images of black women and domestic abuse within the African American community. As Collins notes, healing cannot begin until an abuse is named and thus recognized. Breaking the silence empowers the victims of such abuse by reclaiming their humanity and restoring their status as the subjects or *agents* of their own lives; it also provides a foundation for collective action and group solidarity.[52] In the foreword to *This Bridge Called My Back*, Toni Cade Bambara writes,

> Now that we've begun to break the silence and begun to break through the diabolically erected barriers and can hear each other and see each other, we can sit down with trust and break bread together. . . . For though the initial motive of several sisters/writers here may have been to protest, complain or explain to white feminist would-be allies that there are other ties and visions that bind, prior allegiances and priorities that supersede their invitation to coalesce on their terms . . . the process of examining that would-be alliance awakens us to new tasks.[53]

Claiming authority for the perspectives of radical women of color was a central task of the book, but so too was creating solidarity among and between the different groups represented by the authors of the collection.

Patricia Hill Collins reports that "coming to voice, especially carving out the intellectual and political space that would enable me to be heard," was the motivating concern in *Black Feminist Thought*.[54] Collins goes furthest in thematizing the role of experience as a fundamental element of black feminist epistemologies. Relying in part on the first-person narratives of African American women recorded in John Langston Gwaltney's *Drylongso, A Self-Portrait of Black America* (1980), Collins identifies "lived experience" as a criterion of the credibility of knowledge claims within African American thought systems.[55] The shared historical conditions of black women's work, she argues, "fostered a series of experiences that when shared and passed on became the collective wisdom of a Black women's standpoint."[56] Though *Black Feminist Thought* may sometimes sound essentialist about the role of experience, Collins makes it clear that there is no "homogenous Black *woman's* standpoint" just as there is "no essential or archetypal Black woman whose experiences stand as normal, normative, and thereby authentic."[57] The experiences and knowledges of differently situated African American women will differ, but Collins nonetheless argues that there are core themes and a recognizable black feminist standpoint produced by recurring patterns of discrimination and differential treatment.[58] This experiential, material base is not without its connections to universal, human experiences,[59] and the knowledge produced on this basis needs to be recognized as partial and unfinished, but from Collins' standpoint, acknowledging the partiality of your own position, as well as its connection to a set of political and economic interests and experiences, should be the *condition* of being heard not a reason for having one's claims dismissed or diminished in the arena of knowledge and truth building.[60] Cheryl A. Wall makes a nearly identical point when she writes, "Making our positionality explicit is not to claim a 'privileged' status for our positions. Black and white male critics have written perceptively about black women's texts." Wall goes on to state that nevertheless, "Making our positionality explicit is, rather, a response to the false universalism that long defined critical practice and rendered black women and their writing mute."[61]

The Limits of Experience: The Common Ground with Poststructuralism

Even in the early 1980s, in what might be regarded as the heyday of personalist black feminist writing, the perils of the genre were already being noted. When Gloria Steinem lauds Michele Wallace's *Black Macho and the Myth of the Superwoman*, saying that what Kate Millett's book *Sexual Politics* was for the seventies, Wallace's book might be for the eighties, bell hooks acerbically points out that Wallace's book in fact says "little about the impact of sexist discrimination and sexist oppression on the lives of black women."[62] While hooks acknowledges that Wallace's book is "an interesting, provocative analysis of Wallace's personal life" and draws an insightful portrait of the sexism and "patriarchal impulses of black activists," she vehemently contests the idea that "one can know all there is to know about black people by merely hearing the life story and opinions of one black person."[63] Nonetheless, at the end of the same chapter, hooks describes her own project as a concern "to move beyond racist and sexist assumptions about the nature of black womanhood to arrive at the truth of our experience."[64] Her problem is not with Wallace's appeal to experience so much as it is with a certain way of reading or treating that experience, namely, as having the same epistemological status as a truth arrived at through the critical theoretical and analytical examination of sexual and race politics from a feminist perspective.

In *Talking Back* (1989), hooks' own writing became deeply autobiographical, but at the same time even more skeptical about the "voice" of experience. While empowering black women to tell their *own* stories and working to establish the authority of black women's voices, the tradition of autobiographical writing raises problems, hooks notes, about whose voice can be deemed authentic and when. The only African American in her college creative writing classes, hooks remembers being praised for developing a " 'true,' authentic voice" whenever she wrote in the dialect of southern black speech.[65] This assumption of a single authentic voice betrays not only a racial bias but also a static notion of self and identity that functions to keep black women writers in an assigned slot.[66] "Claiming that only African-American women can invoke the authority of experience to adequately depict 'the Black woman's experience' creates a new form of silencing that, in effect, restricts Black women merely to breaking silence in a narrow box of authenticity."[67] It also keeps black feminist voices corralled in a manner that makes them simultaneously easier to commodify and easier to ignore. When experience is at the core of a work, and an "authentic" voice is one that appeals to that experience, it is easier to assume that black feminists write mainly for other black women and women of color and perhaps for some white feminists. It is also easier to assume that their voices do not then necessarily contribute to general debates in epistemology, literature, or political theory. It is striking, for example, when feminist scholars are held accountable for knowing the work of philosophers, critics, or others in so-called mainstream traditions, but scholars working in those traditions feel no responsibility to acquaint themselves with the basic positions and tenets of feminism—let alone black or third-world feminism. This one-sided interest results in work that, as Patricia Williams comments regarding her own highly interdisciplinary work, can be described simultaneously as "universal, trendy, and marginal."[68]

In her recent work, Collins still distinguishes between dominant and subjugated, public and private "knowledges" but she's less sanguine about the usefulness of appeals to experience in the creation of social and political theory, largely, she says, because she has come to see how quickly the voice of experience can be coopted.[69] When the false universalism of a white male perspective reigned without question, the mere presentation of black female experiences contested dominant paradigms, but "under a new politics of containment wherein Black women can be highly visible yet rendered powerless, breaking silence may not work."[70] "In particular," Collins argues, "whereas breaking silence within an identity politics grounded in concrete experiences has merit for *individuals*, as a *group* politic it contains the seeds of its own limitation."[71] Here Collins's concerns directly parallel those of Scott and in some cases go further. A principal worry for Collins is the cooptation of identity politics by the state such that minorities deemed unable to assimilate become targets for elimination or exclusion or, at best, are simply treated with indifference and neglect. Further, an identity politics based on presumably core experiences contributes to the misleading construction of minority groups as unified and homogenous in themselves and as essentially different from other such groups. Like Scott, Collins notes that identity politics tends to depoliticize historically situated differences by making them seem natural or inevitable—as when it is observed that 'we all like to associate with people who are importantly like ourselves.' This leaves the power of the dominant group largely intact, even as it falsely constructs that group as homogenous and without significant divisions.[72] Identity-based politics can also leave the various groups on the bottom fighting among themselves for supposedly scarce resources in what is thought to be a zero sum game.[73]

Experience as Knowledge, Experience as Resistance

There is thus significant common ground between Scott's Foucauldian-inspired critique and black feminist thought's own self-reflective theorizing concerning the limitations of appeals to experience, especially when they are supposed to form the ground for group-based identity politics. Nonetheless, there remains a crucial point of contention around the epistemological status of appeals to experience and their continued role as forms of political resistance—though this might ultimately need to be located not as a bone of contention between poststructuralism and black feminism, but as an issue *within* black feminist thought itself.

A fundamental question raised by Scott's essay concerns the possibility of seeing experiences of race or gender as an unconstructed given. From the epistemological point of view, the question becomes whether *experiencing* can be *knowing*. A related question concerns the role of experience in the making of identity. Scott's answer is clear: experience is constructed by social forces and creates the subject (or subject position) that then "has" that experience. We are unwise, in Scott's view, to trust experience uncritically or to view it as an unmediated ground for the production of knowledge or social theory. The antiessentialism of Scott's position goes well beyond the acknowledgment that the experiences of members of a certain group or a specific identity will differ because of differences in their circumstances or individual interpretations of those circumstances. Scott would no doubt acknowledge the existence of themes and identifications that are recognized by members of a group as core themes or core aspects of their identity, but she is also looking for genealogical accounts of the social mechanisms and institutions by which those cores were established, at the same time shaping the contours of dominant identities.

Admittedly, there is a problem inherent in this view when it comes to African American women's identities and those of other groups whose history has been suppressed. Scott's account assumes, after all, that the genealogical record *can* be reconstructed. But we may well wonder how this works when one side of the story remained unwritten and unrecorded in anything but the scantest details. Patricia Williams, for example, writes of coming into possession of the contract of sale for her great-great-grandmother. The document specifies nothing about her except that she was an eleven-year-old female; not even the price is noted. At thirteen years of age, she appears on the list of personal assets of an Austin Miller, now with an eight-month-old child. Williams tries to piece together her great-great-grandmother's life, but as her story reveals neither the family lore about this ancestor nor any historical record can say what it was like to stand in this girl's shoes. The girl exists in the historical record only as chattel, and the family story is that she was very lazy and not well liked. Williams imagines her raped and pregnant at thirteen, her children raised as the property of their father and as slaves to their white half-brothers and sisters. "Her children grew up reverent of and obedient to this white man—my great-great-grandfather—and his other children, to whom they were taught they owed the debt of their survival. It was a mistake," says Williams, "from which the Emancipation Proclamation never fully freed any of them."[74] Williams suggests that the stories told about this woman around the kitchen table and passed down from one generation to the next are already compromised stories. They can serve in the production of social theory, to be sure, but *not* in the guise of bedrock experience that needs no further analysis. When experience is *constructed* as given, this is just one more discursive manipulation of the real, and Williams among others suggests that though experience most certainly *does* have a role in theory building, its role is not to serve as unquestioned ground.

What then is the status of appeals to experience in social theory building? Williams's writing is exemplary of a hybrid position that makes important use of personal experience while largely trying to avoid the pitfalls that Scott, Collins, and others have identified. When Williams infuses her own writing with personal experience, interbraiding anecdote and social criticism, it is sometimes to make a point vividly, sometimes to provide the context for a line of inquiry, but mostly to reveal the intersubjective forces and assumptions at work in legal constructions that claim to be plainly evident, universal, and transcendently true.[75] For Williams, experience becomes a source for revealing and contesting the conventions of legal writing, which, like those in many other disciplines, privileges what it takes to be "objective, 'unmediated' voices" that express supposedly unchanging truths.[76] Personal experience thus functions as an element in a consciously employed interdisciplinary methodology and in the service of epistemological goals, but it is not a replacement for either of those. Furthermore, personal experience does not serve in any respect as the whole of Williams's, method nor does it serve as the ground for knowledge claims.

Williams's epistemological commitments are mirrored by the political commitments of her work: antiracist, antisexist, antihomophobic, to be sure, but otherwise not easily categorized. Indeed, as Williams writes in a two-page afterword titled "A Word on Categories," her book is as much about boundaries as it is about the centers of identifiable categories. Williams writes: "While being black has been the most powerful social attribution in my life, it is only one of a number of governing narratives or presiding fictions by which I am constantly reconfiguring myself in the world."[77] The terms "governing narrative" and "presiding fiction" are good ones. They suggest that identity categories are in an important sense *products* of human interaction. They are not in the exclusive control of those who wear them or those who wield them; they are *intersubjectively* produced. In Scott's terms, this means that there is a *history* of their production whose material, human, and social elements can be assembled and a new narrative woven.

To speak of narratives or fictions, moreover, is not at all to deny that these social, intersubjective creations have the power to govern or preside over "real" lives. The agent is an active creator but by no means the decisive interpreter of the narrative of her own life, just as the author is the agent of the fiction but does not have *decisive* control over her creation's meaning or its future lives in various interpretive contexts. Williams's work suggests that race "so profoundly affects" African American lives that "the decision to generalize from such a division is valid,"[78] but she adds that none of the words we have to name that generalization do justice to the complexity of one's experience and to the rich diversity of racial perspectives. As Williams notes, she prefers the term *African American* but mostly uses the term *black* "in order to accentuate the unshaded monolithism of color itself as a social force."[79]

For Williams as for Scott, then, experience is not the ground or the point of departure; rather it indicates somewhere that we have *arrived*, often without having clearly seen the mechanisms of our own conveyance. Williams's work shows the means by which various culturally produced boundaries are made to look like fixed parts of the natural landscape. Using a self-consciously employed diary form that creates entries from television, the newspaper, government policies, social commentary, water-cooler conversations, and personal experience, Williams exposes the reader to a barrage of cultural artifacts that undoes conventional wisdom as surely as Sojourner Truth's arm. Williams's cry of "Look!" is not in the name of a single truth that will become apparent if we only have the eyes to see. It is not the truth of black women's experience that she urges on our attention; or rather it is, but with the understanding that if we want to see this experience in its rich complexity we cannot simply say how things look from where we stand, since we have multiple angles of vision, multiple governing narratives, and multiple presiding fictions.

The poststructuralist critique of experience was initially (though by no means uniformly) dismissed by African American feminists as part of a larger suspicion about postmodernism and its usefulness for the agenda of black feminist thought. I have argued here that the question of experience needs to be disentangled from that more general rejection and that when it is there is much common ground, both epistemologically and politically, between Scott's critique and those of black feminist writers. Moreover, and this point is most in the spirit of Williams's knack for complicating rather simplifying things, the debate that needs to be joined now is not one between poststructuralists and black feminists (categories that would have to be read much too monolithically for there even to *be* any such debate) but one that is already underway though not always made explicit *within* black feminism itself. There is important political work that can still be accomplished by appeals to experience insofar as such appeals function as acts of resistance: they challenge dominant group narratives, discredit 'common' sense, create alternative myths, call to collective action, and imagine communities of opposition and change. But if experience remains a legitimate tool or strategy of black feminist writing, it is not because it is a touchstone of truth but because it is a forceful form of creative political expression. And, like any form of creative expression, it will be open to interpretation, subject to multiple and unexpected appropriations, victim to possible recuperations by dominant forces, and kept alive only as long as we engage it critically.

Notes

1. Simone de Beauvoir, *The Second Sex*, trans. H. M. Parshely (Harmondsworth: Penguin, 1984), 267.

2. Michel Foucault, *Discipline and Punish: The Birth of the Prison*, 2nd ed., trans. A. Sheridan (New York: Vintage, 1995).

3. Judith Butler, *Bodies That Matter: On the Discursive Limits of Sex* (New York and London: Routledge, 1993); Anne Fausto-Sterling, *Sexing the Body: Gender Politics and the Construction of Sexuality* (New York: Basic Books 2000).

4. Scott McLemee, "Think Postpositive: A Latina Cultural Theorist Wrestles with Notions of Identity and Experience," *The Chronicle of Higher Education*, February 13, 2004.

5. Paula Moya *Learning from Experience: Minority Identities, Multicultural Struggles* (Berkeley: University of California Press, 2002), 25; emphasis in original. For an effective and witty defanging of critiques of French poststructuralism, see Ladelle McWhorter's essay "Why I Shouldn't Like Foucault . . . So They Say," in McWhorter, *Bodies and Pleasures: Foucault and the Politics of Sexual Normalization* (Bloomington and Indianapolis: University of Indiana Press, 1999), chapter 3.

6. In Nellie McKay, Patricia Hill Collins, Mae Henderson, and June Jordan, "The State of the Art," *Women's Review of Books* 8, no. 5 (February 23–26): 23.

7. Delany 1988, 173, quoted in Scott, "Experience," in Judith Butler and J. Scott, eds., *Feminists Theorize the Political* (New York: Taylor and Francis 1992a), 22–40. Originally published in a longer version as "The Evidence of Experience," *Critical Inquiry* 17 (Summer 1991): 22.

8. Scott, "Experience," 23.

9. Ibid., 24–25.

10. Ibid., 25.

11. Ibid.

12. Ibid., 34.

13. Ibid., 25.

14. Joan Scott, "Multiculturalism and the Politics of Identity," *October* 61, *The Identity in Question* (Summer 1992b): 15.

15. Ibid., 17.

16. Ibid., 14.

17. Ibid., 18.

18. Ibid., 25–26.

19. Scott, "Experience," 31.

20. Ibid., 33.

21. A rich account of the uses of autobiography in African-American political and social theory can be found in Kenneth Mostern's *Autobiography and B.*

22. bell hooks, *Yearning: Race, Gender, and Cultural Politics* (Boston: South End, 1990), 24.

23. Barbara Christian *New Black Feminist Criticism, 1985–2000*, edited with an introduction by G. Bowles, M. G. Fabi, and A. R. Keizer (Urbana and Chicago: University of Illinois Press, 2007), 24.

24. hooks, *Yearning*, 25.

25. Christian, *New Black Feminist Criticism*, 178.

26. Ibid., 178.

27. Ibid., 45. See hooks's partial response to Christian's critique in *Talking Back* (1989). While hooks appreciates much in Christian's critique she is anxious that black feminists do not devalue or abandon theory. When theory is dismissed as having no relevance to "real" life, this reinforces "the misguided assumption that all theory is and

has to be inaccessible." bell hooks, *Talking Back: Thinking Feminist, Thinking Black* (Boston: South End, 1989), 39. For hooks, a theory can be as complex as the matter at hand requires, but the language in which it is stated needs to remain responsible to a wide audience and thus to remain accessible.

28. Rey Chow "Postmodern Automatons," in Butler and Scott, eds., *Feminists Theorize the Political* (New York: Taylor and Francis, 1992), 102–03.

29. Ibid., 103.

30. Ibid., 104.

31. hooks, *Yearning*, 28.

32. Linda Alcoff, "Cultural Feminism versus Post-Structuralism: The Identity Crisis in Feminist Theory," in L. Nichols, ed., *The Second Wave* (New York: Routledge, 1997), 337.

33. Patricia Hill Collins, *Fighting Words: Black Women and the Search for Justice* (Minneapolis: University of Minnesota Press, 1998), 144; emphasis added.

34. Alcoff, "Cultural Feminism versus Post-Structuralism," 338.

35. Patricia Hill Collins, *Black Feminist Thought: Knowledge, Consciousness, and the Politics of Empowerment*, 2nd ed. (New York: Routledge, 2000), 203.

36. Collins, *Fighting Words*, 145.

37. Beverly Guy-Sheftall 2000, 36.

38. Though Truth's arm by no means has a single meaning. It could just as well reinforce stereotypical images that masculinized black women and, thus, supported dominant views of white women's comparative fragility.

39. Salem, Ohio, *Anti-Slavery Bugle*, June 21, 1851. Truth's speech was only written down, dictated to Olive Gibert, some twenty-five years after she gave it. For a discussion of the historical accuracy of the version of the speech that appeared in Truth's *Narrative* (1875), see Nell Painter's biographical study, *Sojourner Truth: A Life, a Symbol Sojourner Truth: A Life, a Symbol* (New York: Norton, 1997).

40. Quoted in bell hooks, *Ain't I a Woman: Black Women and Feminism* (Boston: South End, 1981), 2.

41. Anna Julia Cooper, "The Status of Woman in America," in Beverly Guy-Sheftall, ed., *Words of Fire: An Anthology of African-American Feminist Thought* (New York: New York Press, 1995), 45.

42. Frances Beale "Double Jeopardy: To Be Black and Female," in Beverly Guy-Sheftall, ed., *Words of Fire: An Anthology of African-American Feminist Thought* (New York: New York Press, 1995), 146.

43. Deborah King, "Multiple Jeopardy, Multiple Consciousness: The Context of a Black Feminist Ideology," in Beverly Guy-Sheftall, ed., *Words of Fire: An Anthology of African-American Feminist Thought* (New York: New York Press, 1995), 297, 44.

45. Barbara Christian, *New Black Feminist Criticism, 1985–2000*, ed. with an intro. by G. Bowles, M. G. Fabi, and A. R. Keizer (Urbana and Chicago: University of Illinois Press, 2007), 165. The context for Christian's remark concerns the role of black women in the 1960s and 70s. During the Civil Rights era African-Americans came to voice in increasing numbers, but as many have pointed out sexism with civil rights movements meant that black women's voices were once again marginalized. The case was the same with movements for women's liberation, as white middle-and upper-class women were increasingly heard, but African-American, Latina, queer, and third-world women's

voices had a much harder time finding a stage on which to be heard. See hooks' account in the "Introduction" to *Ain't I a Woman: Black Women and Feminism.*

46. Beverly Guy-Sheftall, *Words of Fire: An Anthology of African-American Feminist Thought* (New York: New York Press, 1995), xiii. Lest one think that story-telling is just a "natural" part of African-American culture adapted here to the ends of black feminists, it is important to remember that this too has a history. Drawing on an essay by William Andrews, Kenneth Mostern notes the relation of contemporary autobiographical political writing in African-American thought to the requirements of a *white* reading public in the anti-slavery era: "The tradition of African-American writing is thus one in which political commentary necessitates, invites, and assumes autobiography as its rhetorical form. This is simultaneously the result of oppression, where, as Andrews states, the white reading public will not trust anything but the (supposedly) transparent testimony of the slave, who is presumed only to report, not theorize" (Mostern 1999, 11). See William Andrews, "African-American Autobiography Criticism: Retrospect and Prospect" in P. J. Eakin, ed. *American Autobiography: Retrospect and Prospect* (Madison: University of Wisconsin Press, 1991), 195–215.

47. Hortense Spillers, "Interstices: A Small Drama of Words," in C. S. Vance, ed., *Pleasures and Danger: Exploring Female Sexuality* (Boston: Routledge and Kegan Paul, 1984), 74.

48. On Alice Walker's efforts to have Hurston's grave site recognized, see Walker, *I Love Myself When I Am Laughing.*

49. hooks, *Ain't I a Woman.*

50. Combahee "The Combahee River Collective: A Black Feminist Statement," in L. Nicholson, ed., *The Second Wave* (New York: Routledge, 1997), 65.

51. hooks, *Talking Back,* 13.

52. Collins, *Fighting Words,* 48.

53. In Cherríe Moraga and Gloria Anzaldúa, *This Bridge Called My Back: Writings by Radical Women of Color,* 2nd ed. (New York: Kitchen Table: Women of Color Press, 1983), vi.

54. Collins, *Black Feminist Thought,* xii–xiii.

55. Ibid., 257. Hortense Spillers likewise makes use of the women's voices recorded in Gwaltney's work to argue for the construction of a Black feminist position that draws together critical academic discourses and the testimony of those who live through the experiences which the theory also addresses (Spillers, "Interstices").

56. Collins, *Black Feminist Thought,* 256.

57. Ibid., 28.

58. Ibid., 26.

59. Ibid., 268.

60. Ibid., 270.

61. Wall, *Changing Our Own Words: Essays on Criticism, Theory, and Writing by Black Women* (New

Brunswick and London: Rutgers University Press, 1989), 2.

62. hooks, *Ain't I a Woman,* 11.

63. Ibid.

64. Ibid., 13.

65. hooks, *Talking Back,* 11.

66. Ibid., 11–12.
67. Collins, *Fighting Words*, 54.
68. Williams 1991, 7.
69. She acknowledges the shift in perspective in the preface to the second edition of *Black Feminist Thought* (xiii).
70. Collins, *Fighting Words*, 56.
71. Ibid., 52.
72. Ibid., 52–53.
73. Ibid., 53.
74. Williams 1991, 18.
75. Ibid., 7.
76. Ibid., 9.
77. Ibid., 256.
78. Ibid.
79. Ibid., 257.

Works Cited

Alcoff, Linda. 1997. "Cultural Feminism versus Post-Structuralism: The Identity Crisis in Feminist Theory," in Nichols, L., ed. *The Second Wave*. New York: Routledge, 330–355.

Beale, Frances. 1995. "Double Jeopardy: To Be Black and Female" in B. Guy-Sheftall, ed. *Words of Fire: An Anthology of African-American Feminist Thought*. New York: The New York Press, 146–155.

de Beauvoir, Simone. 1984. *The Second Sex*. Trans. H.M. Parshely. Harmondsworth: Penguin.

Butler, Judith. 1993. *Bodies That Matter: On the Discursive Limits of Sex*. New York and London: Routledge.

Chow, Rey. 1992. "Postmodern Automatons," in Butler, J. and J. Scott, eds. *Feminists Theorize the Political*. New York: Taylor and Francis, 101–117.

Christian, Barbara. 2007. *New Black Feminist Criticism, 1985–2000*. Edited with an introduction by G. Bowles, M.G. Fabi, and A.R. Keizer. Urbana and Chicago: University of Illinois Press.

Collins, Patricia Hill. 1998. *Fighting Words: Black Women and the Search for Justice*. Minneapolis: University of Minnesota Press.

———. 2000. *Black Feminist Thought: Knowledge, Consciousness, and the Politics of Empowerment*, Second Edition. New York: Routledge.

Combahee River Collective. 1997. "The Combahee River Collective: A Black Feminist Statement" in Nicholson, L., ed. *The Second Wave*. New York: Routledge, 63–70.

Cooper, Anna Julia. 1995. "The Status of Woman in America," in B. Guy-Sheftall, ed. *Words of Fire: An Anthology of African-American Feminist Thought*. New York: The New York Press, 44–49.

Delany, Samuel R. 1988. *The Motion of Light in Water: Sex and Science Fiction Writing in the East Village, 1957–1965*. New York: New American Library.

Fausto-Sterling, Anne. 2000. *Sexing the Body: Gender Politics and the Construction of Sexuality*. New York: Basic Books.

Foucault, Michel. 1995. *Discipline and Punish: The Birth of the Prison*. Second edition. Trans. A. Sheridan. New York: Vintage.

Guy-Sheftall, Beverly, ed. 1995. *Words of Fire: An Anthology of African-American Feminist Thought*. New York: The New York Press.

Gwaltney, John Langston. 1980. *Drylongso, A Self-Portrait of Black America*. New York: Vintage.

hooks, bell. 1981. *Ain't I A Woman: Black Women and Feminism*. Boston: South End Press.

———. 1989. *Talking Back: Thinking Feminist, Thinking Black*. Boston: South End Press.

———. 1990. *Yearning: Race, Gender, and Cultural Politics*. Boston: South End Press.

King, Deborah. 1995. "Multiple Jeopardy, Multiple Consciousness: The Context of A Black Feminist Ideology" in B. Guy-Sheftall, ed. *Words of Fire: An Anthology of African-American Feminist Thought*. New York: The New York Press, 294–317.

McKay, Nellie, Patricia Hill Collins, Mae Henderson, and June Jordan. 1991. "The State of the Art." *Women's Review of Books* 8 (5), February: 23–26.

McLemee, Scott. 2004. "Think Postpositive: A Latina Cultural Theorist Wrestles With Notions of Identity and Experience." *The Chronicle of Higher Education*. February 13, 2004.

McWhorter, Ladelle. 1999. *Bodies and Pleasures: Foucault and the Politics of Sexual Normalization*. Bloomington and Indianapolis: University of Indiana Press.

Moraga, Cherríe and Gloria Anzaldúa, eds. 1983. *This Bridge Called My Back: Writings by Radical Women of Color*. Second edition. New York: Kitchen Table: Women of Color Press.

Mostern, Kenneth. 1999. *Autobiography and Black Identity Politics*. Cambridge: Cambridge University Press.

Moya, Paula. 2002. *Learning from Experience: Minority Identities, Multicultural Struggles*. Berkeley: University of California Press.

Painter, Nell. 1997. *Sojourner Truth: A Life, A Symbol*. New York: W.W. Norton & Sons.

Scott, Joan. 1992a. "Experience," in Butler, J. and J. Scott, eds. *Feminists Theorize the Political*. New York: Taylor and Francis, 22–40. Originally published in a longer version as "The Evidence of Experience," *Critical Inquiry* 17 (Summer 1991).

———. 1992b. "Multiculturalism and the Politics of Identity," *October*, vol. 61, *The Identity in Question*, (Summer), 12–19.

Spillers, Hortense. 1984. "Interstices: A Small Drama of Words," in C.S. Vance, ed. *Pleasures and Danger: Exploring Female Sexuality*. Boston: Routledge and Kegan Paul, 73–100.

Walker, Alice, ed. 1979. *I Love Myself When I Am Laughing.*.

Wall, Cheryl A., ed. 1989. *Changing Our Own Words: Essays on Criticism, Theory, and Writing by Black Women*. New Brunswick and London: Rutgers University Press.

2

Sartre, Beauvoir, and the Race/Gender Analogy

A Case for Black Feminist Philosophy

Kathryn T. Gines

The discipline of philosophy leaves much to be desired when it comes to black feminism. Although white feminism (especially French feminism in the continental tradition) is making strides, this is often to the exclusion or marginalization of women of color. Similarly black male philosophers and scholars have left their imprint on continental philosophy (for example, in the critical philosophy of race), but often to the exclusion of the woman question. Considered from another perspective, continental philosophy has been a resource for feminist philosophy and the critical philosophy of race, but perhaps less so for what we might call a "critical" philosophy of black feminism. Although the few black women philosophers who work in the areas of feminist philosophy and critical philosophy of race (and some black men) are beginning to bring black feminism into the philosophy canon, we still do not have a fully developed black feminist philosophy.[1]

In the chapter that follows, I demonstrate the need for black feminism in philosophy (and for a black feminist philosophy), by looking at specific cases of its absence. I begin by critically examining the conspicuous lack of a black feminist account of the intersectionality of race and gender in what I call the "race/gender analogy." Toward that end, I am especially interested in the shortcomings of this analogy in general as well as the usage of this analogy in Jean-Paul Sartre's *The Respectful Prostitute* (1946) and Simone de Beauvoir's *The Second Sex* (1949) in particular. The chapter continues by highlighting the influences of Richard Wright on these two prominent continental philosophers. While Wright offers Sartre and Beauvoir insights into racial oppression, still missing from their accounts is a black feminist analysis of the interlocking systems of racial and gender oppression. The remaining portion of the chapter underscores the development of black feminist theory in the United States and the ways in which black feminism fills this void by confronting both sexism and racism. Concentrating on the scholarship of Anna Julia Cooper (with mention of other philosophical black feminist thinkers and texts), I call for the expansion of the philosophy canon to include these scholars in an effort to help pave the way for a black feminist philosophy.

The Race/Gender Analogy

Simply stated, the race/gender analogy is the use of racial oppression as an analogy for gender oppression. One shortcoming of the analogy is that it usually emphasizes black men and white women while ignoring the situation of women of color. Like this analogy, historically, white feminism has often ignored the ways in which black women experience sexist oppression differently because of the added burden of racism. Take, for example, the 1848 Seneca Falls Convention that signaled the emergence of the first wave women's movement in the United States. Among the mostly white and female suffragist attendees there were not any black women on record. It seems that Frederick Douglass was the only black person present, and his name is included on the "Roll of Honor containing all the signatures to the Declaration of Sentiments set forth by the First Women's Right's Convention held at Seneca Falls, New York July 19–20, 1848."[2] Key organizers of the convention included Elizabeth Cady Stanton and Lucretia Mott, two white women who "felt a striking similarity between themselves as white women, and black slaves, a common theme in early white feminist discourse."[3]

But the loose usage of institutionalized and racialized slavery and antiblack racism as an analogy for other forms of oppression proves to be problematic. The race/gender analogy often codes race as black man and gender as white woman, neglecting the situation of women of color. Another shortcoming of the analogy is that it is frequently exploited to support members of groups and their causes even when those groups are often themselves participating in or complicit with some form of antiblack racism. For instance, although prominent black leaders such as Sojourner Truth, Ida B. Wells-Barnett, and Frederick Douglass were active in the women's movement and active in seeking women's suffrage, this and other movements for women's liberation have historically limited their focus to liberating white women while ignoring the oppression of women of color (who suffer from both racial and gender oppression), or people of color more generally.

Angela Davis examines racism in the women's suffrage movement in "Woman Suffrage at the Turn of the Century: The Rising Influence of Racism," where she begins with some conflicts between Ida B. Wells-Barnett and Susan B. Anthony. According to Davis, "Wells' admiration for Anthony's individual stance against racism was undeniable . . . But she unhesitatingly criticized her white sister for failing to make her personal fight against racism a public issue of the suffrage movement."[4] Davis also notes that Anthony "pushed [Frederick] Douglass aside for the sake of recruiting white Southern women into the movement for woman suffrage," and "she refused to support the efforts of several Black women who wanted to form a branch of the suffrage association."[5] In her analysis Davis is drawing from Ida B. Wells-Barnett's autobiography *Crusade for Justice: The Auto-Biography of Ida B. Wells* and from *Up from the Pedestal: Selected Writings in the History of American Feminism.*[6]

The pushing aside of Douglass is significant in part because Douglass was an advocate and activist for women's suffrage. The *North Star* was among the few newspapers to advertise the Seneca Falls Convention, and he interceded at the convention on the resolution on women's suffrage so that it would pass. He also wrote "The Rights of Women" in the *North Star* (July 28, 1828), in which he discusses the convention and argues for equal political rights for men and women. By 1869 Douglass and white feminists would disagree about the order of priorities regarding race and gender (Douglass prioritizing the former and white feminists the latter). In spite of these conflicts, his commitments to women's suffrage and rights are still expressed in two 1888 speeches "Give Women Fair Play" and "I Am a Radical Woman Suffrage Man."[7]

The issues at the axes of race and gender are raised again at one of the subsequent meetings to the 1848 Seneca Falls Convention (held in 1851 in Akron, Ohio) by the "Ain't I a Woman?" remarks attributed to Sojourner Truth. While there is now some controversy surrounding the commentary, it remains significant because it asserts that the category "woman" is not monolithic.[8] Furthermore it underscores how the use of the general term *woman* often really means white women in particular, excluding black women and ignoring our intersectionality. Throughout the commentary, the question is asked repeatedly and rhetorically, "Ain't I a Woman?" even as it is noted that black women are never helped into carriages like white women, and black women labor as intensely and are beaten as violently as black men. In a later speech (1867) Truth complicates the notion of race versus gender rights and states, "There is a great stir about colored men getting their rights, but no word about the colored women; and if colored men get their rights, and not colored women get theirs, there will be a bad time about it."[9] Another implication of this claim, though it is not explicitly stated, is that if white women get their rights and not black women (and black men), then there would also "be a bad time about it."

The debate about black men's versus women's rights (again, both sides ignoring black women's rights and reinforcing the implicit whiteness of women's rights) was reignited in the recent (2008) historic democratic primaries in which Senators Barack Obama and Hillary Clinton emerged as the front-runners. White feminist icon Gloria Steinem wrote a controversial op-ed piece in the *New*

York Times titled "Women Are Never Forerunners."[10] Steinem begins by claiming that if Senator (now President) Obama were a black (biracial) woman, he would not be where he is today, inferring that this is evidence that sexism is more pernicious than racism. But it does not seem to occur to Steinem that if Hillary Clinton were a black (biracial) woman, she also would not likely be where she is today. In other words, Clinton is as much (if not more so) a beneficiary of her whiteness as Obama is of his maleness. While Steinem acknowledges, "The caste systems of sex and race are interdependent and can only be uprooted together," her remarks throughout the piece do not reflect this understanding.

Like other white feminists before her, Steinem privileges gender oppression above other forms of oppression and declares, "Gender is probably the most restricting force in American life, whether the question is who must be in the kitchen or who could be in the White House?" She questions, "Why is the sex barrier not taken as seriously as the racial one?" and replies, "[B]ecause sexism is still confused with nature as racism once was." When Steinem asserts, "Black men were given the vote a half-century before women of any race were allowed to mark a ballot, and generally have ascended to positions of power, from the military to the boardroom, before any women," she does not mention the white terrorist violence that prevented both black men and black women from exercising their right to vote and other political rights even after they attained them legally. Steinem also neglects to acknowledge how white women have benefited from, and have often consciously chosen, white supremacist patriarchy at the expense of both gender and racial equality and liberation.

All of this does not mean that comparisons between systems of racial oppression and systems of gender oppression are altogether unfruitful.[11] The comparison may point to interesting common ground between black men and white women. It has been said that while black women experience double damnation (i.e., two "strikes" against us because of race and gender), black men and white women each have one strike: the former, his race, and the latter, her gender. Of course this is a grossly oversimplified understanding of race and gender that still ignores other intersecting aspects of identities (including nationality, ethnicity, culture, class, sexual orientation, religion, etc.). Nonetheless, this idea of a common ground between white women and black men looms in the background of the race/gender analogy as Sartre and Beauvoir use it.

Sartre, Wright, and *The Respectful Prostitute*

Prominent continental philosopher Jean-Paul Sartre's *The Respectful Prostitute* (*La Putain respectueuse*) was presented for the first time on November 8, 1946, in Paris at the Theatre Antoine.[12] The play was inspired by the Scottsboro case of the 1930s in which nine black males (ranging in age between twelve and twenty) were accused and convicted of raping two white women.[13] Eight of the nine were sentenced to the death penalty. The accusations came in the aftermath of a fight between several black males and a gang of white males on a freight train in Alabama. The white males filed a complaint with the sheriff in Scottsboro, Alabama, that resulted in the arrest of the nine black males and the discovery of two white females (ages seventeen and nineteen, both thought to be prostitutes), all of whom were taken to Scottsboro. According to James Sellman, "Although the women initially denied that any assault had taken place, under the pressure of a lynch mob that filled the streets that evening and after repeated goading by a local prosecutor, they conceded that they had been raped by the black youths."[14] After the initial convictions, the Communist Party of the United States of America (CPUSA) and the party's International Labor Defense (ILD) assisted the Scottsboro nine and appealed their convictions and death penalties to the U.S. Supreme Court.[15]

Sartre incorporates many elements from the Scottsboro case into his play: the fight, the white female prostitute who insists that she has not been raped until she is coerced into signing a false statement, and the lynch mob in the streets. What immediately strikes me about this play is the way in which situations of the black man and the white woman are presented as overlapping or intertwined. For example, Fred (a white male) says to the white prostitute Lizzie, "You are the devil. The nigger is a devil, too."[16] Later Lizzie sees similarities between herself and the Negro (the unnamed black character in the play accused of raping her). On one occasion, in response to the Negro's claim that he can't shoot white folks because "they're white folks" she states, "Jesus, you're like me! You're a sucker too."[17] On another occasion Lizzie says to the Negro, "Well, look at us now! Aren't we alone in the world? Like two orphans."[18]

Also striking is the way that Sartre is able to capture American capitalism, antiblack racism, anti-Semitism, anti-Communist sentiments, and white male patriarchy in a play with only one act and two scenes. The senator describes Thomas to Lizzie as "a hundred percent American . . . a firm bulwark against Communists, the labor unions and the Jews."[19] In his appeal to Lizzie to sign the statement that she had been raped by the Negro, Fred proclaims, "We have made this country, and its history is ours. . . . Are you going to kill the whole United States?"[20] It will suffice to say that the play was not well received by many Americans who saw it as anti-American. In his own defense against critics, Sartre asserts, "I am not anti-American. I don't even know what the word means. I am anti-racist because I do know what *racism* means."[21] Appealing to his track record for writing against oppression, Sartre adds, "The writer cannot accomplish much in this world. He can only say what he has seen. I have attacked anti-Semitism. Today in this play I attack racism. Tomorrow I shall devote an issue of my magazine to attacking colonialism."[22]

One reason that Sartre can identify racism is that he was in contact with and/or had relationships with black intellectuals (e.g., Richard Wright, Aimé Césaire, Frantz Fanon, and Leopold Senghor), all of whom experienced racism firsthand. Sartre and Beauvoir cite Wright in their own publications and featured Wright's work in several volumes of *Les Temps Modernes*. In addition to writing the introductory note that appears with Sartre's play in *Art and Action*, Wright also wrote a very detailed response to a manuscript version of the play. After reading the play in French with his French instructor, Wright responded, "The characters are well-drawn and the overall atmosphere in the USA is very well caught. There are, of course, several minor mistakes which are natural when a Frenchman tries to depict the US scene, but they are minor."[23] Some of the details that Wright has in mind include the Negro (whom Wright refers to as Sidney, though the character is nameless in the finished version of the play) going to Lizzie's home. Wright explains that "this simply would not happen in the United States" (i.e., a black man accused of raping a white woman would not go to the white woman's home).[24] In addition to recommending more development of the original characters, adding in several new characters, and altering the manner in which events unfold, Wright also emphasized the fact that segregation signs should be clear throughout the script. He states, "It is absolutely necessary that it is indicated that the toilets are sexually separated and that they are marked: FOR WHITE WOMEN, FOR WHITE MEN, FOR COLORED MEN, FOR COLORED WOMEN, etc. In fact, this fact ought to be observed in the whole script, in the railroad station and other public places."[25]

Although Sartre did not take up most of Wright's suggestions (if he had it would have resulted in an entirely new play), Wright is still very positive about the finished product. In an interview with Michel Gordey in 1947, when asked what French literary expression struck him most, he replies that he is most interested in *The Respectful Prostitute* because, "[Sartre] seems to perceive deeply the realities of my country. This acute perception is felt in his play to such a point that, in my opinion, many American writers could use it as an example of the treatment of American realities. . . . Better than any writer who dealt with the [Scottsboro] case, Sartre has been able to pinpoint the crux of the situation."[26] In his introduction to the play in *Art and Action*, Wright describes it as "a calculated challenge to those who feel that America is a finished democracy . . . [I]t deals with a reality which is all-too-familiar to the citizens of a nation living under the banner of White Supremacy."[27]

Other Influences: Beauvoir, Sartre, and Wright

Although it is frequently suggested (at times by Simone de Beauvoir herself) that Beauvoir followed Sartre's philosophical lead, scholars have attempted to prove that the opposite was the case. For example, in *Simone de Beauvoir and Jean-Paul Sartre: The Remaking of a Twentieth-Century Legend* (1994), Kate and

Edward Fullbrook analyze Sartre's *War Diaries* and Beauvoir's *Letters to Sartre* to make the case: "It is now utterly clear to us that Beauvoir was the driving intellectual power in the joint development of the couple's most influential ideas. The story of their partnership has been told backwards. Our detailed work on the genesis of *She Came to Stay* shows, incontrovertibly we believe, that the major ideas behind *Being and Nothingness* were fully worked out by Beauvoir and adopted by Sartre before he even began his famous study."[28]

In *Beauvoir and the Second Sex: Feminism, Race, and the Origins of Existentialism* (1999), Margaret Simons problematizes the traditional view of Beauvoir as a mere follower (and companion) of Sartre. Simons explains: "From the standpoint of feminist theory, a most serious aspect of this sexist view of Beauvoir's relationship to Sartre is the discounting of Beauvoir as an original thinker and a refusal to acknowledge, analyze, and critically study her work as social theory and social philosophy. This view fails to recognize the originality of Beauvoir's insights and is thus unable to appreciate her considerable influence on Sartre's development of a social philosophy of existentialism, and on contemporary feminist theorists as well."[29]

Simons points out that Beauvoir's 1927 diary gives an account of her "struggle against despair and the temptation of self-deception, which anticipates her later concept of 'Bad Faith' " along with "the opposition of the self and the other," both major themes in *The Second Sex* and *Being and Nothingness*.[30] These claims that Beauvoir was not only a philosopher in her own right, but also that she influenced Sartre's philosophical development, are significant. While Sartre is readily embraced within the continental philosophy tradition, Beauvoir is still relatively marginalized or relegated to feminist philosophy anthologies and readers. In addition to being an influence on Sartre, Simons argues that Beauvoir also had significant influences on her work, especially her use of racial oppression as an analogy for gender oppression in *The Second Sex*. Two particular influences on this aspect of Beauvoir's scholarship include European theorist Gunnar Myrdal and again, Richard Wright.

In *Anti-Semite and Jew* Sartre correctly attributes the claim that America does not have a Negro problem but rather a white problem to Wright. Gunnar Myrdal also takes this position in *An American Dilemma: The Negro Problem and Modern Democracy* (1944). Simons outlines Myrdal's influence on Beauvoir's *Second Sex* and concludes: "Myrdal can thus be seen as influencing Beauvoir's theoretical framework in *The Second Sex* in four ways: by encouraging the use of an analogy with racism, providing a model for the encyclopedic scope of *The Second Sex*, introducing the concept of caste as a substitute for the biological category of race, and grounding her understanding of social constructionism in science and in the African American intellectual tradition."[31] Not only was *An American Dilemma* influential on Beauvoir's work, but it is also frequently referenced by Sartre in "Revolutionary Violence" (from *Notebooks for an Ethics*), where he offers an analysis of oppression, racism, and slavery in the United States. While Simons thinks that Wright probably introduced Beauvoir to Myrdal's work, biographer Deirdre Bair points out that Beauvoir received a copy of the text from Nelson Algren in 1947. It is likely that Sartre had access to this text (along with *What the Negro Wants* edited by Rayford Logan, which Sartre also references) through Beauvoir.[32]

Concerning Richard Wright, Simons reveals that "Wright's influence on Simone de Beauvoir's philosophy, [consisted of] . . . providing her with a theory of racial oppression and liberation that she utilized as a model in constructing the theoretical foundations for radical feminism in *The Second Sex*."[33] Simons later adds, "Wright, as the intellectual heir of W. E. B. Du Bois, introduces Beauvoir to the concept of the 'double-consciousness' of blacks under racism, which serves as a model for Beauvoir's concept of woman as the Other in *The Second Sex*. Wright's phenomenological descriptions of black experience of oppression provide a methodological alternative to both Myrdal's objectifying social science methodology and the economic reductionism of Marxist orthodoxy."[34] But Simons is also clear about the shortcomings of the race/gender analogy and explains that "separating racism and sexism as distinct, though analogous, categories can be problematic, denying the experience of African American women, for instance, for whom the effects of racism and sexism are often inseparable."[35]

What I appreciate most about Simons' analysis is her thorough research, clear arguments, and emphasis on Wright's philosophical contributions and impact. She indicates that "Wright's philosophical influence on Beauvoir's theory of oppression is in their shared concept of the oppressed Other, and their focus on the importance of social relations and recognition in the formation of the self."[36] And she adds, "The second area of Wright's philosophical influence on Beauvoir is a subjectivist, phenomenological approach to the study of oppression . . . describing the lived experience of American racism from the standpoint of the oppressed. Wright provided a phenomenology of racial oppression to challenge the claims by segregationists that blacks are happy and contented with their naturally inferior place in society, much as Beauvoir, in the second volume of *The Second Sex* (entitled *Lived Experience*), relies on a phenomenological description of women's experience to challenge the oppressive stereotypes of popular myths and Freaudian psychology."[37]

We need not depend on Simons' examination of Wright and Beauvoir to see Wright's impact on her work. Beauvoir, who had read much of Wright's literature, would make multiple references to Wright in *The Second Sex*. For example, comparing the plight of the American Negro with the plight facing (white) women, Beauvoir cites Wright at the end of the second book of *The Second Sex*: "In *Black Boy* Richard Wright has shown how the ambitions of a young American Negro are blocked from the start and what a struggle he had merely to be posed for whites. Negroes coming to France from Africa also find difficulties—with themselves as well as around them—similar to those confronting women."[38] Here Beauvoir is not only comparing the ways in which the ambitions of black (men) and (white) women are discouraged and/or denied, but she is also bringing our attention to the internal struggles within oppressed groups including women and Africans in France.

Another race/gender comparison is made earlier in her analysis when Beauvoir cites Wright again and explains:

> It is a strange experience for an individual who feels himself to be an autonomous and transcendent subject, an absolute, to discover inferiority in himself as a fixed and preordained essence: it is a strange experience for whoever regards himself as the One to be revealed to himself as otherness, alterity. . . . This situation is not unique. The American Negroes know it, being partially integrated in a civilization that nevertheless regards them as constituting an inferior caste; what Bigger Thomas, in Richard Wright's *Native Son,* feels with bitterness at the dawn of his life is this definitive inferiority, this accursed alterity, which is written in the color of his skin: he sees airplanes flying by and he knows that because he is black the sky is forbidden to him. Because she is a woman, the little girl knows that she is forbidden the sea and the polar regions, a thousand adventures, a thousand joys: she was born on the wrong side of the line. There is a great difference: the Negroes submit with a feeling of revolt, no privileges compensating for their hard lot, whereas woman is offered inducements to complicity.[39]

What is significant about this analysis is not just the comparison Beauvoir makes between the Negro (man) and the (white) woman, but also the fact that she highlights "a great difference," namely, the privilege and complicity of (white) women. With this note, Beauvoir anticipates criticisms of white feminism and white female privilege by later black feminists such as Audre Lorde, who declares that "the master's tools will never dismantle the master's house. . . . And this fact is only threatening to those women who still define the master's house as their only source of support. . . . The failure of academic feminists to recognize difference as a crucial strength is a failure to reach beyond the first patriarchal lesson."[40] Unfortunately, while Beauvoir and Sartre do recognize problems of white privilege, neither of them explicitly engages black women intellectuals or a black feminist analysis in the texts here discussed. Consequently, their usage of the race/gender analogy results in the erasure of black women who experience both racial and gender oppression.

Sartre and Beauvoir (along with Wright, and even Myrdal) would have been able to offer a richer analysis of racial and gender oppression if they had taken black feminist theory into account. Rather than framing racial oppression as exclusively male or gender oppression as primarily white, a black feminist analysis would have introduced the drawbacks and advantages of race and gender intersectionality into their philosophical frameworks. Thus, a black feminist analysis would have provided a space for black women (and other women of color) alongside the black men and white women situated within these frameworks.

Black Feminism and Intersectionality

Lacking from Sartre's and Beauvoir's accounts here are two among many of the staple issues that black feminism has addressed from its inception, namely, the ways in which black women are, in the words of Anna Julia Cooper, "confronted by both a woman question and a race problem, and [are] as yet an unknown or unacknowledged factor of both."[41] Cooper's collection of essays and speeches in *A Voice from the South by a Black Woman of the South*, published in 1892, has been identified as the first book-length black feminist text.[42] It transcends the limitations of the race/gender analogy previously outlined. Like other black feminist scholarship spanning from the nineteenth and into the twenty-first century, Cooper is quite critical of the *sexism* of black and white men as well as the *racism* of white men and women.

Analyzing, confronting, and overcoming these dual-operating systems of oppression are important, even central, to a black feminist project. And while the multifaceted oppression against black women is often analyzed as a hindrance, it is less frequently studied from the perspective of the peculiar position in which it places us, giving us a particular standpoint from which we can observe, judge, and experience the world. Standpoint theory or standpoint epistemology has gained popularity among contemporary feminist theorists, but Cooper asserted over a century ago that woman's experience, particularly black woman's experience, places her in a unique position to have a distinctive voice, influence, and contribution to make to the race, to America, and to the world at large. Given Cooper's emphasis on the importance of her own voice and black women's voices, I quote her at length in the following section in an attempt to honor and accurately represent this voice.

Cooper introduces *Voice* with the short but powerful opening statement "Our Raison d'Être" where she explains that while the voice of the Negro (man) of the South has been but a muffled chord, "the one mute and voiceless note has been the sadly expectant Black woman."[43] Using the analogy of a courtroom trial about "the race problem," Cooper explains that the plaintiff's and defendant's attorneys: "have analyzed and dissected, theorized and synthesized with sublime ignorance or pathetic misapprehension of counsel from the black client. One important witness has not yet been heard from. The summing up of evidence deposed, and the charge to the jury have been made—but no word from the Black Woman."[44] Cooper underscores how the black (male) client, the muffled voice, has at least been consulted, even if only with "ignorance" and "misapprehension." But the "one important witness," that is, the "Black Woman," has been rendered mute or voiceless. She asserts that the white man cannot speak for black men's experiences and furthermore that black men cannot speak in place of black women.[45] In "Womanhood: A Vital Element in the Regeneration and Progress of a Race" (1886), Cooper made the now famous declaration, "Only the BLACK WOMAN can say 'when and where I enter, in the quiet, undisputed dignity of my womanhood, without violence and without suing or special patronage, then and there the whole *Negro race enters with me.*' "[46]

Critiquing the gender politics of black men, Cooper states, "As far as my experience goes the average man of our race is less frequently ready to admit the actual need among the sturdier forces of the world for women's help or influence."[47] The point here is that black men were not sufficiently supportive of the struggles of black women, and furthermore, black men did not acknowledge the numerous contributions that black women made toward the progress of the race. And in "The Higher Education of Women" (1890–1891) Cooper admits, "It seems hardly a gracious thing to say, but it strikes me as true, that while our men seem thoroughly abreast of the times in almost every other subject, when they strike the woman question they drop back into sixteenth century logic."[48] Cooper is claiming that while black men were aware of issues such as racial uplift, they largely ignored the problems specific to black women, that is, the other "half" of the race that they were supposedly uplifting.

Just as she is critical of black men for their sexism, Cooper is equally critical of white women's racism, particularly the racism expressed by white women's organizations that claimed to be tackling the oppression of *all* women. She challenges the tendency in the (white) woman's movement to fight for (white) women's rights at the expense of, or instead of, others' rights. Taking a strong stand against all forms of oppression in "Woman Versus the Indian" (1891–1892) she declares: "Woman should not even by inference, or for the sake of argument, seem to disparage what is weak. For woman's cause is the cause of the weak; and when all the weak shall have received their due consideration, then woman will have her 'rights,' and the Indian will have his rights, and the Negro will have his rights, and all the strong will have learned at last to deal justly, to love mercy, and to walk humbly.[49] It is noteworthy that Cooper rejects exclusionary reasoning (by inference or by argument) stating, "All prejudices, whether of race, sect, or sex, class pride, and caste distinctions are the belittling inheritance and badge of snobs and prigs."[50] Cooper's disdain for such thinking is thoroughly communicated. She adds, "The *philosophic* mind sees that its own 'rights' are the rights of humanity."[51] Cooper is denouncing oppression against all persons, "The white woman does not need to sue the Indian, or the Negro, or any other race or class who have been crushed under the iron heel of Anglo Saxon power and selfishness."[52] For Cooper, it is necessary to reject and speak out against various forms of oppression. She petitions: "It is not the intelligent woman versus the ignorant woman; nor the white woman versus the black, the brown, and the red—it is not even the cause of woman versus man . . . [W]oman's strongest vindication for speaking is that the world needs to hear her voice . . . when race, color, sex, condition, are realized to be *accidents*, not the substance of life . . . then woman's lesson is taught and woman's lesson is won—not the white woman not the black woman nor the red woman, but the cause of every man or woman who has writhed silently under a mighty wrong."[53] She pleads the cause of every man and woman who is wronged, rejecting oppression against the ignorant, various races, and women.

Cooper's intellectual legacy is shared by other nineteenth- and early twentieth-century black women thinkers and activists such as Maria W. Stewart, frequently cited as the first black woman to speak publicly about women's issues, or more specifically, black women's issues in the United States; Sojourner Truth, abolitionist and women's rights advocate; Ida B. Wells-Barnett, crusader against lynching (even while being harshly criticized by black men for being too much on the front lines), who offered insights into the political, racial, and gendered implications of lynching in America; and Mary Church Terrell, founder and president of the National Association of Colored Women who often emphasized the strides made by black women in difficult circumstances—to name a few.

Almost a century would pass before the crux of Cooper's analysis; specifically, a theoretically nuanced articulation of black women's intersectionality would be taken up again and be more fully developed in transformational book-length texts. Beverly Guy-Sheftall notes that 1970 marked a reemergence of (manuscript-length) black feminist writings with the publication of Toni Cade Bambara's *Black Woman: An Anthology*, Shirley Chisolm's *Unbought and Unbossed*, and Toni Morrison's *Bluest Eye*.[54] The foundation that Cooper and others laid would continue to be built upon by classic black feminist texts, including anthologies such as *All of the Women Are White, All of the Blacks Are Men, But Some of Us Are Brave: Black Women's Studies* (1982) edited by Gloria Hull, Patricia Bell Scott, and Barbara Smith, as well as Guy-Sheftall's collection of black women's scholarship that spans over one and a half centuries *Words of Fire: An Anthology of African American Feminist Thought* (1995).

Some of the seminal single-authored black feminist texts include bell hooks' *Ain't I a Woman: Black Women and Feminism* (1981) and *Feminist Theory from Margin to Center* (1984); Angela Davis' *Woman, Race, and Class* (1983); Alice Walker's *In Search of Our Mother's Gardens* (1983); Audre Lorde's *Sister Outsider:*

Essays and Speeches by Audre Lorde (1984); Paula Giddings' *When and Where I Enter: The Impact of Black Women on Race and Sex in America* (1984); Hazel Carby's *Reconstruction Womanhood: The Emergence of the Afro-American Woman Novelist* (1987); and Patricia Hill Collins' *Black Feminist Thought: Knowledge, Consciousness, and the Politics of Empowerment* (1990). All of these texts and many others that have been published in the last twenty years offer insights and resources that should be drawn upon in the expansion of the philosophy canon and the development of a black feminist philosophy. Black feminism in general, and the development of black feminist philosophy in particular, would help to foster a more inclusive and pluralistic continental philosophy.

Conclusion: Toward a Black Feminist Philosophy

It is clear that black male intellectuals have been influential in the development of what we now call the "continental philosophy" tradition, for example, in the cases of Sartre and Beauvoir outlined in this chapter. It is also the case that other philosophy traditions including African American/Africana philosophy and the critical philosophy of race have made hedge way in expanding the philosophy canon by emphasizing the philosophical insights of black male intellectuals whether or not these intellectuals' academic training have been in philosophy. In 1903 Thomas Nelson Baker[55] became the first African American to earn a Ph.D. in philosophy (Yale University), and in 1918 Alain Locke earned a Ph.D. in philosophy (Harvard University). But examples of frequently cited philosophical thinkers who did not earn doctorates in philosophy include Frederick Douglass, Alexander Crummell, Martin Delaney, Edward Blyden, W. E. B. Du Bois, Richard Wright, Ralph Ellison, Frantz Fanon, and C. L. R. James. Including these thinkers in the philosophy canon shows that we are slowly (and at times reluctantly) making strides in this discipline that are vitally important for its survival and progress.

The first African American woman to earn a Ph.D. in philosophy was Joyce Mitchell Cook (Yale University).[56] But black women philosophers and other black women intellectuals with philosophical insights have not yet been fully embraced and brought into the philosophy canon, continental or analytic, like their black male intellectual counterparts. Like African American philosophy and the critical philosophy of race, the development of a black feminist philosophy can draw from several sources both within and beyond traditional disciplinary boundaries of philosophy. Anna Julia Cooper is slowly being brought into the canon through the work of philosophers such as Joy James, Kathryn Gines, Anika Mann, Lewis Gordon, and Ronald Sundstrom. Contemporary black feminists such as Audre Lorde, bell hooks, and Patricia Hill Collins are also gradually trickling in. Furthermore, as the numbers of black women and others entering the discipline of philosophy (and interested in contributing to building black feminist philosophy) begin to write and publish in this area, progress will continue to be made. It is hoped that this chapter along with the others collected in this anthology turn this trickling of progress into a flood.

Notes

1. A few of the black women philosophers who have worked on black feminism that I have in mind here are more senior philosophers such as Angela Davis (*Women, Race, and Class*) and Joy James (*Transcending the Talented Tenth*) along with recently emerging philosophers such as Donna Marcano, Anika Mann, and Kathryn Gines, each of whom is a contributor to this anthology. Editors James A. Montmarquet and William Hardy published *Reflections: An Anthology of African American Philosophy* (California: Wadsworth, 2000) with the section "Feminism, Womanism, and Gender Relations." Tommy Lott's anthology *African American Philosophy: Selected Readings* (New Jersey: Prentice Hall, 2002), features an essay by Anna Julia Cooper under the heading "Assimilation and Social Uplift" and one from Angela Davis under the heading "Rebellion and Radical Thought." The section "Contemporary Black Feminist Thought" includes essays from Patricia Hill Collins, bell hooks, Kimberlé Crenshaw, and Audre Lorde. Additionally, Lott includes a section titled "Black Women Writers on Rape," with contributions from Ida B. Wells-Barnett, Alice Walker, Valerie Smith, and Joy James. Lewis Gordon's *Introduction to Africana Philosophy* (Cambridge: Cambridge University Press, 2008) includes the section "Anna Julia Cooper and the Problem of Value" in the chapter "Three Pillars of African-American Philosophy." He also includes the section "Black Feminist and Womanist Thought" in the chapter "Africana Philosophical Movement in the United States and Britain." Also, Maria del Guadalupe Davidson (trained in rhetoric) and George Yancy have edited a forthcoming collection of essays that offers philosophical readings of bell hooks' scholarship.

2. Beverly Guy-Sheftall, *Words of Fire: An Anthology of African American Feminist Thought* (New York: New, 1995), 4. For a digital image of the "Roll of Honor," see the American Treasures of the Library of Congress online at http://www.loc.gov/exhibits/treasures/images/vc006195.jpg. Also available is a digital image of an article published on the convention in the *North Star* at http://www.loc.gov/exhibits/treasures/images/vc006197.jpg.

3. Guy-Sheftall, *Words of Fire*, 4.

4. Angela Davis, *Women, Race, and Class* (New York: Vintage Books, 1981), 111.

5. Ibid., 111. Davis later asks, "How could Susan B. Anthony claim to believe in human rights and political equality and at the same time counsel the members of her organization to remain silent on the issue of racism?" (121).

6. *Crusade for Justice: The Auto-Biography of Ida B. Wells*, ed. Alfreda M. Duster (Chicago: University of Chicago Press, 1970). *Up from the Pedestal: Selected Writings in the History of American Feminism*, ed. Aileen Kraditor (Chicago: Quadrangle, 1968).

7. Both speeches are available in *Traps: African American Men on Gender and Sexuality,* ed. Rudolph Bird and Beverly Guy-Sheftall (Indiana: Indiana University Press, 2001). Douglass had already been a major advocate of women's rights decades prior to giving these addresses where he goes beyond the issue of political rights and asserts that women have both the ability and the agency to articulate their own cause, their problems, and the best way for those problems to be remedied. Furthermore, Douglass expresses the need for black men to shut up and take a back seat on these points because women are the most qualified to address women's issues. By this Douglass is not asserting that men should not be involved in providing any assistance they can in women's progress, rather, he is arguing that men are not to determine *what* women's issues are and *how* they are to be addressed. The white woman's suffrage movement becomes more silent about racism and violence against blacks in the 1890s at the very moment when such violence is escalating.

8. For more on the controversy see Neil Painter's "Sojourner Truth in Life and Memory: Writing the Biography of an American Exotic," in *Gender and History* 2 (1990): 3–19. See also Painter's full biography of Truth, *Sojourner Truth: A Life, a Symbol* (New York: Norton, 1997).

9. Sojourner Truth, "When Woman Gets Her Rights Man Will Be Right," in *Words of Fire*, 37.

10. See Gloria Steinem, "Women Are Never Front-Runners," *New York Times*, January 8, 2008.

11. In fact, a comparison of racial and gender oppression, or more specifically an examination of how the two forms of oppression reinforce one another is very productive. A recent example of the insights that come from seeing racism and sexism as reinforcing one another is provided in *Contract and Domination* by Carole Pateman and Charles Mills (New York: Polity, 2007).

12. Jean-Paul Sartre, *No Exit and Three Other Plays* (New York: Vintage International, 1989), 244.

13. See David Aretha, *The Trial of the Scottsboro Boys* (Greensboro, NC: Reynolds, 2007), and Dan Carter, *Scottsboro: A Tragedy of the American South* (Baton Rouge: Louisiana State University Press, 1979).

14. James Sellman, "Scottsboro Case," in *Africana: The Encyclopedia of the African and African American Experience*, ed. Anthony Appiah and Henry Louis Gates, Jr. (New York: Basic Civitas Books, 1999).

15. Darlene Clark Hine, *The African American Odyssey* (New Jersey: Pearson Prentice Hall, 2006), 479.

16. *Art and Action, Tenth Anniversary Issue, Twice a Year-1938–1948, A Book of Literature, the Arts, and Civil Liberties* (New York: Twice a Year Press, 1948), 34.

17. Ibid., 58.

18. Ibid., 61.

19. Ibid., 48.

20. Ibid., 64.

21. Ibid., 17.

22. Ibid.

23. See Michele Fabre, "Reactions to the Script of *La Putain Respectuese*," in *Richard Wright: Books and Writers* (Jackson and London: University Press of Mississippi, 1990), 238.

24. Ibid., 238.

25. Ibid., 239.

26. Kenneth Kinnamon and Michele Fabre, *Conversations with Richard Wright* (Jackson and London: University Press of Mississippi, 1993), 119.

27. *Art and Action*, 14.

28. Kate Fullbrook and Edward Fullbrook, *Simone de Beauvoir and Jean-Paul Sartre: The Remaking of a Twentieth Century Legend* (New York: Basic Books, Harper-Collins, 1994), 3.

29. Margaret Simons, *Beauvoir and the Second Sex: Feminism, Race, and the Origins of Existentialism* (New York: Rowman and Littlefield, 1999), 2.

30. Ibid., xiv.

31. Ibid., 171.

32. Deirdre Bair, *Simone de Beauvoir: A Biography* (New York: Summit Books, 1990), 364, 368.

33. Simons, *Beauvoir and the Second Sex*, 168.

34. Ibid., 176.

35. Ibid., 170.

36. Ibid., 176–77.

37. Ibid., 178.

38. Simone de Beauvoir, *The Second Sex* (New York: Vintage Books, 1989), 698. Originally published in France by Librarie Gallimard in two volumes, *Le Deuxieme Sexe: I. Les Faits et Les Mythes, II. L'Expe'rience Ve'cue*, 1949.

39. Ibid., 298. The notion that the girl is born on the "wrong side of the line" echoes Du Bois' analysis of the color line.

40. Audre Lorde, "The Master's Tools Will Never Dismantle the Master's House," in *Sister Outsider: Essays and Speeches by Audre Lorde*, (Freedom, CA: Crossing, 1984), 112. Lorde quotes Beauvoir in another part of this essay on page 113. Also see bell hooks, *Ain't I a Woman: Black Women and Feminism* (Boston: South End, 1981), and Aida Hurtado, *The Color of Privilege: Three Blasphemies on Race and Feminism* (Ann Arbor: University of Michigan Press, 1996).

41. Anna Julia Cooper, "The Status of Women in America," in *A Voice from the South* (1892), reprinted and ed. Charles Lamert and Esme Bhan, *The Voice of Anna Julia Cooper* (Lanham, MD: Rowman and Littlefield, 1998), 112–13.

42. Guy-Sheftall, *Words of Fire*, 43. For an excellent critical engagement with Cooper's scholarship (including *A Voice from the South* and other writings), see Vivian M. May, *Anna Julia Cooper, Visionary Black Feminist: A Critical Introduction* (2007). See also a review of May's book by Kathryn T. Gines in *SIGNS* 34, no. 2 (2008).

43. Anna Julia Cooper, "Raison d'Etre," in *A Voice from the South* (1892), reprinted by eds. Charles Lamert and Esme Bhan, *The Voice of Anna Julia Cooper* (Lanham, MD: Rowman and Littlefield, 1998), 51.

44. Ibid., 51.

45. Anna Julia Cooper, "The Status of Women in America," in *A Voice from the South* (1892), reprinted and ed. Charles Lamert and Esme Bhan, *The Voice of Anna Julia Cooper* (Lanham, MD: Rowman and Littlefield, 1998), 112.

46. Anna Julia Cooper, "Womanhood: A Vital Element in the Regeneration and Progress of the Race," in *A Voice from the South* (1892), reprinted and ed. Charles

Lamert and Esme Bhan, *The Voice of Anna Julia Cooper* (Lanham, MD: Rowman and Littlefield, 1998), 63; emphasis in original.

47. Cooper, "The Status of Women in America," 113.

48. Anna Julia Cooper, "The Higher Education of Women," in *A Voice from the South* (1892), reprinted and ed. Charles Lamert and Esme Bhan, *The Voice of Anna Julia Cooper* (Lanham, MD: Rowman and Littlefield, 1998), 85.

49. Anna Julia Cooper, "Woman versus the Indian," in *A Voice from the South* (1892), reprinted and ed. Charles Lamert and Esme Bhan, *The Voice of Anna Julia Cooper* (Lanham, MD: Rowman and Littlefield, 1998), p 105. Cooper is responding in part to an essay by Ann Shaw with the same title. Shaw's essay, as the title suggests, places the issue of women's rights against the rights of American Indians.

50. Cooper, "Woman versus the Indian," 105.

51. Ibid.; my emphasis. This is not an abstract humanism because Cooper has already demonstrated her insight into the way men and women and blacks and whites (and Indians) experience oppression differently.

52. Cooper, "Woman versus the Indian," 108.

53. Ibid.; my emphasis.

54. Guy-Sheftall, *Words of Fire*, 14.

55. For an essay on Baker's life and philosophy, see George Yancy, "On the Power of Black Aesthetic Ideals: Thomas Nelson Baker as Teacher and Philosopher," in *A.M.E. Church Review* (October–December 2001).

56. On the life and philosophy of Cook, in her own words, see "Joyce Mitchell Cook," in George Yancy's *African American Philosophers, 17 Conversations* (New York: Routledge, 1998).

3

The Difference That Difference Makes

Black Feminism and Philosophy

Donna-Dale L. Marcano

Introduction to the Problem of Being Black, Woman, and Philosopher

To ask after the existence of black feminist philosophy is to ask after the tools, resources, and skills attached to the characteristics specific to the discipline of philosophy. The question of whether or not there is room in philosophy for a subtopic and experience so particular as a black feminist philosophy also returns us to the question, What is philosophy? This latter question remains a battleground for feminist philosophers and philosophers of race. The fact is that we are still required to argue that philosophy of race and feminist philosophy are philosophically significant in the sense that it locates the specific social and historical context of race or gender within the larger, fundamental questions of philosophy. What is even more interesting to consider is that the question of what constitutes philosophy and the answers given have been and continue to be given by white, male philosophers. We are certainly in a moment in time where the discipline of philosophy has had to expand its understanding of what counts as philosophy due to increased presence of individuals other than white men. This movement both expands and breaks down the boundaries of philosophy such that specificity and particularity can be included in its discourses. Yet we can still ask after the extent to which some particularities are so particular that philosophy resists its presence. Or we may still need to contemplate whether philosophy remains so unequivocally detached from particularities that anything like a black feminist philosophy is unable to indulgently use its tools, skills, or resources. While it is not my intention here to redefine philosophy such that students of philosophy, in whatever shape they take, will and can recognize the connections of particular lived experiences with philosophy qua philosophy, the goal of this chapter is to understand what it might mean to have a black feminist philosophy, that is, a creation of black feminist thought that is consciously tied both to black women and to the traditions of philosophy, including feminist philosophy.

Of course, black feminist thought exists, and black women, in academia as well as within political activism, have sought to promote past and contemporary black female writers, activists, and thinkers in order to explore and illuminate the experiences of black women in their attempt to address their place in a sexist, racist, classist society. This suggests that there is no shortage of black feminist thought or analyses. They are out there, and they sometimes use philosophy. But black feminist thought or attempts to figure out what that might mean have primarily occurred in other disciplines, such as sociology, English, literature, history, and even law. The discipline of philosophy itself has not seemed to open up the necessary space in which theoretical frameworks for black feminist thought can develop. As a philosopher, the contribution of other disciplines to theorizing black women's experiences really struck me. It forced me to consider my role and place in philosophy as a philosopher and as a black woman.

This is an especially interesting task for someone, like me, who takes herself to be working within the "continental" tradition. Continental philosophy's unabashed and thorough link to Germany and France and thus to Europe and whiteness, even in its feminist locutions, makes a philosopher interested in theorizing the experiences of being black and woman hard-pressed to find suitable resources with which to philosophize. The tension, here, is really one between philosophy as a discipline, which attempts to address the "human" condition, and the potential of a particular kind of theorizing we might call "black feminist philosophy," which locates its source in the experience of a not-yet-universalizable subjectivity. In order to find writers who theorize the concerns of black women, one must work outside the tradition. However, women who do this find themselves displaced into categories other than philosophy. In contrast, merely using the resources of philosophy, including feminist philosophy, leads to the systematic and continued privileging of white philosophers as a source of philosophizing. This leaves black feminist thought so particular that it exists outside the realm of philosophy or so universally white and male that one's work remains parasitic on the tradition without creating something new.

Today, I would like to share two fundamental challenges to developing black feminist philosophy in the hopes that in articulating these challenges we philosophers can be more attentive to philosophy's silent exclusions, that is, to the way philosophy and philosophizing inhibits and discourages the presence and voices of black women. First, I will discuss the challenge of the social construction thesis to the possibility of theorizing black women's experience as black. Second, I will discuss the challenges to the use of the analytic tool of "difference" in articulating black women's thought and experience as theorizable.

The Social Construction Thesis

According to Ian Hacking, the social construction thesis has a primary premise: "X need not have existed or need not be at all as it is. X, or X as it is at present, is not determined by the nature of things; it is not inevitable."[1]

The social construction thesis is a critical thesis that challenges an assumed given or natural reality. To say that an object or concept is socially constructed is to argue it is neither inevitable nor necessary but rather contingent. In this way, establishing a concept or object as socially constructed is a rejection of naturalization and most important the concomitant effect of essentialism.

The problem of essentialism in the social/political realm is two-fold: (1) that others outside of Group X codify attributes of members of the group in such a way that one is forced to be both a member X of the group X and a member in a particular way; and, (2) member X is forced by others within group X to express group identity in a particular way. If we recognize that characteristics, behaviors, and tendencies of a group, and most important as individuals are constructed through social, though normalizing, concepts or forces, then we can disengage individual identity from notions of an essential nature ascribed to whole segments of the population. Additionally, we are ultimately forced to reconsider the basic premise of a unified collective.

In the contemporary discourses of gender and race, both reject essentialism and the natural reality that underwrites it. Both aim to liberate individuals as well as groups historically deemed as marginal and other from effects of oppressive ideologies prevalent in society; both aim to liberate individuals as members within a group from their own oppressive and exclusive tendencies, what Anthony Appiah has called "identity imperialism." A significant effect of social construction discourses is that these discourses question and destabilize the notions of sexual and racial identities even as they show the constituted nature of those identities.

I argue that despite the framing of the discourse of social construction as a revolutionary and liberatory discourse that disrupts the relationship between biology and gender or biology and race, the social construction thesis as a strategy in the discourses on race and gender have contrary effects. Or maybe a better way of saying this is that the conclusions of these discussions have led to fundamentally different understandings of what is liberatory. Both discourses entail the political promise of overcoming oppressive hegemonies whose supports have required exclusion, violence, and domination. However, I would argue that while the feminisms that have engaged the social construction thesis have yielded (despite problems) an opportunity for gender complexity, the strategy of social construction of race as it has been taken up in philosophy, other academic disciplines, as well as in the common culture has instead yielded a turn to nonreality or an eliminativist tendency.

I am proposing that the strategy of the social construction thesis has yielded two different effects, which I will call "the effect of expansion" implicated in the discourse on the social construction of sex and "the effect of poverty" implicated in the discourse on the social construction of race.

One can argue that the application of the social construction thesis to two different objects or "things" would reasonably lead to two different effects. That the social construction thesis is applied to two different things and thus *could* have different effects seems true. However, we should not be too quick to assume that because there are two different things—sex and race—then it *should* lead to two different effects. We should ask ourselves, rather, why it should lead to different effects or, from another approach, what motivates these distinct outcomes. I take seriously, as Judith Butler has warned, that race and gender ought not to be treated as simple analogies. Nonetheless, I believe it fruitful to look at the operation of these discourses inasmuch as they have strategic links.

What I mean by an effect of expansion as it relates to feminist discourse is that such a discourse leads or intends to lead the reader to a more complex model of the category of woman or the concept of sex or gender. In the disruption of the unified nature of sex, gender, or woman, the reader is expected to understand the exclusions necessary for the wholesale determination and formation of the category or concept. The result is that the discourse produces more thought concerning these categories and concepts as they become fecund with possibilities for various manifestations of what it means to be sexed, gendered, or woman. The ambiguities illuminated and the exclusions revealed force inclusion and the expansion of the boundaries of the given even as the category is destabilized. We can even say that the role of ambiguity and disruption results in the production of more complex reality.

The discourse on the social construction of race, however, much of it generated in the analytic tradition, effects a discourse of poverty where the same strategies of disruption and ambiguity result in impotence, conceptual barrenness, or a paucity of options. We can say similarly to gender that such a discourse aims to complicate our notions of race, or what it means to be a particular race, as well as show the exclusion necessary for the wholesale determination and formation of the unified categories of race. However, the discourse has not left us with a description of a complex reality but rather has led quite directly to the insistence upon nonreality. As such, ambiguities, revelations of exclusions, and the disruption of race have led to the nonreality of race where ambiguity of sex or gender leads to a complex reality that must be confronted.

In fact one can say that the leading literature on the social construction of race leads the reader to accept the complexity of race only to do away with it. One is left with only one mantra, one conclusion: race does not exist. And while this is an undoubtedly complicated conclusion in itself, one is left merely to do battle within the metaphysical realm over exactly what reality or realities there are. If fighting metaphysical battles is unappealing, one is pushed back into the subjective realm.

I want to suggest that the different discourses of race and sex/gender in fact have different phenomenological impacts insofar as each makes different claims upon the lived experience of individuals. While feminism's concern is to denaturalize the body, sex, and gender in response to sexism, its goals revolve around liberation as enabling a variety of sex and gender expressions. In this way, the feminism I have discussed here forces self-examination; I must think about the preconceptions I hold and perform that limit possibilities for my own and others' sexual and gender expression. However, when we turn to race, what is seen as liberatory has most often included a rejection of racial categories, racial expression, and racial identities, especially for those historically raced. Even as theorists Naomi Zack and Anthony Appiah acknowledge the social presence and impact of racial categories and identities, they also envision a postracial future, one in which the burden of racial identities is displaced in favor of a subject position closer to the "view from nowhere" or from "everywhere"—a view they believe will transcend difference for a vision of a race-less humanity.

Now, given this rather reductive and simplistic narrative of the two discourses in which one appears positive and the other a negation of sorts, I would like to complicate this story for you. Sources in continental feminist philosophy have been tied to the men of the tradition. Feminist philosophers were able to return to texts written by canonical figures and find themselves even in the awkward absences. By virtue of race, black women do not even exist, not even in the silences of our most revered texts in which white women have been able to find themselves. In philosophy of race, theorists (mostly men) returned to texts of canonical figures to address the problem of race as one that has already existed as a philosophical problem. It would seem, then, that the cross-pollination of these discourses could and should include black women and the possibility of black feminist philosophy. Plainly said, that is not the case.

The most radical social constructionists of the feminist philosophical canon, feminist philosophers such as Monique Wittig, Collette Guillamin, and Judith Butler to name a few, aim to challenge and deconstruct the 'givenness" of the concept of 'sex' and the category of "woman" in such a way that "recognizes multiplicity, indeterminancy, and heterogeneity of cultural meaning and meaning production. They criticize gender as a fixed, binary structuring of reality and replace it with an ideal of ceaseless textual play."[2] Initially, these critical feminist theories were developed in order to avoid the ethnocentrism, unconscious racial biases, and heterosexism within the feminist movement and regarding the category of woman. Thus, any generalizations regarding gender are critiqued as a priori essentialist. Claiming sexual difference, or racial difference for that matter, by those oppressed becomes problematic because the maintenance of group difference not only reinstitutes binary constructions of reality but also reinstitutes hierarchy and oppression which are based on the very use of the concept of 'difference' as a tool for oppressive and hierarchical society.

Thus, while the discourse of social construction leads to an expansion of sex and gender expressions, it does so while destabilizing all collective experience. Difference becomes heterogeneity as absolutely fluid and individual. This tendency toward what Susan Bordo describes as a postmodernist gender skepticism leaves little room for attempting to articulating or theorizing from a collective voice regarding black women's voices within philosophy as black and as women, more specifically as black women. As Bordo argues this postmodern gender skepticism neglects that "while in theory totalizing narratives may be equal in the context of Western history and of the actual relations of power characteristic of that history, key differences distinguish the universalizations of gender theory from the meta-narratives arising out of the propertied, white, male, Western intellectual tradition. We must remember that that tradition reigned for thousands of years and was able to produce powerful works of philosophy, literature, art and religion before its hegemony began to be dismantled."[3] Alongside a discourse of race that accepts race as an illusion, that race does not exist, the postmodernist deconstruction of gender in "current academic feminist philosophy ultimately neglects concerns regarding professional and institutional mechanisms through which the politics of exclusion operate most powerfully."[4] In other words, these discourses lend themselves to the continued marginalization of black women and black feminist thought, for neither black nor women exist or can be theorized. But this is not the only problem facing a philosopher attempting to think through black feminist thought.

The Invasion of Philosophy on Black Women's Theorizing

One can count many reasons for philosophy's failure to contribute people and theories to black feminist thought—what is a large body of thought. First, of course, is that few black women have opted for graduate degrees in philosophy. Let me be clear, that is not to say there aren't any. I too was under the illusion that black women with philosophy degrees could be counted on one hand. I have since realized that black women in philosophy have given up their connection to the academic and social spaces of philosophers. They are out there, publishing, teaching, lecturing, but in other, more welcoming spaces. Which leads us to a second reason: philosophy remains downright hostile to the presence of black women in its ranks. Thus, consequently, philosophy remains downright hostile to black women's thought, especially if these women think about the historical and social conditions of black women. Fourth, while black female theorists use philosophers, philosophical tools, and vocabulary, they nonetheless find that philosophy exhibits an entrenched abstractness that fails to acknowledge, recognize, include, or capture the lives and concerns of black women. In this section, I would like to discuss a critique of philosophy and thus theory from a black woman literary critic, Barbara Christian.

In an essay entitled "Race for Theory," Christian openly resents the influence of philosophy on literary theory. This particular essay articulates the problem a black feminist philosopher must confront—one who understands herself to be working within the tradition of philosophy and wants to work within that tradition to create, think, and write about black women as raced, as women, as human beings.

Christian, herself at one time interested in philosophy, admits she "raced" from what she calls the "metaphysical language" of philosophy to literature, "since the latter seemed to me to have the possibilities of rendering the world as large and as complicated as I experienced it, as sensual as I knew it was. In literature I sensed the possibility of the integration of feeling/knowledge, rather than the split between the abstract and the emotion in which Western philosophy inevitably indulged."[5] Whatever one might think of Christian's characterization of philosophy or her needs, it is clear that philosophy itself is not alien to black women, that black women do find their interests there, but that nonetheless philosophy seems to fail in its capacity to express the complex nature of their lives.

What is more important to this chapter is Christian's concern that philosophers, dare I say—those giants of continental philosophy—have infiltrated and influenced literary theory such that they, those she calls the "New Philosophers," "eager to understand a world that is today fast escaping their political control, have redefined literature so that the distinctions implied by that term, that is, the distinctions between everything written and those things written to evoke feeling as well as to express thought, have been blurred. They have changed literary critical language to suit their own purposes as philosophers, and they have reinvented the meaning of theory."[6] Christian describes this reinvention of the meaning of theory as the "race for theory," which has subordinated and diminished the relationship of critic as writer—poet, novelist, or playwright. In effect, philosophy has taken over the literary world, and in doing so, the primary goal is to create theory. The price paid in this race for theory is the coercion of "potentially radical critics, those black, women, and third world into speaking a language and defining their discussion in terms alien to and opposed to our needs."[7] Since theorizing in historically oppressed communities of color occurs through a variety of means, including narrative, riddles, stories, language play, theorizing is more dynamic than fixed. The emphasis on theory also places an emphasis on a fixed constellation of ideas, which Christian argues is often manifested as linguistic jargon, "biblical" exegesis, preoccupations with mechanical analyses of language, and gross cultural generalizations.[8] For Christian, the new theoretical emphasis arises from the power of the reigning academic elite who produce the terms, definitions, and language that ultimately relegates the types of theorizing done in black writings as "minority discourse"—a term that casts some theories as universal and central and others as minor.[9]

As Christian views it, this drive to theory reinstitutes hegemony even as it portends to critique a tradition of hegemony. Mystifying, incomprehensible language and the prevalent return to and study of Western male texts are first inhibiting spaces for those writers interested in hitherto neglected works of past and present third-world literatures as the obsession with literary theory increases; and second, these texts are then used as norms that are transferred onto third-world, female texts.[10] Indeed, for Christian, the exaltation of theory diverts the attention and needs of black third-world women who have an interest in reclaiming and claiming ignored black writers of the past and present. As a critic of contemporary African American women's writing, Christian worries that the preoccupations of the New Criticism, with its focus on reading as well as its emphasis on the absence of the author leads quite frankly to further neglect and ignorance of the literature of blacks.

> Now I am being told that philosophers are the ones who write literature, that authors are dead, irrelevant, mere vessels through which their narratives ooze . . . ; rather, they produce texts as disembodied as angels. . . . In other words, the literature of blacks, women of South America and Africa, etc., [previously seen] as overly "political" literature was being preempted by a new Western concept which proclaimed that reality does not exist, that everything is relative, and that every text is silent about something—which indeed it must necessarily be.[11]

Christian's critique of the rise of literary theory, influenced, at least as she sees it, by a new philosophy, presents two problems to the black feminist philosophical project. The first is the problem of philosophy itself. Is philosophy so inherently abstract, so inherently totalizing, that it may be incapable of capturing the complexities of what it might mean to be black and woman for all the variations of black women out there? Theory, it seems, tends to create monolithic discourses which operate not only in predominantly Western-focused theoretical projects but also in the spaces, like the black arts movements, where unheard, ignored voices, talents, and so on were supposed to have a voice.[12] From a viewpoint such as Christian's, philosophical theory leads to abstract frameworks that inherently reduce, totalize, and exclude.

Second, a related problem of theorizing black women's lives arises with regard to these very lives. Indeed, Christian suggests that the very heterogeneity of black women's lives should give one pause in any theoretical attempt. In a criticism of feminist theorists, especially French feminist theorists, Christian suggests that if feminist theorists were able to note the distinctions and complexities of women of many races, histories, and culture, they could *not* articulate a theory.[13]

> I and many of my sisters do not the see the world as being so simple. And perhaps that is why we have not rushed to create abstract theories. For we know there are countless women of color, both in America and in the rest of the world, to whom our singular ideas would be applied. There is therefore, a caution we feel about pronouncing black feminist theory that might be seen as a decisive statement about third world women. This is not to say we are not theorizing. Certainly our literature is an indication of the ways in which our theorizing, of necessity is based on our multiplicity of experiences.[14]

Though I would argue that Christian assumes a unity of black women's consciousnesses that she never fully articulates, she nonetheless elucidates the way theoretical frameworks have often worked against black women in both feminist and black literature. Black women become forced to participate in a discourse but always only to the extent that they exercise language and expression of often alien theoretical frameworks. Additionally, because black women often work within political and from political concerns, the emphasis on theory can be a deflection of the real problems black women face. Furthermore, as Christian indicates, the heterogeneity of black women's lives may also elude theoretical framing.

So What's a Black Chick Philosopher to Do?

An interesting secondary though nonetheless significant question regarding these challenges to black feminist philosophy is, Will the philosophical community develop such that black feminist philosophy becomes an authoritative discourse?; that is, will it become a discourse in which the experiences of black women are in the forefront but does so in such a way that it appeals to understanding that as a philosophy, it is telling us something about the world, about experiences, about philosophy, for black women but also for philosophers in general. This universality is what it means to be an authoritative discourse, but it also requires that first the philosophical establishment must recognize the significance of such a subtopic as vital to its understanding of itself. As a consequence, black feminist philosophy must by necessity appear monolithic, in the worst light, or at least universal in its most positive expression. This is exactly the problem Hill Collins elucidates in her construction of the debate over the naming of the black women's standpoint.

Hill Collins argues that the debate between naming black women's standpoint as "womanist" or "black feminism" reflects both the current preoccupation in black women's intellectual production with questions of individual and group identity within academia as well as a "concern with crafting a Black women's standpoint that is sensitive to differences among Black women yet grounded in solidarity."[15] These concerns imply a reconsideration of "longstanding notions of racial solidarity that have been central to Black women's community work." Additionally, the attempt at naming "not only demonstrates the heterogeneity among Black women but also highlights ongoing and contested functions of self-definition in developing adequate political analyses of current social conditions."[16]

The debate over naming a black women's standpoint, if that's possible, as Hill Collins reconstructs it, reveals black women's recognition of their own diversity. This recognition is both its creativity and its possible undoing. The constant reminder of difference within black women's individual and communities of experience denoted by the often-used label *black feminisms* may offer black women more opportunities "to synthesize emancipation theories on race, gender, sexuality and class, [and thus] black feminisms improvise, constructing integrative analyses in limbos toward their own constructions."[17] But as Hill Collins points out, overemphasizing differences among black women while rarely, if ever, situating analyses in a context of black women's distinctive group-based oppression in the United States is, at best, politically naïve. "African-American women benefit much less from critical social theories organized around difference than do other groups."[18] The very deconstruction of the category "woman," which aims to uncover racial and sexual biases within feminist theory and thus create alliances between women of historical markers of difference, may not be so beneficial to women of color in its application to differences among women of color.[19]

Collin's concern is two-fold. First is that black women's intellectual production organized around difference and individuality may inadvertently eliminate black feminist thought and thus "weaken black women's ability to resist injustice as a collectivity."[20] But just as important, given that the academic infrastructure sees black women's thought as minority or unmarketable to a wider audience, black women intellectuals are faced with the challenge of having to balance the interests of their communities with the interest of gaining access to institutional platforms and therefore a voice.[21] Related to this concern is that black women intellectuals become less and less involved with the lives of a variety of black women and black civil society, a particular concern that haunts my very own daily life.

In the institution of philosophy, black women especially carry all these burdens. One must keep up and know the traditional mainstream discourses while at the same time attending to the necessities for learning, creating, or developing intellectual work and practices of black feminisms. One must attend to levels of knowledge deemed as authoritative and universal; that is, one must go through feminism, which entails a predominance of white feminists who are themselves in dialogue with white men. Finding the space to return to, or explore, black women's thoughts or one's own thought as a black woman and a philosopher borders on living a schizophrenic intellectual life. And despite the trends of terms such as *fractured, schizophrenic,* or *multiplicities*, this life, experienced a thousand fold by black women in philosophy, does little to address the injustices, segregation, sexism, and racism we inevitably face in academic philosophy. Without an infrastructure that acknowledges black feminist thought as philosophy, without a real sense of the presence of African American females in our midst, black feminist philosophers will continue to be underdeveloped and marginalized.

So, what is a black chick philosopher to do? The answer is to recreate philosophy, to be the one that asks the question, What is philosophy? and attempt an answer that can and does incorporate the concerns and experience of black women. But philosophy must continue to rethink itself through the lens of different subjectivities, different interests that are not about merely parlaying French or German or ancient Greek male philosophers into a lens through which we can abstractly consider the experiences of women of color. We must allow that though black women's experiences cannot merely be collapsed into each other, they nonetheless, as Hill Collins wants to argue, have a commonality: the search for justice.[22] The trick will be if philosophy and the philosophers who constantly produce more philosophers who in turn reinstitute the marginalization of black feminist discourse can see in black women's thought important questions of philosophy. We must begin to understand that the theorizing done by black women is unique but nonetheless bears on the gamut of philosophical speculations that confront everything from democracy to subjectivity to the role of reason. There is a history of black women theorizing, and philosophy must do more to contribute to it. This means recognizing its potential for universality while at the same time recognizing that it arises out of the experiences of black women. Finally, this means that we must understand that philosophy—including the question of philosophy and its various answers—also arises from a particular experience.

Finally, I would like to echo Susan Bordo's caution in engaging postmodernist deconstructions. Bordo warns that while postmodern skepticism challenges the disembodied knowledge of the Cartesian cogito, it nonetheless escapes from human locatedness by supposing that the critic can become wholly protean, adopting endlessly shifting, seemingly inexhaustible vantage points.[23] This sensibility, she argues, retains the philosopher's fantasy of transcendence by adopting a new configuration of detachment, a new imagination of disembodiedment, a dream of being everywhere.[24] Despite the insistence that there is no escape from the human perspective, from the process of human making and remaking the world; despite the body no longer being conceived as an obstacle to knowledge, the postmodern body, shattered by multiplicity, shape-shifting, and indeterminancy, also obscures the located, limited, inescapably partial, and always personally invested nature of human story making.

"Appreciation of difference requires the acknowledgement of some point beyond which the dancer cannot go. If she were able to go everywhere, that would be no difference, nothing eludes. Denial of unity and stability of identity is one thing. The epistemological fantasy of becoming multiplicity, the dream of limitless multiple embodiedment, allowing one to dance from place to place and self to self is another. One is always somewhere."[25]

Notes

1. Ian Hacking, *The Social Construction of What?* (Harvard University Press, 1999), 6.

2. Susan Bordo, *Unbearable Weight: Feminism, Western Culture, and the Body* (Berkeley: University of California Press, 1995), 222.

3. Ibid., 224.

4. Ibid.

5. Christian, Barbara, "Race for Theory," in *The Black Feminist Reader,* ed. Joy James and Denise Sharpley-Whiting (Malden: Blackwell, 2000), 16.

6. Ibid., 11.

7. Ibid., 12.

8. Ibid., 14.

9. Ibid., 13.

10. Ibid., 17.

11. Ibid., 16–17.

12. Ibid., 18–19.

13. Ibid., 19.

14. Ibid., 20.

15. Patricia Hill Collins, *Black Feminist Thought: Knowledge, Consciousness, and the Politics o f Empowerment* (New York: Routledge, 2000), 60.

16. Ibid., 60–61.

17. James, Joy. "Black Feminism: Liberation Limbos and Existence in Gray," in *Existence in Black: An Anthology of Black Existential Philosophy,* ed. Lewis Gordon (New York: Routledge, 1997), 218.

18. Hill Collins, *Black Feminist Thought,* 71.

19. Ibid., 72.

20. Ibid.

21. Ibid.

22. Ibid., 75.

23. Bordo, *Unbearable Weight*, 225.

24. Ibid., 226.

25. Ibid., 228.

4

Antigone's Other Legacy

Slavery and Colonialism in *Tègònni: An African Antigone*

Tina Chanter

In the wake of G. W. F. Hegel's understanding of *Antigone* in terms of a conflict between the ethical demands of the family on the one hand and the state on the other, feminist commentary on Sophocles' Greek tragedy has tended to privilege Hegel's terms of reference.[1] Luce Irigaray's response to *Antigone* is heavily overdetermined by its Hegelian reception, while Judith Butler frames her important discussion of *Antigone* as a response to both Hegel and Jacques Lacan.[2] The focal point of my argument concerns the need to expand the debate over the significance of Antigone's challenge to Creon beyond the concerns of family, kinship, and gender, themes that have come to dominate the post-Hegelian critical literature. This chapter is part of a larger project that contends that there is another discourse in which the oedipal cycle, and particularly *Antigone*, is implicated, one that has been overlooked, in part due to the colonial commitments of the tradition of German idealism that have dominated interpretation of Greek tragedy. This discourse is one in which definitions of citizenship, political rights, foreigners, slavery, and enemies figure writ large. A rich, international tradition of postcolonial dramatic appropriations, of *Antigone*, including African appropriations, brings to light these concerns. In what follows I focus in particular on Fémi Òsófisan's *Tègònni: An African Antigone*, a Nigerian play that transposes the concerns of Sophocles' *Antigone* into a colonial context. Instead of Polynices's burial being prohibited by King Creon, it is the burial of Tègònni's brother that is banned by the colonial regime, and it is Tègònni, rather than Antigone, who flouts the prohibition. Òsófisan also introduces the issue of interracial marriage into the plot, at the same time as he confronts the complex and problematic ways in which the mythological figure of Antigone has held sway over the philosophical, literary, and psychoanalytic imagination of the West through the ages.

"It was a brother, not a slave [δουλος], who died," Antigone says to Creon in Sophocles' *Antigone* (517).[3] While a good deal of scholarly attention has been devoted to the sense in which Antigone claims Polynices is irreplaceable, such that he is distinguished from a future husband or son of Antigone, there is very little consideration of the ease with which Antigone seems ready to dismiss slaves.[4] It would seem that what is decisive for Antigone is not Polynices' act, not any significance, political or otherwise, attached to what he has or has not done in life, but rather the importance of acknowledging his blood relationship to her—or, more specifically, as she says at line 466, the fact that he is born of the same mother [μητρὸς]. In specifying Polynices as a son born of a mother she shares with him, Antigone is distancing herself from Creon's judgment of Polynices in more ways than one. In contrast to Antigone, Creon emphasizes the lineage from her father, rather than stipulating Polynices as her mother's son, and construes Polynices as an enemy, a traitor to the state, rather than a friend or family member.[5] At the same time, however, as Antigone aligns herself with *philia*, Antigone appears to be endorsing a problematic view of slaves, apparently writing them off as not worthy of burial.

Earlier in the play Creon had suggested that Polynices had tried to "enslave" [δουλώσας] the Thebans (202) by attacking the city, and later he will call Haemon a "woman's slave" [δούλευμα].[6] By insisting that Polynices is not a slave, Antigone is repudiating Creon's association of him with slavery. Yet she, no more than Creon, brings into question the status of slaves as inferior. Critics have observed the extent to which Creon associates Polynices, Antigone, Ismene, and Haemon with "slaves and animals" but have not problematized Antigone's own implicit assumption that had Polynices been a slave, he would have been unworthy of burial.[7] O'Brien cites Goheen as having explored the extent to which Creon labels others as slaves and animals but does not put into question the assumption that Antigone and Creon appear to share, namely, that the House of Labdacus is human in some way that slaves and animals are not.[8] The closest O'Brien comes to confronting this issue is when she observes that Creon treats Ismene and Antigone as "less than slaves" (531–33), as females not allowed to 'range abroad' (579).[9] The reference is to Creon's simile comparing Ismene to a "viper."[10]

The unstated presupposition here is that while slaves are still recognizably human, animals are not. The question arises then as to what precisely differentiates Polynices from a slave. Is the humanity of slaves questionable in a way that is not reducible to their animality? Is it the deprivation of their freedom that brings into question their humanity? Is there not a sense, then, in which treating them as if they lacked humanity, rather than putting them on a par with animals, in fact brings into question the humanity of those who enslave them? In this sense, perhaps there is a way in which those who refuse to question enslavement fail to match up to animals, since at least animals do not deprive some humans of their freedom, while retaining for themselves the right to freedom. Of course, crucial questions have been raised about the ease with which humanist discourse appeals to animality, as if the animal were a coherent concept, one that could be unproblematically distinguished from humanity (as if not only all animals were animal in the same way, and all humans were human in the same way, but also the humanity of the latter were somehow established in relation to a boundary or divide such that all animals line up on one side and all humans line up on the other).[11] Could it be that those who have insisted upon associating Antigone with monstrosity have fallen prey to some of the metaphysical misconceptions Derrida and others have brought into question, not the least of which is the reduction of multiple animals to an animality, the construction of which serves to contain many a human anxiety about how questionable our own humanity might be?[12]

By distinguishing between the kinship bonds that link her to her brother and the ties that link her to objects and to slaves that also constitute the *oikos* or household, is Antigone attempting to establish the right to bury Polynices, and at the same time her own right to be included within the polis, her right to be considered human? Is she trying to demarcate those who are included within the *oikos* because of family ties from those included as possessions? Does the reference to a slave serve to demarcate those who do not share her bonds of kinship from those who do? Perhaps the status of a slave serves to differentiate not only Antigone's kinship relation to her brother but also Polynices' freedom as decisive for his humanity? If Polynices is human as a free man in a way that a slave, by definition, would not be, does not slavery become the unthought ground on the basis of which Antigone rests her claim to enact the bonds of humanity, to recognize her brother as human by consecrating his memory as such?

How, then, is Antigone's effort to discriminate between a slave and a brother to be read, and how are we to account for the consistency with which it has not been read, the extent to which an entire tradition of scholarship has been able to read over it? Could it be that the tradition of German idealism that idealized the Greeks, even while it sought to distinguish itself from them, was unable to attend to this reference to slavery because to do so might have led to introspection about its own complicity with new world slavery?[13] Is the failure to notice or attend to the assumptions Antigone imports into her defense of her brother a direct result of the impossibility of a white, European tradition confronting its own failure to see its endorsement of slavery and colonialism as an indictment of its claims to be civilized?[14] As Robert Bernasconi has shown, even as Hegel decries slavery, he also ascribes to it a certain necessity.[15] Hegel, as Bernasconi argues, justifies colonialism and denies that "all people are peoples in the sense of world historical entities," suggesting that "not all races develop into world historical peoples." For Hegel, Africans "show no inner drive to culture and . . . make no progress."[16]

How would sustained attention to the dynamic of slavery in *Antigone* have altered the reception of *Antigone*, for which Hegel's reading has been decisive, and how would the tradition that has celebrated Antigone have been altered by it? What would that tradition have looked like, had it been capable of attending to Antigone's apparently unproblematic endorsement of slavery? How do plays that take up *Antigone* in a postcolonial context allow us to renew the philosophical and psychoanalytic tradition that has taken up *Antigone*? How do plays such as Òsófisan's *Tègònni* complicate Antigone's legacy as a freedom fighter, by implicating her in colonialism, even as she embodies a certain spirit of defiance? How does Òsófisan allow us to problematize the Western legacy of *Antigone*, rather than to repeat its blindspots? How might such a problematization ramify throughout this tradition of tragic interpretation, and how might it intervene in this history, even to the point of recasting it, revising it, or rewriting it?

While family or kinship remains an important reference point for Sophocles' *Antigone*, and for many of his prominent Western commentators, Hegel, Lacan, and Judith Butler, for example, it has not always been the focal point for dramatists who have found inspiration in the figure of Antigone.[17] Or rather, perhaps one should say that the ways in which kinship itself is delineated by racialized discourses and assumptions about slavery have been rendered invisible.[18] Let us grant, for now, the plausibility of Lacan's assumption that the very possibility of linguistic communities is bound up with the prohibition of incest and that therefore any meaningful exchange—including the exchange of marriage vows—must take place in a context that presupposes the inauguration of the symbolic order or perhaps is synonymous with it. Even on its own terms, Lacan's account of the symbolic could be rewritten to take account of the sense in which not only sexual but also racial categories might be infused into the very possibilities of recognition it facilitates. If there is a sense in which the kind of recognition at stake in kinship laws presupposes a prior recognition of an other as human (rather than nonhuman), and if there are some cases in which the humanity of some racialized group is rendered dubious in advance, by some feature that would seem to mark it out as less than human, would this more primordial sense of recognition not operate at a level that is even more fundamental than—or at least as fundamental as—kinship?[19] When certain groups, classified according to the color of their skin, are denied basic human rights, when laws are erected in order to prevent them enjoying the protection of those laws from which other racially classified groups benefit due to the color of their skin, this deprivation of human rights signals a failure to recognize both groups as equally deserving of legal rights. Racial taboos that rest upon neglecting to concede that certain individuals qualify as properly human, taboos that acquire legal authority under certain conditions, such as apartheid, do not afford those individuals protection under laws that other groups can assume, including the right to marry regardless of skin color. If there are certain humans whose humanity is in question, humans who do not unequivocally signify as human, and if their failure to qualify as unambiguously human puts them off limits as sexual/marriage partners, this would appear to prescribe that only those whose humanity is not in question are acceptable sexual partners.[20] If skin color becomes a mark of race, and race becomes a way of distinguishing between those who qualify unproblematically as human, and those who barely qualify as human, then racial taboos would seem to function as inarticulate conditions, invisibly built into the incest prohibition.

Racial taboos limit the potential pool of marriage partners by imposing an endogamous rule that constitutes whiteness as the criterion for inclusion within the group. Incest prohibitions specify particular individuals as out of bounds, but they do so by appealing to more or less explicit racial taboos, which specify entire groups as out of bounds. Racial taboos thus operate as hidden conditions of incest prohibitions, by designating racially homogenous groups as permissible candidates for marriage. Put another way, incest prohibitions create an exception to the general rule articulated by racial taboos. Racial taboos, in effect, specify a pool of potential marriage partners as those worthy of being considered, those whose humanity is not rendered questionable by their race. They function as positive incitements to marry, as injunctions to marry within this group, rather than another. From this perspective, incest prohibitions can be construed as endorsing the racial incitement to marry within a group that constitutes itself as not racially contaminated but specifying certain exceptions within that group. Not only is there a taboo against homosexuality built into kinship structures, but the symbolic is infused with kinship structures that assume both heteronormative and miscegenating biases.

In what follows I propose a reading of Òsófisan's African version of Antigone, *Tègònni,* a play that confronts the impossibility of definitively separating out incest prohibitions from racial taboos.[21] I suggest that Antigone's impact is not limited to exposing, in Butler's words, "the socially contingent character of kinship" but that she also exposes the socially contingent character of laws under apartheid, or that of postcolonial practices.[22] In calling for a renewal of the political that is not premised on apartheid, or for a future that is not determined by the history of colonialism and imperialism in plays such as *The Island* or *Tègònni,* Antigone precisely throws into crisis, again in Butler's words, the "reigning regimes of representation" (24), but such regimes are not limited to prevailing kinship structures. Rather, they extend to the racially inflected regimes that inform postcolonial relations or the hierarchies that structure apartheid regimes. Both Butler and Lacan tend to conflate the legitimacy of the symbolic with the existence of the incest prohibition—or with its violation—and to privilege kinship relations in doing so. Yet what if the origin/possibility of the symbolic is irrevocably bound up with racial taboos?

In violating a racist taboo against miscegenation, a taboo that has all the trappings of colonial ideology, Tègònni (Antigone's double) disrupts two very different traditions, both of which oppose her marriage to Captain Allan Jones (the metaphorical equivalent of Sophocles' Haemon). On the one hand there is the tradition to which Isokun refers, and on the other hand there is that to which Governor Carter-Ross (the metaphorical equivalent of Sophocles' Creon) appeals. Isokun thinks Tègònni will be making a "tragic error" (22) in marrying the district officer and wants Tègònni to find a husband "among us, among her own people" (20). He points out, "It's never been heard of, that a woman of our land, and a princess at that, would go and marry one of those ghosts from across the seas (21), and, "No one here accepts it, except . . . her friends" (22). In terms of kinship lines, Isokun represents a traditional view, advocating racial closure. At the same time, he supports Tègònni in her quest to become the first female carver and encourages her to petition Jones. Isokun wants to preserve the racial homogeneity of his own people as a basis for a cultural identity that, however, is not based on an atavistic ideal, but that is rather open to progressive influences. His reason for wanting Tègònni to marry among her own has to do with forging a cultural identity that submits neither to colonialism nor to an allegedly pure, idealized cultural tradition that preceded colonial oppression.

Isokun wants Tègònni to remain among her own, rather than marry a foreign invader, while Governor Carter-Ross sees Jones's impending marriage to Tègònni as an inappropriate act of insubordination that flies in the face of everything he has been working for. Here is what he says to Jones: "You thought you were being a fucking hero, didn't you! You'll marry a nigger woman and show us all! Teach us a lesson perhaps on the equality of races! Rebuild the world with your penis! . . . You want to undo, in one single day, the work it took me years to accomplish here! Undermine our authority! And you think I'd let you!" (120–21). Accordingly, Carter-Ross arranges for the corpse of Tègònni's brother to block the path of the wedding celebrants, who are prevented from reaching the palace, where they intended to honor the grave of Tègònni's late father, Oba (Sophocles' Oedipus), as was the custom (see 45). As a result, Tègònni's wedding day is cursed. Prince Oyekunle (Sophocles' Haemon), who was killed in battle, defending his people against the British, must remain unburied by order of the governor. Just as Sophocles' Antigone buries Polynices, so Tègònni insists on burying her brother and is arrested for doing so. Her wedding is thereby effectively disrupted.

In putting her love for Jones above her loyalty to her own people—or perhaps in looking to a future that sees beyond racial divisiveness—and in putting aside any misgivings she might have about marrying a "ghost from across the seas," Tègònni acts on her belief, in Yemisi's words, that "he was always different" (46) from other white men. As Kunbi says, he "decided to do what other white men have never done—he went and paid the dowry!" (45–46). Unlike others "who fought their wars in the beds of our women," he "was polite and gentle" (46); he respected the traditions of the people in whose country he was living, traditions that had so often been violated, as is clear from the following exchange.

> *Yemisi*: Yes, he was always different! Because white men, we have known them before, those the missionaries said they brought to end the slave raids—
>
> *Kunbi:* And who fought their wars in the beds of our women—
>
> *Faderera*: And made adulterers of our mothers!
>
> *Yemisi*: Oh yes, white men have trampled past here, and created havoc among our virgins—
>
> *Faderera*: Leaving several unfathered children!
>
> *Kunbi:* But this time, for the first time, this white man on the hill, abandoned his guns and boots, came blushing all over, got himself a go between as is proper.(46)

In her desire to see beyond the racial divisions created by colonialism, Tègònni decides to marry Jones; her desire is also a desire for peace, for an end to the war; for the "whiteman" in Kunbi's words to be an "ally" rather than an "invader" and "antagonist" (22). If the aggression of colonialism was justified by the assumption that the British knew what was in the best interests of the Nigerians better than they did themselves, it was also buttressed by the assumption of the inherent inferiority of black-skinned peoples. Hence the racial taboos against whites marrying blacks. When Tègònni decides to marry Jones, she brings into question the validity of such racial taboos and at the same time affirms herself as equal to Jones. In effect, she contests the law that dictates that neither whites nor blacks should marry outside their race, but only inside, positing a new law that affirms the right to marry across racial boundaries, irrespective of skin color.

Rather than reaffirming a prohibition that had been violated, as is the case with Sophocles' Antigone, when, on Mary Beth Mader's reading, she reinvokes the law that Oedipus had transgressed, Tègònni brings into question the validity of a racial taboo that prohibits marriage across racial lines.[23] She acts in such a way as to discredit such racial prohibitions and the social hierarchies from which they stem, hierarchies that might originate from British colonialism, but that African tribal leaders have exploited. In this way, we might say, she calls for a reconceptualization of the polity, one that does not appeal to racist assumptions.[24]

Tègònni engages at least three different timeframes, that of Sophocles' "story of Antigone," the "British colonization of Nigeria and the defeat of [Òsófisan's] ancestors" in the late nineteenth century, and finally the imperialist exploitation of late twentieth-century Nigeria by Western powers such as Britain, Germany, and France, who, still in Òsófisan's words, "lend support to military dictatorship, just as long as their vast economic interest in oil exploration, telecommunications, the construction industry, and so forth are protected" (10). While Òsófisan sets the play in colonial Nigeria, drawing on the "well-known format of Sophocles' *Antigone*," his main concern is the "problem of political freedom" in Nigeria at the time he writes the play, in the 1990s (11). Straddling twentieth-century and nineteenth-century Nigeria, *Tègònni* comments on the abuses of power committed by imperial Britain on the one hand and those of African leaders on the other hand. The play contrasts the assumption of rights by British subjects with the complete absence of rights for colonial subjects (see 120), while at the same time it decries the maltreatment of its own people by corrupt military regimes. Isokun, the official town poet in *Tègònni*, exclaims, "Tell me, what cruelties have we not inflicted on ourselves, we black people, as agents in service of others!" (108).

The triple referentiality of the play's historical frames allows Òsófisan to engage the figure of Antigone in their interplay. When Antigone suggests that it is her story that is being told, Yemisi responds, "Your story! Sorry, you're mistaken. This is the story of Tègònni, our sister. Funny, the names sound almost the same" (25). Neither Tègònni nor Antigone is Sophocles' Antigone, but both of them are inspired by her, a fact that Òsófisan problematizes even as he draws on the Antigone of Greek mythology. As Yemisi contests Antigone's assumption that it is her story, insisting that it is in fact Tègònni's story, Òsófisan confronts the question of how a postcolonial nation fosters a culture that is neither a mere repetition of its colonial heritage nor merely a reactive rejection of it. The story is familiar enough—theorists such as Homi Bhabha and Frantz Fanon are among those to have exposed the dangers of anticolonialism, when it appeals to an inert, fossilized, atavistic politics in an attempt to resist the excesses of colonialism.[25] While colonial powers justify their subordination and exploitation of colonies by maintaining that they represent a civilizing influence (a view that can only be maintained on the basis of a highly selective account of its own dynamic), there is a tendency for anticolonial forces to formulate versions of their national identity that require less privileged members of the polity to play the role of stabilizing forces of purity. As often as not, as Uma Narayan and Gayatri Chakravorty Spivak, among others, have shown, this burden falls disproportionately on women, who are expected to safeguard mythical, imaginary versions of a national culture that are themselves called into being largely in reaction to Western imperialism, but that are celebrated as if they represented a return to some pristine, authentic, precolonial national identity, which was violated and disrupted by the invasion of colonial powers.[26]

In these terms, the attempts by the elders, including Isokun, to persuade Tègònni to apologize for defying orders by burying her brother, Oyekunle (Polynices), against the orders of Carter-Jones, the British colonial Governor, can be seen as a measure of their successful inculcation of colonial ideology. The efforts of the elders to bring Tègònni and her supporters back into line are met with the following refusal by her sister, Kunbi: "After surrendering our land, they want us to surrender our spirit too into the bargain" (90).

In the program notes to the first performance of *Tègònni*, at Emory University in Atlanta, Georgia, in 1994—the occasion for which Òsófisan wrote the play—Òsófisan highlights the way in which the apartheid regime in South Africa was used by the political leadership of other African nations as a diversion to mask the corruption of their own regimes. He observes that the "struggle against South Africa's apartheid" served as a "smokescreen to mask th[e] . . . villainies" of African leadership, which, he says, "kept our people in abject misery, easy prey to diseases and natural disasters, while, without compunction, they sent ambassadors everywhere to beg for aid" (8). Citing the influence of "foreign multinational business interests" (8) and widespread corruption of democratic processes, Òsófisan states that "the fight for freedom remains a concrete, and burning, issue for our deprived populations," and he calls on "the world to listen" (9). Òsófisan wants to add his voice "to the millions of other small voices in Africa, all shouting unheard and pleading to be set free—voices that are waiting desperately for help from friends in the free world" (10). *Tègònni* is written, then, as an appeal to "friends," those in the international community in a position to listen and respond to the plight of the poverty-stricken people of Nigeria. It is worth remembering, in the context of this appeal, the Sophoclean Antigone's appeal to *philia*, an appeal that has stepped beyond the pages of the ancient Greek tragedy that Sophocles named *Antigone*, to reach, among others, African dramatists and their audiences in the late twentieth century. In the absence of democracy and in the presence of corrupt military regimes that threaten the viability of his country in the 1990s, Òsófisan turns for inspiration to the "story of Antigone" (10).

When Antigone arrives on the scene in Òsófisan's *Tègònni*, she is late. Having traveled "a very long way, through the channels of history," traversing a road that "at many points is unsafe" (25), she arrives with bodyguards, and asks, "Has the play started? . . . we hurried as fast as we could. We wanted to catch the beginning" (25). While the play appears to have begun without her, the form that it takes is in fact predicated on her very existence as a literary figure who refuses to be confined to the annals of history. In one sense, the story that is told in *Tègònni* is one more variation of Antigone's myth, and in this sense, it owes its shape to the lasting impact her character has had in its multiple "incarnations" (26). Yet *Tègònni* is neither reducible to Sophocles' *Antigone*—"a story goes on, no matter when one arrives in it" (28)—nor to its rich historical and performative legacy. If *Tègònni* takes its place in a long tradition of interpretative drama that has turned for inspiration to ancient Greek tragedy, and to *Antigone* in particular, it is at the same time just as firmly embedded in the history of British colonialism and European imperialism, which prepared the ground for the series of military dictatorships that dominated the political landscape of Nigeria at the end of the twentieth century.

Of course, insofar as the champions of colonialism are convinced of their inherent superiority to the natives they conquer, and are thus able to rationalize their actions by reference to their civilizing influence, they are content to emphasize the continuity between the achievements of the golden age of fifth-century BCE Athens and their own cultural supremacy. As the British governor puts it,

> I grew up in an age when certain things were taken for granted. We did not need to write the rules down, everybody knew what you had to do, and the options were simple. You came with the gun in one hand, and the whip in the other. You barked out orders, and you punished summarily. You knew you were right, because you were white, and you believed in the Cross and in the Empire. You hammered the Union Jack down their throats, and made them sing "God Save the Queen"! For if you didn't do that, they would quickly resort to barbarism, to cannibalism, to living like apes. (133)

Bayo, a colonial priest, sees things rather differently. Pointing out that the implacable belief of the British in their civilization is undermined by their means of securing power, Bayo exclaims: "Yes, you've built an Empire, as you boast to us. You've conquered our people. But so what? That's the power of guns not of civilization. Any brute with a gun can give orders!" (55). Inscribed into the play in the figure of Bayo is a reference to slavery: in the words of the governor, Bayo "[e]scaped from slavery in Georgia" (61). The governor claims to have stopped the slave trade but fails to acknowledge that replacing it with colonialism is merely to substitute another form of tyranny.

Òsófisan employs a framing device at the opening of the play in order to introduce one of the mainstays structuring the colonial history of Africa, namely the question of race relations. The question arises in terms of which actors are available to play the parts of certain characters in the ensuing drama, the beginning of which has been delayed due to the fact that the director has been unable to find any white actors for the roles of the British governor Carter-Ross his aide-de-camp (ADC), and his district officer (DO), Allan Jones. Impatient to have the play underway, an actor volunteers his services, only to be rejected by the director because he doesn't have a white skin. Using the occasion as an opportunity to introduce a question about the status of theatre vis-à-vis realism, Òsófisan has the actor retort to the director, "But use your imagination, man! Theatre is all about illusion, isn't it?" (14). When the director acquiesces to this idea, the actor presses his advantage, and Òsófisan makes the actor complicit in his solicitation of the audience's cooperation: "All is illusion here, and everyone in the audience has come to play his or her own part in a dream. And dreams are where anything can happen. So give me a costume, anything to mark me out from the others, and this evening's dream begins" (14). At the same time as thematizing the illusory, dreamlike, utopian quality of theatre—a quality that the political realities of Nigeria's colonial legacy that Òsófisan sets out to explore belie, even as the play sounds a note of resistance to this legacy—the actor's observation draws attention to the arbitrary status of skin color as a signifier of racial oppression. If "anything"—a costume, a wig—can serve to "mark" him off from the others, so that the costume or wig becomes a symbol signifying his race, then skin color no longer seems to retain its overdetermined significance in relation to racial signification. If racial signification can be displaced from the skin onto a wig in a play, then perhaps a similar displacement can occur in "real life." While the displacement of racial signifiers in and of itself does not necessarily dislodge the power of racial discrimination, it does make it much more difficult to attribute racial signification to inherent traits, by suggesting that race is a phenomenon that becomes attached to socially agreed-upon conventions. Yet the overdetermination of race by skin color proves not to be as easy to dislodge as the actor might have hoped. Accordingly, myths of racial disparities, such as the one Tègònni invokes when she ironically exclaims to the governor, "How can I be black and intelligent! You're slipping?" (81) are not as easily dispelled as we might have hoped, resting, as they tend to do, on deeply embedded assumptions about the natural inferiority of some races in relations to others.

Once the costume manager has handed wigs to the actors who are to play the white characters, the governor, the ADC, and the DO, the dream can begin to unfold, but not before another actor receives her wig: Antigone. Òsófisan thus sets up the encounter between Antigone and the friends and sisters of Tègònni as one in which their expectation that the color of Antigone's skin be white can be thwarted. In a moment that conforms to the historical overdetermination of race by skin color—a moment that will, however, once again be deflected, Kunbi exclaims to Antigone, "But you . . . you're black!" (26). Having been prepared in advance by Òsófisan's framing device, the audience is already in on the secret, as it were. On cue, then, Antigone laughingly reacts to the suggestion that she must be an "imposter" because she is black (26) by posing the question, "What colour is mythology?" (27). Harking back to the opening scene of the play, in which a black actor has insisted on the need to use one's imagination in the theater, Antigone's crew chimes in, "We always come in the colour and the shape of your imagination" (27). As the play proceeds, it becomes clear that Antigone and her entourage have taken part in many other plays, also inspired by Sophocles' *Antigone*: they have taken on many different hues throughout the ages. Having transcended the particulars of Sophocles' play, Antigone and her crew thus come to take part in a script that is "well rehearsed . . . the story we rehearsed, as it's happened at other times, in other places" (29).

Taking advantage of her status as both inside and outside of the play, as a mythological figure who comes from elsewhere, and yet one who has come to take part in Tègònni's story, Antigone plays the role of director at times, moving in and out of her part. She tells her bodyguards that they may as well play the soldiers of the Hausa constabulary, since they are already dressed for the part, and anyway they have been well rehearsed (see 29). For the most part, the soldiers obediently play the roles assigned to them, adopting a characterization reminiscent of the metaphorical stand-ins for Nazi guards in Anouilh's *Antigone*, repeatedly uttering the refrain that "orders are orders."[27] Yet if the soldiers in Anouilh's *Antigone*, in Ismene's words, "do exactly as they've been told, without caring about right or wrong," the bodyguards playing the solidiers in *Tègònni* object to playing soldiers, as the following exchange reveals:

> 2nd Sol: You've got to find us another role. This one's no fun at all!
>
> Antigone: You're tired of being soldiers?
>
> 4th Sol: Demoralised. All we do is carry corpses.
>
> 2nd Sol: Or build execution platforms—
>
> 4th Sol: Or terrorise people—
>
> 2nd Sol: Burn and plunder houses—
>
> 4th Sol: Collect bribes!
>
> 3rd Sol: We're so ashamed! Is this all that soldiers do in this country?
>
> 2nd Sol: Not even one act you could call humane?

Unlike Anouilh, whose portrait of the soldiers remains true to Hannah Arendt's well-known analysis of Eichmann as succumbing to the "banality of evil," Òsófisan uses Antigone's crew to pass judgment on the excesses and injustices of colonial rule.[28] Yet at the same time, since Jones and Carter-Ross are played by black actors, the audience is encouraged to see the African leaders of the 1990s as mimicking the abuses of colonialism.

Òsófisan's Antigone becomes a critical commentator on the impact that her mythological character has had throughout the ages. In her metatheatrical role, she takes it upon herself to test the mettle of Tègònni. The exchange that follows articulates one of the central issues at stake in this work, namely, how and whether those who have suffered injustices can avoid perpetrating new injustices in their own turn, thereby perpetuating a cycle of oppression. Antigone can be read as a figure who brings into question and reworks her status as abject, that is, her status as the excluded but constitutive other. Under Òsófisan's pen, she calls for a freedom that is not premised on the subjugation of others. If Sophocles's Antigone fails to problematize slavery, Òsófisan's Antigone is implicated in colonialism and slavery, yet works to overcome that legacy, showing herself willing to learn from Tègònni. A genuine exchange takes place between Antigone and Tègònni. Òsófisan's play celebrates Antigone as a figure whose rebirth throughout the ages keeps alive the hope of freedom, even in the face of implacable obstacles. Antigone declares, "Freedom is a myth," insisting, "Human beings throw off their yokes, only for themselves to turn into oppressors" (125). Tègònni retorts, You say freedom is a myth. But where do you think we'd be without such myths? . . . Freedom is an undying faith, the force which underwrites our presence here on earth, as human beings. When we lose that faith, we die!" (125). "To this, Antigone responds, "Come, my sister, embrace me! I was testing you. And now I find you're a true believer, like me! Yes, it is true that many tyrants have marched through history. That for a while, people have been deprived of their freedom. But oppression can never last. Again and again it will be overthrown, and people will reclaim their right to be free!" (125). This assertion will itself be tested when at the end of the play shots ring out, and the violence of force appears to win the day against freedom. Yet the bond that unites Antigone and Tègònni, making them sisters across the ages of history, is one that ensures that Antigone and Tègònni will "rise again" (see 127 and 147), and that the spirit of freedom, on which neither of them—despite being tested—will renege, lives on. In the epilogue of the play, despite the fact that Tègònni has been shot, both Tègònni and Antigone sail off with the Yoruba water goddess, Yemoja—with whom Antigone had arrived at the beginning of the play. We are reminded of the dreamlike quality of theater to which our attention had been drawn at the beginning of the play and in which we had become complicitous. Anything can happen in a play.

Antigone attests, "There's only one Antigone," only to concede a couple of lines later that "Antigone belongs to several incarnations" (26). As the play proceeds, we are offered a way of understanding the tension involved in sustaining these two claims, as the singular spirit of freedom Antigone embodies refuses to be quelled and is rather reincarnated with each rebirth of the play, including Òsófisan's *Tègònni*. As a character in a story that is both her own and not her own, Òsófisan's Antigone is able to reflect on how and why Sophocles' Antigone has lent her name to so many struggles, in so many epochs. The promise that both her character and that of Tègònni hold out is that many more Antigones are to come. Of course, this also implies that there will be many more threats to freedom. Yet each time an oppressive regime comes to power, an Antigone—whether it is under her own name or under another name—will rise again to call its abuses into question.

As excluded from, but necessitated by, the regime of colonialism, Tègònni rises up to change her status, and in doing so, she challenges and rewrites the law that prohibits her marriage to Jones. As such she calls for a future not specified by racial taboos, not determined by a conflictual racial past, a future in which the invisible racial taboos that structure incest taboos comes to the fore, which is a condition for their overcoming. As long as they remain tacit, unspoken, invisible, and as long as the suffering they promote remains unseen, racial taboos remain resistant to change, the hidden condition of incest prohibitions, and the hidden condition of the kind of (white) psychoanalytic theory that writes them out of its technical apparatus, while secretly appealing to them.

If Hölderlin and Hegel, in different ways, saw tragedy as signaling epochal shifts, recent appropriations of Antigone have focused upon conflicting interpretations of such shifts. Paradoxically, then, the tragedy of *Antigone* has come to embody the hopes of those who appear to be hemmed in by implacable forces, who turn to Antigone, again and again, as a way of renewing their hope precisely when injustice might seem to have won the day. If tragedy, in Timothy Reiss's words, "fulfills the role of making a new class of discourse possible," and if its appearance as a literary form occurs "at the moment of a shift in the discursive order that rules a society," perhaps we must say not merely that we no longer have any need for tragedy, having hypostasized it into the tragic, where it has come to refer to those events that do not consort with everyday realities, but which disrupt the humdrum existence that tends to characterize the flow of everyday life.[29] Perhaps we should say, at least in the case of *Antigone*, rather that tragedy has been transformed into a vehicle of protest for those whose interpretation of everyday life as tragic is systematically delegitimated or not given a proper hearing. When the banalities of what has come to appear as the everyday for some rest upon systematic racial injustices for others, when business as usual for the white ruling classes of South Africa is premised upon apartheid, or when postcolonial, imperial practices of European powers exploit the natural resources of Nigeria through their support of multinational conglomerates, is it accidental that the casualties of those practices have found literary dramatists who have turned to *Antigone* to expose the injustices to which those who justify the systems of oppression from which they benefit can remain, if not oblivious, at least defensive and uncaring? Perhaps dramatists have turned to *Antigone* again and again because it explores so effectively not only the impact of systemic blindness, how competing value systems can come to operate as absolute grounds, so that individuals become inured to acknowledging or being able to see any other meaning than their own, but also how such grounds acquire authority. When competing views point out that the absolutism of these grounds is premised on the dual condition of usurping others at the same time as systematically failing to acknowledge this usurpation, these views fall on deaf ears. It is ironic, then, that in commenting on *Antigone*, so many critics have passed over the reference to slavery, and the ways in which the oedipal myth is entrenched in a discourse about outsiders, about foreigners, about those, like Antigone, who are considered apolitical, outside the polis not only due to their gender, but also due to their "barbarian" status.

The influence of Greek tragedy on African dramatists is part of a complex dynamic. As Barbara Goff points out, "the very presence of Greek and Roman classics within African culture, however fruitful for creative endeavour, testifies to the disruption of African history by decades of colonial exploitation."[30] Òsófisan's choice of Sophocles' *Antigone* is surely a highly self-conscious one, which might, in part, be attributed to the fact that *Tègònni* was written initially for an American audience. *Tègònni* can be read as drawing attention to a thread that runs through the fabric of Sophocles' oedipal cycle but one that has been rendered invisible by translators and commentators alike, one that has become submerged not only by the themes that Hegel and Lacan have seen fit to privilege, but also in influential feminist readings that remain somewhat overdetermined by the Hegelian and Lacanian reception of *Antigone*. Òsófisan foregrounds the colonial legacy with which his country is trying to come to terms, in a way that also confronts gender conflicts at the same time as acknowledging the history of slavery that helped to shape his country. He appropriates Antigone as a figure whose dramatic reincarnation throughout the ages presents her as a freedom fighter, but he also problematizes her Western heritage as one that has become implicated in colonialism. Òsófisan thereby opens up both *Antigone* and the philosophical tradition of commentary that the play has spawned in a new way. He allows us to return to Sophocles' text in a way that renews it and demands a rethinking of that tradition. He requires us to ask what kind of readers we want to be and which tradition we want to privilege. Do we want to be the kind of readers who, with Hegel and his devotees, read over Sophocles' reference to slavery and who justify colonialism, whether in the name of recuperating Antigone as a feminist or queer heroine or in some other cause? Or do we want to attend to Antgione's acquiescence to the idea that her brother deserves to be honored by a proper burial, but a slave does not? What do even apparently progressive appropriations of *Antigone* leave unthought, when the status of a slave is relegated to the untranslatable, illegible, unintelligible, to the point where generations of readers remain oblivious to the invitation inscribed in Sophocles' text to think about its implications? How does our continuing unease about slavery and colonialism inform the ease with which commentators and translators of *Antigone* erase the need to think about Antigone's casual endorsement of slavery?

Notes

1. G. W. F. Hegel, *Phenomenology of Spirit*, tr. A. V. Miller (Oxford: Oxford University Press, 1981).

2. Luce Irigaray, *Speculum of the Other Woman*, tr. Gillian C. Gill (Ithaca: Cornell University Press, 1985); *Speculum de l'autre femme* (Minuit: Paris, 1974); Judith Butler, *Antigone's Claim: Kinship between Life and Death* (New York: Columbia University Press, 2000); Jacques Lacan, *The Ethics of Psychoanalysis 1959–1960: The Seminar of Jacques Lacan*, ed. Jacques-Alain Miller, book 7, tr. Dennis Porter (New York: Tavistock/Routledge, 1992).

3. Elizabeth Wyckoff, "Antigone," in *Sophocles I*, ed. David Grene; *The Complete Greek Tragedies*, ed. David Grene and Richmond Lattimore (Chicago: University of Chicago Press, 1954). F. Storr translates the line, "The slain man was no villain but a brother," *Sophocles in Two Volumes*, vol. 1 (Cambridge: Harvard University Press, 1981), 353; while Reginald Gibbons has, "It was no slave—it was my brother who died," *Antigone*, tr. Reginald Gibbons and Charles Segal, *The Greek Tragedy in New Translations*, ed. Peter Burian and Alan Shapiro (Oxford: Oxford University Press, 2003), 76.

4. See, for example, Samuel Weber, "Antigone's Nomos," *Theatricality as Medium* (New York: Fordham University Press, 2004), 138, 383–84 n. 17. See also Lacan, *Ethics*, p. 254–56. See also Mader, Mary Beth. 2005. *Antigone's Line. Bulletin de la société Américaine de philosophie de langue Francaise*, 14:2.

5. See Wyckoff, *Antigone*, line 199. Joan V. O'Brien comments that Creon speaks of " 'the land of his fathers and the gods of his race' [Gēn patroiān kai theous tous engeneis], i.e., the gods and ancestors not just of this father's house of Labdakos but those revered by the whole Cadmean people" *Guide to Sophocles'* Antigone (Carbondale and Edwardsville: Southern Illinois University Press, 1978), 40. O'Brien goes on to note, however, that while one could see the differences between Antigone's and Creon's outlooks as "relics of the matrilineal and patrilineal outlook of an earlier age," Antigone also "invokes the gods 'of our fathers (848) and hopes for reunion with both her mother and her father (898ff)," suggesting that Antigone does not align herself exclusively with a matrilineal tradition.

6. See Gibbons, *Antigone*, 62; Storr, *Sophocles*, 373; and Wyckoff, *Antigone*, 185. See also O'Brien, whose commentary in this regard is valuable (see *Guide*, 41). She makes the point that the abstract noun *douleuma*, "a slave-thing," is a more insulting word than the world *doulos*, the concrete noun "slave" (*Guide*, 92).

7. See O'Brien, *Guide*, 41.

8. See Robert F. Goheen, *The Imagery of Sophocles' Antigone* (Princeton: Princeton University Press, 1951), 28–35.

9. O'Brien, *Guide*, 41.

10. See Storr, *Sophocles*, 355.

11. See Jacques Derrida, *L'animal que donc je suis*, ed. Marie-Louise Mallet (Paris: Galilée, 2006).

12. For readings of Antigone that emphasize her monstrous, uncanny dimension, see Martin Heidegger, *An Introduction to Metaphysics*, tr. Ralph Manheim (New Haven and London: Yale University Press, 1959. See also Lacan, *Ethics*, 263. Lacan appears to distance himself from understanding Antigone as monstrous, only to read her as beyond Atē, beyond all limits.

13. For the formulation of this particular point, and for help in thinking about the issue of slavery more generally in relation to *Antigone*, I am grateful to Sabine Broeck.

14. Katie Geneva Cannon makes a related point with respect to the allegedly civilizing mission of Christianity and the ways in which scriptural interpretation was coopted in order to justify slavery: "Being enslaved in a Christian country was considered advantageous to Africans' physical, intellectual, and moral development." See "Slave Ideology and Biblical Interpretation," in *The Black Studies Reader*, ed. Jacqueline Bobo, Cynthia Hudley, and Claudine Michel (New York: Routledge, 2004), 416.

15. See Robert Bernasconi, "Hegel at the Court of the Ashanti," in Stuart Barnett, ed., *Hegel after Derrida* (London and New York: Routledge, 1998), 58. See also Bernasconi, "Hegel's Racism: A Reply to McCarney," *Radical Philosophy* 119 (May/June 2003): 5.

16. Robert Bernasconi, "With What Must the Philosophy of History Begin? On the Racial Bases of Hegel's Eurocentrism," *Nineteenth Century Contexts*, 2000 22 (2000): 171–201. See esp. pp. 185 and 189–90.

17. Butler, for example, in a phrase that clearly evokes her earlier *Gender Trouble*, reads Antigone as eliciting "kinship trouble." *Antigone's Claim: Kinship between Life and Death* (New York: Columbia University Press, 2000), 62.

18. The failure to attend to how assumptions about slavery inform questions of kinship is, perhaps, especially surprising given that Hegel's analysis of the master-slave relationship has taken center stage in many important discussions of Antigone.

19. That recognition is something that must occur between two humans, rather than something that can proceed from inanimate objects, is one of the lessons that issues in the master-slave dialectic. Patchen Markell's discussion of the master-slave relationship in this regard is illuminating. See *Bound by Recognition* (Princeton and Oxford: Princeton University Press, 2003), 103–05. The importance of this dialectic for Lacan is well established. Of course, the questions raised by Derrida in *L'animal que donc je suis* throw into crisis the assumption that one should ever appeal to a definitive boundary separating animality from humanity, yet this has not prevented racialized, orientalizing, homophobic, and classist discourses benefiting from precisely such metaphysically problematic appeals.

20. Butler makes the point that from the restriction of certain familial relations it does not follow that other familial relations should follow a specific normative pattern: "From the presumption that one cannot—or ought not to—choose one's closest family members as one's lovers and marital partners, it does not follow that the bonds of kinship that are possible assume any particular form" (Butler, *Antigone's Claim*, 66).

21. Fémi Òsófisan, *Tègònni, an African Antigone* (Ibadan, Nigeria: Kenbim, 1999).

22. Butler, *Antigone's Claim*, 6.

23. See Mader, "Antigone's Line."

24. Charles W. Mills makes a similar point, in a different context. See *The Racial Contract* (Ithaca and London: Cornell University Press, 1997).

25. Homi K. Bhabha, *The Location of Culture* (London: Routledge, 1994); Frantz Fanon, *Racism and Culture: Toward the African Revolution*, ed. Haakon Chevalier (New York: Grove, 1967).

26. Uma Narayan, *Dislocating Cultures: Identities, Traditions and Third World Feminism* (New York: Routledge, 1997); Gayatri Chakravorty Spivak, "Can the Subaltern Speak?" in *Marxism and the Interpretation of Culture*, ed. Cary Nelson and Lawrence Grossberg (Urbana: University of Illinois Press, 1988).

27. Jean Anouilh, *Antigone: A Tragedy by Jean Anouilh*, tr. Lewis Galantière (London: Methuen, 1951), 20.

28. Hannah Arendt, *Eichmann in Jerusalem: A Report on the Banality of Evil* (New York: Viking, 1963).

29. Timothy J. Reiss, *Tragedy and Truth: Studies in the Development of a Renaissance and*

Neoclassical Discourse (New Haven and London: Yale University Press, 1980), 2.

30. Barbara Goff, "Antigone's Boat: The Colonial and the Postcolonial in Tegonni: An African Antigone by Femi Osofisan," in *Portraits for an Eagle: Essays in Honor of Femi Osofisan*, ed. Sola Adeyemi (Bayreuth: Bayreuth African Studies, 2006), 111–21, esp. p. 11.

5

L Is for . . .

Longing and Becoming in the L-Word's Racialized Erotic

Aimee Carrillo Rowe

This chapter deploys the work of Judith Butler in an effort to theorize the trans- associated with transgender theories of subjectivity as a productive intervention into theories of race and whiteness. Butler's account of the lesbian phallus, which denaturalizes the link between the penis and the phallus, enables us to imagine sources and sites of sexual pleasure in ways that exceed and indeed rewrite compulsory heterosexuality. While the lesbian phallus multiplies sites of pleasure and, in turn, identifications across sexual boundaries, it also retains the whiteness of such phallic displacements. Audre Lorde's "uses of the erotic" enable a productive rereading of queer *and* racialized erotics that allow us to mobilize the trans to intervene in the essentialisms of racial identities. Here I develop a theory of subject formation that is based not first in identities but in longing, erotic encounters and the contingent becomings that gain their charge through queer and racialized erotics. Identifications and desires across racial lines—particularly those that empower racialized subjects to critique power relations—offer a new way of thinking about, and more important, *feeling* relations of race and power. Just as transgender bodies and theories of subject formation denaturalize and render fluid gender relations, so too, I argue here, transracial bodies and sites of desire potentially remake subjects and reinscribe power lines.

I situate my argument within the contemporary historical moment, with its emphasis on the "post": postracism, postfeminism, postidentity, postmodernism. The organizing principle through which these posts cohere is the loosening of boundaries of difference, a slide into a potentially productive, and potentially dangerous, uncertainty about the politics of difference. This move functions not through the suppression of difference but through a proliferation of difference.[1] So the popular is saturated with images of interracial relationship and mixed-race figures such as Barack Obama, Jennifer Beale, and Halle Barry. Yet in spite of the proliferation of difference, or perhaps because of it, the moment is also one that insists on a color-blind investment in *not* seeing power.[2] Cultural and feminist critics have demonstrated the danger of the temporal slide into the post by excavating the gap between the real lived experience of multiple forms of oppression and the power-evasive discourse that enables the premature celebration of some kind of arrival to a power-neutral, democratic America. Within this context I consider the ways in which the racial is necessarily implicated in postracism, even as its difference to itself allows for disidentifications that span power lines. In this chapter, then, I want to consider another side of postracism that locates its motility and mobility in the category of the transracial.[3]

The study of gender and sexuality has gained some productive theoretical and political ground by loosening the relationship between identity and identification, between dimorphic sex and the constitution of the sexed subject, that might inform theorizations of racial difference. The study of race might be also productively mobilized by attending to the politics of the trans—the movement across categories of difference, the loosening of the relationship between the racialized body and categorical racial difference. At stake in such a motility is the capacity of the racialized subject to conduct a series of reverse interpellations[4] that hail the differently (de)racialized subjects to reimagine their positionality vis-à-vis racial difference in the capacious space-time of the trans. The trans is the movement across racial categories and identifications, a movement enabled through desire, (reverse) interpellation, and identification. Such crossings might be conceived as a "movement beyond the stasis attributed to 'positions' located on a closed map of social power" by establishing a "connection or continuity."[5]

For the purpose of mobilizing such queer and colored (dis)identifications, I am drawn to popular texts featuring mixed-race figures and interracial relationships that confuse any easy assignations of racialized difference by foregrounding the politics of belonging. Such texts invite viewers to make sense of the ambiguously racialized character by tracking the politics of relation through which the texts' racial and sexual politics unfold. This is not to suggest that such texts are necessarily progressive, and indeed, there is much work to suggest the danger in too facile celebrations of postracism.[6] Still such readings might also lend themselves to productive antiracist work that ambiguously racialized bodies-in-relation might enable us to theorize. Writing from a mixed-race location, my interrogation is one of my own subject position, of my own identification with and through the transracial, and how the movement across power lines that necessarily informs my subject formation might be theorized and recast as an invitation to coalitional subjectivity. My queer Anglo-Chicana perspective has prompted me to develop a theory of racial and sexual difference that is configured not through our essentialized identities but through our longings—how we insert ourselves into community.[7]

In this chapter I develop this category of transracial as a critical reading practice through which to engage popular texts through a study of race and the erotic in the popular lesbian drama, *The L-Word*. I focus on the character, Bette, a woman of mixed-race, Anglo–African American origin, whose racial identity is mediated through her relationships with other, differently racialized characters. I explore how Bette's identity moves and slides as her ambiguously racialized body gets mobilized to do political work through her relations with others. Her black identity[8]—signified variously in different episodes, but perhaps most clearly in her desire for an African American sperm donor and in her relationships with her sister and her Latina lover—is marked through these relations to open up productive questions about racial identity and the politics of belonging. Bette's location is alternately whitened and racialized in her partnership with her white partner, Tina, and in her affair with a Latina, Candice. Bette and Tina's partnership serves as a tenuous marker of normativity within the lesbian community as their seven-year relationship and hopes to build a family mark a particular lesbian future that is constantly deferred by Bette's racialized and queer longings. Thus the racialized erotic haunts and dislocates the show's complicity with straight time, generating a queer and colored temporality that dwells in the ambivalent and unanticipated spaces of the erotic.

L Is for . . . : Looking, Longing, Dis-Locating the Subject

In the premier episode of *The L-Word,* Jenny, a twenty-something fiction writer from the East Coast, arrives in Los Angeles to join her boyfriend, Tim. Presumably the couple will build a life together. When they arrive to their home from the airport, Tim takes Jenny to the backyard to show her a writing studio he built for her, a converted garage that is spatially and ultimately metaphorically removed from the main house. When Tim goes to work, Jenny is left alone in her studio, when a commotion in the neighbor's yard catches her eye. Curious, she presses her face to the slatted wooden fence that divides the backyards and, through the cracks, watches as two women strip their clothes, jump in the pool, and then begin to make out with such an intensity that Jenny finds she cannot look away.[9] Later that night, Jenny recreates the erotic spectacle for Tim:

> "Do you know the neighbors next door?" Jenny asks. "Are they a gay couple? I saw them having sex in their pool this afternoon," she says, flirtation animating her voice.
>
> "Are you sure you saw them getting down?" Tim asks playfully.

> "I saw them getting way down," Jenny assures him.
>
> "Why don't you tell me about it?"
>
> "There was this girl with short black hair. She walks out and takes off her clothes in like two seconds flat."
>
> "Like this?" Tim asks, removing Jenny's shirt.
>
> "I think it was a little faster," Jenny offers as she kisses Tim, raising the stakes of the queer erotic wager. "Then there was this blonde girl who had these beautiful breasts. I wasn't watching that closely."
>
> "Oh I think you were," he returns.
>
> "Then she begins to fuck her," Jenny finishes, placing herself on Tim.
>
> "Like this?" Tim asks, moving into her.
>
> "Oh, fuck," she gasps. The scene closes as the camera pans up from the couple, over Jenny's face as she rolls her head back in pleasure.

This sequence is only the first of a series through which Jenny's character becomes thoroughly queered, her heterosexual subjectivity unravels, and the straight temporal line—one which would have moved from her arrival in Los Angeles to her marriage with Tim to a presumed future of familial reproduction—gets bent. Soon after her scopofilic encounter with the lesbians next door, she will be aggressively pursued, and ultimately undone, by Marina, the beautifully cosmopolitan and ambiguously European, or Latin, player. If the subject that is Jenny gains her coherence through a series of foreclosures that circumscribe how she might relate to another ("I am not homosexual"), the fictions of her bounded self are composed through the organization of social space and intimate relations that segregate difference. "We seek forms of segregation and phobic forms of organizing social reality that keep the fiction of those [heterosexual and white] subjects intact," Butler explains. And yet, at the visual encounter with her lesbian neighbors and through the ensuing erotic encounters that the spectacle animates, Jenny must "submit to an undoing by virtue of what spectrally threatens," reinstating her subjectivity "on a new and different ground."[10]

I begin with this sequence to attend to *The L-Word*'s framing device: viewing becomes doing becomes the reinstatement of the subject on a new and different ground. To the extent that the viewer identifies with *The L-Word*'s characters, plot, and actions and, by extension, this sequence of seeing and doing and becoming, the act of looking interpellates the audience to queer her own subject position as the boundary between performance and spectatorship become blurred. A queer intimacy that circulates through the erotic charge between audience and performer risks remaking the social through the invitation, the look, the queer production of desire that moves from the screen to the social, or in which the screen provides an erotic landscape that animates the social.[11] Thus the signifier *lesbian* that serves as *The L-Word*'s most obvious "L" might productively be understood as not an essentialized identity but rather a place holder for the possibility of multiple, queer, and gynocentric forms of the erotic. "Erotic comings-together," Audre Lorde writes, "are almost always characterized by a simultaneous looking away, a pretense of calling them something else, whether a religion, a fit, mob violence, or even playing doctor."[12] This is when the erotic loses its power, contained within the abjected category of the pornographic. And yet in *The L-Word* we, the viewers, are encouraged not only to indulge our desire to look, but also to allow the look to work on us, to move through us, to invite us to dwell, through the imaginary, in a series of female erotic comings-together. "And this is no soft-focus, *Personal Best*, stolen-glances-in-the-shower-room treatment of lesbianism," one critic writes. "The characters are brazenly lusty, and the show never flinches when the clothes start coming off."[13] By dwelling in the shameless spectacle of the lesbian erotic, *The L-Word* invites the viewer to queer her own viewing practice as the phallocentrism of what constitutes sexual pleasure is displaced through the mobility of the lesbian phallus[14] through the multiplicity and reterrotitorialization of the female body and what constitutes an erotic exchange between those bodies.

It is the reconstitution of the gendered and racialized form of sexual power and pleasure—which can be derived from a whole host of body parts—that allows the erotic to be wrested from its alignment with compulsory heterosexuality and, as we shall see, whiteness. This disarticulation and its attendant realignments, in turn, generates an expansive erotic imaginary for queer and colored identifications. Judith Butler accounts for this capacity of the lesbian phallus to reconstitute identifications: "If the heterosexualization of identification and morphogenesis is historically contingent, however hegemonic, then identifications, which are always already imaginary, as they cross gender boundaries, reinstitute sexed bodies in variable ways. In crossing these boundaries, such morphogenentic identifications reconfigure the mapping of sexual difference itself." Even as the lesbian phallus multiplies and displaces sites of pleasure and, in turn, identifications across sexual boundaries, the concept circulates within a frame that presumes and produces the particular of Europe or Euro-America as the universal. In what follows, then, is an effort to think this vital move of queering identification through a racial discourse in which subject is constituted through not only queer but also colored imaginaries, interpellations, and potential sites of belonging.

This movement might be cast as a piece of a much larger, more diffuse, and less mainstream project of queer world-making or those efforts to infuse the social with queer imaginaries and sites of belonging that might create space for the formation of new queer subjects and communities.[15] The rhetorical force of queer performance in the formation of queer counterpublics arises through the constitution of the relational imaginary, wherein I am no longer who I thought I was in relation to you within a heterosexual landscape. The queer "performance permits the spectator, often a queer who has been locked out of the halls of representation or rendered a static caricature there, to imagine a worlds where queer lives, politics and possibilities are representable in their complexity," José Muñoz writes, underscoring, "The importance of such public and semipublic enactments of the hybrid self" as invaluable to "the formation of counterpublics that contest the hegemonic supremacy of the majoritarian public sphere."[16] The erotic capacity of queer public performance is contained to the extent that the queer erotic becomes equated with the pornographic, in which it might be reduced to a titillation aroused through lesbian sex for the purpose of male gratification. In this case, the male spectator imagines himself at the center of the female erotic; yet the lesbian erotic within which *The L-Word* dwells is one in which the female, even in the form of a male body, and particularly the female erotic, is at stake in its production. Thus *The L-Word* might be said to gain its queer rhetorical force from its capacity to wrest the lesbian erotic from its articulation to the pornographic.

Lorde's "uses of the erotic" seek to mobilize female power through "the assertion of the lifeforce of women; of that creative energy empowered, the knowledge and use of which we are now reclaiming in our language, our history, our dancing, our loving, our work, our lives."[17] Yet the space of the erotic has been colonized by the heterosexual social imaginary. As Lorde explains, "the erotic has often been misnamed by men and used against women. It has been made into the confused, the trivial, the psychotic, the plasticized sensation. For this reason, we have often turned away from the exploration and consideration of the erotic as a source of power and information, confusing it with its opposite, the pornographic."[18] Thus the erotic—particularly the queer female erotic—becomes a powerful resource in queer world-making, in cultivating an imaginary in which women are empowered, desiring, and fully embodied. The cultivation of a queer erotic, then, serves to interpellate queer counterpublics into such an alternate imaginary, to and through queer modes of belonging.

But is the formation of queer counterpublics a space, or an imaginary, only or exclusively *for* "a queer who has been locked out of the halls of representation"? I want to suggest that a spectator's identity and her identification do not necessarily or so easily need to align with one another. Feminist film theory and cultural studies often assume an equivalence between identity and identification: the "male gaze" is for or conducted by (presumably white, straight) men; the "female gaze" is for (presumably white, straight) women; the "black gaze" is for the heterosexual black male. While the ways in which the gaze has been theorized in relation to gender and race have provided invaluable insights into the relationship between looking and subject formation, it has had to rely on rather blunt essentialisms in order to do so. Here I want to open up the relationship between identity and identification and by extension to consider the moment of viewing as far more constituative, even if fleetingly so, of the viewer's subjectivity. Thus the value of the lesbian erotic in the formation of lesbian counterpublics coexists with the possibility for the "straight" viewer to undergo a queer interpellation, to be hailed by the lesbian erotic into a certain unraveling of those foreclosures through which the subject was imagined to be coherent in the first place. Thus there is no "queer" or "straight" viewer *prior* to the encounter with the lesbian erotic; rather, the subject is formed, performed, deformed through the act of looking. This move seeks to make room for the interaction between text and audience, which may be as fleeting as it is profound in the work that the encounter does on subject formation.

At stake in this loosening between identity and identification is the alliance potential of how we imagine and theorize the subject through the movement across power lines. We might consider, for instance, the conditions under which the "white straight male" might cultivate a "queer and colored" gaze, sensibility, or affinity and if he would still *be* a "white straight male" if he were truly to be undone through the affective encounter with (an) other(s). Or might a "black gay male" subject identify, imagine, or become interpellated by a racialized lesbian erotic? At stake are a decentering and a destabilizing of the subject of privilege through the unraveling of the spatial and relational segregations through which that subjectivity had been formed on the previously unexamined ground of hegemonic belonging. The lesbian erotic hailing I am imagining takes the queer woman of color feminism as its point of departure for theorizing what Chela Sandoval calls a "differential consciousness." Differential consciousness arises from the mobility of U.S. third-world feminists within and across race, class, and sex liberation movements, a mobility that arises from her multiple displacements and which enables her to cultivate an oppositional consciousness.

It is precisely this movement "between and among" oppositional ideologies—never resting comfortably in one or another, using the rhetorical force of one with and against another, locating the transformative power and limitations within each through the movement among oppositional sites—that constitutes a uniquely U.S. third-world feminist criticism.[19] Sandoval offers differential consciousness as a theoretical formation designed to move the privileged subject of oppositional consciousness, the male continental critical theorist—figured in the work of Fredrick Jameson and Roland Barthes, among others—from his despair within the abyss of postmodernism and imperialism onto a new theoretical ground based on a decolonial politics of affinity across lines of difference. Thus U.S. third-world feminism, and in particular, the experience of women of color vis-à-vis social justice movements, becomes not the peripheral site of marginality that always haunts cultural theory but the point of departure for a mobile imaginary and politics that moves theory and political praxis from the power and poetics that have allowed U.S. third-world feminists to survive and thrive. Marginality itself becomes mobilized as a tactic, ironically centering that which is other, not for a new essentialism, but for the cultivation of a fluid and political savvy sensibility that informs and inspires a methodology of the oppressed.

What kinds of imaginaries might a differential relationship between viewer and text enable? If the differential is that movement across sites of power and resistance that have enabled women of color to cultivate a flexible political intelligence, how might such methodologies for engaging the political be shared with others? How might we cultivate a framework for assessing what is at stake in such crossings, in the destabilization of the subject, for the formation of a differential politics? And, to move this differential analytic, animated here through the queer erotic, to the politics of transracial crossings, what risks and dangers are transgressed?

Race and the Erotic: Toward a Queer Antiracist Politics of Relation

This section seeks to bridge the uses of the erotic in queer world building with the formation of differential consciousness that might be cultivated in the direction of antiracism or of critical race consciousness. If *The L-Word* does some work in the direction of interpellating viewers into queer spectatorship that potentially destabilizes the subject, what work, if any, does its racialized performance undo in the viewer's investment in whiteness? It is certainly the case that queer studies and queer texts are overwhelmingly white, as multiple queer of color critiques have argued. How might a queer of color reading, then, invite a disidentificatory posture in relation to *The L-Word* that allows us to locate moments of resistance and recuperation vis-à-vis the segregation and color-blind discourse that inaugurates and sustains white racial hegemony? This section explores a series of *L-Word* scenes in which racial categories, belongings, and identifications become blurred through the power of the racialized erotic. The *erotic* is a term marked by its ambiguity, paradox, and transformative potential.

Bette's racialization is fluid and, for all purposes, could remain a silent subtext of *The L-Word.* Actress Jennifer Beale's beautiful tawny body can slide easily enough into a sea of whiteness, can go unremarked as a racial text and thus, unwittingly sanction a politics of color-blind assimilation. "Prior to taking this role on *The L Word,* in fact, only two of the dozens of characters Beals played over the years have been biracial," one critic explains. "The rest have been white women or women whose race was unspecified but assumed to be white."[20] Bette's character, however, is actively and strategically crafted to work against this "unspecified" whiteness. One review describes the process, and Beals's efforts to recast the script for these very purposes, as follows:

> After green-lighting *The L Word*, Showtime approached Beals about playing one of two characters: Bette, a headstrong, temperamental workaholic, and Tina, Bette's slightly more well-adjusted domestic partner. Beals took to Bette, but she wanted Chaiken to complicate the character's life in one additional way—by making her explicitly bi-racial. Beals, the daughter of a white mother and a black father, felt this would make the role more attractive to her. So Chaiken wrote that into the part. Pam Grier's character, Kit, was originally supposed to be Bette's friend, but her role was rewritten as Bette's half-sister. 'I wanted to explore what it means to be bi-racial in a larger cultural context and what it means within the gay community,' Beals said.[21]

And the queer erotic, in its multiple manifestations, becomes a vehicle through which her racialized positionality is marked and the deracialization of her light-skin privilege comes under scrutiny and through which, in turn, the whiteness of the space of *The L-Word* is marked and displaced. This is to suggest that the show plays with the postracist preoccupation with mixed-race figures such as Beals, but instead of merely deploying the ambiguous body, mobilizing the post in ways that both critique and reify the logics of white inclusion/exclusion.

I realize that mobilizing the queer erotic to do the work of the (trans)racial is treacherous territory. I do not wish to conflate racism with homophobia or to unwittingly conflate the modes of resistance that arise from each experience of displacement. Nor do I wish to argue that the destabilization of the (straight) subject through a queer (dis)identification is somehow transferable, or parallel, to the destabilization of the (white) subject through a racialized (dis)identification. Certainly there are countless distinctions between and among forms of oppression and the modes of resistance that arise from those particular experiences. And certainly there are phobias *across* these lines of oppression that challenge any easy affinity or alliance-based theorizing and political praxis. Mary Louise Fellows and Sherene Razack argue that the "race to innocence," a politics based in a hierarchy of oppression, compels us to invest in our particular marginality through the erasure of our complicity in oppressing others. "Given the benefits and necessity of concentrating on the sources of our own subordination," they write, "it is not surprising that each of us does not easily endanger our place on the margin by an examination of our complicity in the oppression of others. To acknowledge that we oppress other women not only *feels* like a risk; it *is* a risk. Our own claim for justice is likely to be undermined if we acknowledge the claims of Others—competing claims that would position us as dominant."[22]

Indeed, my sense is that it is precisely the ways oppression in which critical race and queer theory are often segregated from one another—a segregation inseparable from the phobias, ism's, and complicities that potentially animate each project—that compels me to risk the conflation of different differences in an effort to trace the convergences and intersections among them.

In *The L-Word* premier episode, Beals's efforts to "complicate" her "character's life" by marking Bette as explicitly biracial sets the frame for the show's ongoing exploration of the motility of racialized (be)longings in relation to multiple sites of the erotic. One such theme is lesbian motherhood, as Bette locates a sperm donor for the couple but fails to tell Tina he is black. When he arrives at their house, Tina opens the door, looks up at the tall black man, and stammers, "Marcus, right? Um, I have to get something out of the bedroom," she says, buying herself some time as she tries to recover her composure. "Have a seat then we'll go to the Chryobank." Tina escapes to her bedroom. She perches on the edge of the bed breathing hard, and cries out in a whisper, "Fuck! OK." She grabs her purse and joins Marcus, casually asking him "Ready?" But Marcus refuses to let the awkward moment pass, marking instead with a gentle prompt:

> "Tina, did Bette not tell you I was black?" he asks.
>
> "No, not at all," Tina replies, "but she didn't not tell me, 'cuz it doesn't matter either way, right?"
>
> "I can't answer that for you," he responds. "Well ready to go?"

Ready to go indeed. The scene marks as insipid Tina's efforts to erase the color line in the couple's choice of donor and the beginning of a process through which Tina's whiteness will be destabilized in relation to Bette, even as Bette's blackness will be marked as a resource in the project of queer and mixed-race family building.

Later Tina will confront her on not "preparing" her for the blackness Bette had unilaterally introduced into their family-to-be. Bette insists that they had discussed it, that is, Tina was to be the birth mother, and they should find an African American donor, "so the child could be more like our child," as Bette puts it.

> "But I wasn't prepared," Tina pleads, recycling her original complaint.
>
> "I don't understand other than being committed to spending the rest of your life with me. What more do you need to do to prepare?" Bette returns.

> "Look at me, Bette," Tina says, holding up her hands. "I don't feel qualified to be the mother of a child who's half African American. I don't know what it means to be black."
>
> "I think I can make a contribution in that department," Bette's tone is at once sharp and vulnerable.
>
> "And don't you think, on top of everything else, to also have two moms, that is a lot of otherness to put on one child?" Tina volleys back as the scene closes.

Here it is precisely the intersection between race and sexuality in the formation of their mixed-race lesbian family that becomes the tangible marker not only of heterosexual but also and simultaneously of white privilege. The interchange destabilizes the identities of both characters, as Bette is compelled to slip from her privileged racial ambiguity to stand firmly in her African American identity, and Tina retreats to the innocence and incompetence of whiteness when threatened with the specter of crossing racial lines. Further, that the couple is lesbian and in need of a donor serves as the condition of possibility for this interchange. That is, the queer erotic that binds the couple and that animates their family-building desires, in turn, becomes the site of the transracial encounter that renders palpable that fact of whiteness and blackness that constitutes their relation. The permeability of the boundaries of race and sexuality upon which categories of difference and the potential to hierarchize oppressions ruptures in this scene. Both Bette and Tina are undone by the encounter. Bette seeks refuge and advice from her sister, but Kit reminds her that it is her of her own complicity in her light-skinned privilege that allows her to gain white acceptance, including Tina's: "When she looks at you she doesn't see a black woman or a white woman. She sees what she wants to see. Maybe she sees what you let her see. Maybe it wasn't that important before. Maybe what's worked best for you all these years, you getting all your pretty things, and you know putting together your pretty life, is that you let people see what you want them to see." Thus, even as Bette seeks to regain the unspoken loss of her previously unmarked biraciality, Kit pushes her a step further, holding her to account for her strategic deployment of whiteness, or race invisibility, in "putting together" her "pretty life." Bette is offended by Kit's charges and starts to leave, creating a point of entry for the white viewer to identify with Bette through an impulse to reject charges of privilege. The scene closes as Kit encourages Bette to recognize the love in her life and how that love "cuts across all our realities." Bette cries in the arms of her sister.

This sequence draws on the queer racialized erotic to allow for the collusion of multiple interventions through intersecting modes of power and privilege: interracial family building; lesbian motherhood; white privilege; woman of color consciousness, insight, and love. White intolerance for interracial coupling marks the limits of color-blind racism's tolerance for difference in the name of protecting the child.[23] A similar hegemonic logic is deployed against lesbian mothers—that they shouldn't parent because it is unfair to the children. The convergence of these two injunctions is ironically marked by Tina, who echoes these complaints in her worry that their choice will place "too much otherness" on their child. But ultimately this complaint is revealed to be a ruse to cover for her fear that she will be disadvantaged as the mother of a biracial child, which, in turn, critiques the fear of white and heterosexual displacement that animates the complaint. Indeed, the innocence upon which the injunction relies becomes untenable as Tina, and by extension, the white viewer grapples with the fact that her reaction to the possibility of having a mixed-race child is based in the effacement of her lover's African American identity. We also feel the effects of this effacement as Bette expresses her pain to Kit. And yet Bette herself must be held accountable for her complicity in this racial erasure as the wage she will pay for the benefits of whiteness, which has enabled her material gain at the expense of her identity. Indeed, her black identity becomes a resource in the imaginary of mixed-race family building, just as Kit's race critique, coupled with her vision that love bridges us across lines of difference, provides a new ground for transracial love that merges the critique of power with the transformative possibilities of love. While Kit's critique is "softened" by her evocation of love, the coupling between "love" and "critique" is quite productive in cultivating transracial feminist alliances. The critique is configured here *as* an act of love, such that critique and love become intertwined in ways that make room for women of color to voice alternative visions and for white subjects to hear critique not as a rejection but as a gesture of love.[24]

The power of the racialized erotic to destabilize and remake Bette's identity moves outward from this opening episode as her relationships with other women of color become more prominent. As Bette begins to question her relationship with Tina, she meets Candice, to whom she is immediately and erotically bound. The erotic encounter between them begins with a look: sideways, not necessarily straight on, fleeting and then direct and then it evaporates as if it never happened, only to return like the sun in the height of summer or the moon in new spring. When Candice and Bette meet, it all seems very casual. The woman who introduces them had gone off on Bette in a group therapy session, accusing her of downplaying her blackness. But Bette, in all of her competitive ambition and not to be outdone, out-maneuvered, out-politicized by anyone did not miss a beat; she outed the woman as a lesbian to the whole group. Race and sexuality play against each other in the scene as two queer women of color spar over the politics of inclusion and pride before an audience primarily of white straight therapy-goers. So it is surprising that when the women meet in a bar weeks later, they seem happy to see one another. The woman introduces Bette to her friend, Candice. That is when it happens: the look. Bette and Candice look too long, then have to look down and smile, or look away and change the subject, or look around the bar to dissolve the sexual tension that would otherwise be too much too soon. It is like arriving at a cocktail party and downing a vodka or going to a buffet and going straight for the roast beef, something carnal and sensual and utterly satisfying, or perhaps a sign of being out of balance. The camera work follows Bette's gaze as she watches Candice walk away, suturing the viewer into the racialized erotic between them.[25]

Candice watches as Bette walks away; Bette turns to catch her eye one more time. It is a dark and sensual look, one shared by dark women who are moved by longing that pulls their bodies toward one another without their consent, shamelessly. It is not the evasion of a look, not the mask of self-hatred displaced upon another queer colored body, but a look that is at once hot and warm and cold, a look that consumes even as it feeds, a look that compels even as it restrains the bodies that are moved by the exchange. And even though it has passed, for now, the look lingers and burrows and finds its way to all of the soft spots and the hard spots that long to be softened until it returns, only this time intensified by the work of the erotic imaginary since the last encounter. The look will return again and again between Bette and Candice, interpellating the audience into the racialized erotic through performative repetition. Soon Bette, a museum director, will hire Candice, a construction worker, to renovate her museum in preparation for the opening of the big gay art show, Provocations. Bette will hire Candice in spite of this look, or because of it, in spite of the fact that she and her life partner, Tina, are trying to get pregnant and build a family, are trying to commit to a life partnership. The look is so dangerous and so compelling, or so compelling because it is so dangerous, that Bette finds herself moved and transformed by it. All of her efforts to control her life and her partner and her life partnership begin to unravel in the movement of the look. The look becomes a kiss; the kiss becomes an erotic force that connects their bodies without even touching. Finally, the look becomes the kiss becomes this erotic force becomes an irresistible fuck that neither Bette nor Candice can contain. Tina need only see the two together to know. As with the figure of Jenny, who is moved in the premier episode from looking to longing to unraveling, the look between Bette and Candice is saturated in longing that acquiesces to a series of intense erotic encounters that move Bette from her placement in a predominantly white world to and through a racialized erotic that she finds irresistible, that unravels her subjectivity and in turn, the viewer's.

The desire that through which Bette and Candice are bound to one another through the look mirrors the process of queer interpellation outlined in the previous section. So while Bette stands firmly in her African American identity in relation to Tina and the prospect of raising a mixed-race child, she is challenged by another African American woman for eliding her racial identity. Yet this challenge to her passing and privilege does not become a ground for rejection or division. As with the encounter between Bette and Kit, the critique of unmarked racial privilege serves both to inspire her defensiveness and as a ground for Bette to build transracial community with other women of color. This is vital to the formation of transracial consciousness for, as with the woman of color love put forth by Kit, in which love and critique intermingle, the convergence of love and critique creates the ground for transracial alliances. Here Bette serves as a figure of identification, placed between whiteness and color—responding with both defensiveness *and* love to critiques that emerge from an impulse for accountability that is also inseparable from love—in ways that provide viewers a methodology for transracial love.

The compelling attraction that animates Bette and Candice's desire might be productively understood as Bette's desire for her own darkness, for racialized belongings that move through a complex articulation of love and critique and desire. "Erotic attraction is not physical but metaphysical," David Halperin writes, as "it intends an object that cannot be grasped without a finely calibrated knowledge of the kinds and degrees of being. Desire ultimately aims not at bodily contact but at self-transcendence. It means more than human beings realize, and it exceeds what can be realized within the limits of any human life."[26] What, then, of the uses of the erotic that cross racial lines and that queer those of sexuality? My argument is that something profoundly unsettling and potentially transformative is at stake when the erotic animates the project of difference-based encounters. In the case of Bette and Candice, their relationship will be as fleeting as it is destabilizing. As Bette follows the path of racialized belonging, she distances herself and in turn is distanced from the unmarked whiteness that characterized her relationship with Tina. Indeed, *The L-Word* takes the destabilization of the whiteness of Bette and Tina's family-building project as its point of departure and proceeds to follow Bette as she explores her racial identity through her erotic confrontations and encounters with other women of color.

In one scene Bette and Candice are placed together as cell mates when they join forces to combat homophobic protesters seeking to shut down *Provocations*. After the two, along with all of Bette's friends, clash with prolife picketers outside of the museum, the whole crew ends up in jail. The white female guard leads Bette and Candice to a separate cell because, the guard asserts, they are "dangerous ring-leaders." Left alone in a closed space, the desire that Bette has been trying to squelch becomes an unbearable force that charges the entire space of the cell with a queer and racialized erotic. The site of discipline and control of the racialized body, the cell as the interior holding point of the prison industrial complex is reclaimed by the racialized erotic that saturates the space. To contain this energy, the women decide to draw an imaginary line down the middle of the cell—dividing space to contain the animating force of the erotic. Bette leans up against the wall while Candice lies back on the cot, and they undergo an erotic exchange that overcomes the dividing line they have erected between their bodies. That they make love without touching marks a significant move in the racialized erotic imaginary into which the viewer—also compelled into the drama by looking and longing, but divided from the action by the imaginary line of the television screen—is sutured.

This moment might be productively read through an erotohistoriographic frame. Erotohistoriography, Elizabeth Freeman writes, is "a politics of unpredictable, deeply embodied pleasures that counters the logic of development. . . . As a mode of reparative criticism, then erotohistoriography indexes how queer relations complexly exceed the present. It insists that various queer social practices, especially those involving enjoyable bodily sensations, produce form(s) of time consciousness, even historical consciousness, that can intervene upon the material damage done in the name of development."[27] The erotic force that animates the love-making scene works against the progress narrative and family-building work that organize Bette's lifeworld—a project in which the audience invests, but by which we also feel constrained. The encounter erotically exceeds the time-space relations through which the "present" is constrained as their desire transgresses the distance that divides their bodies, loosens the scene's relation to time, and reworks the prison site of women-of-color bondage as one of overwhelming woman-of-color pleasure. The action strives neither toward a developmentalist telos nor toward an easy resting point of narrative closure. Rather, it opens a space-time for the erotic to work on and through the characters, binding and combining their energies for nothing more than "enjoyable bodily sensations" that potentially "produce new form(s) of consciousness" in the viewer.

Conclusion: Toward a Queer Transracial Erotic

What kinds of lifeworlds might we imagine as we intersect the queer with the transracial and as we queerly eroticize the racial? I want to suggest that to the extent that critical race feminist and queer feminist projects come to life in and through one another holds tremendous potential for recasting both projects. Our efforts might be well suited if we, following Audre Lorde, mobilize the uses of the erotic at work in one on behalf of the other. This is to suggest that the erotic might be activated as the lifeforce through which the queer and the racial come to join the forces of their critiques and visions for a "new and more possible" imaginary.[28] The constant processes of overturning and undoing that animate queer theory and lived experience of queer erotics work through a kind of movement and fluidity in racialized imaginaries and belongings might open up the ways critical race feminists theorize identity, politics, and resistance. That is, this queer movement across boundaries of difference might productively be mobilized to transgress the binary of whiteness and color to allow subjects some latitude to internalize different modes of racial consciousness, belonging, and desire.

The post that saturates the current historical moment works through a loosening and even an erasure of boundaries that risks erasing the very conditions of subordination and privilege that antiracist, feminist, and decolonial activists have worked so hard to raise consciousness about. Indeed, there is something ultimately unsatisfying about the queer racial erotic between Bette and Candice as the relationship is short-lived, and when it ends, Candice disappears from the show, Bette kidnaps her child from Tina, and Tina hooks up with a white man. Thus the queer racial erotic is so fleeting as to be potentially read as a racial fetish. And yet, if we are to cultivate a queer racialized reading practice, such moments—even if they are contained within the larger narrative—become luscious sites in which to dwell (see Gopinath). While one prong of the cultural work to be done is to struggle against color-blind racism's erasures and the kinds of regressive, nostalgic, and supremacist projects that a power-free imaginary might enable, another aspect of this cultural work might involve playing within the space of this loosening to see what kinds of queer and colored interpellations might be possible—deploying the power of the racialized erotic to unhinge subjects from their imagined fixity within their locations. The progress narrative that drives assimilation, for instance, presumes a forward and linear movement of time. Yet many of those who come from assimilated roots—whether mixed-race, white, or of color—we might also queer that linear movement through the racialized erotic. Time need not flow in any particular direction, and we need not feel bound to the politics of assimilation that follows a developmentalist model of time.

The politics of transracial belonging, in which we find deep and intimate connections that span racial lines, holds tremendous potential to rework multiple cultural maps. As we become intimately involved in the lives of differently located others, we gain access to ways of thinking, knowing, and becoming that are organized by a different set of power relations. If our cinematic encounters interpellate us to cross racial, gender, and sexual lines, then it plants those seeds in our imaginaries that cultivate the desire to travel outside of the restrictions of belonging into which we have been born. This examination of *The L-Word* seeks to generate such a reading. By attending to the move from looking to longing to becoming, I seek to render tangible the transgressive potential of consuming the queer and racialized erotic, not just for the pleasure of eating the other (hooks), but for the purpose of remaking the subject on a new and more possible ground, on a ground *inclined* toward the other, not so certain of or invested in its own coherency, but rather, willing, wanting to be moved in the direction of something beautiful and dark and powerful.

Notes

1. Banet-Weiser 2006.

2. This blurring of racialized difference inaugurates a moment of color-blind racism that accounts for "contemporary racial inequality as the outcome of non-racial dynamics." Eduardo Bonilla-Silva, *Racism without Racists: Color-Blind Racism and the Persistence of Racial Injustice in America* (Lanham, MD: Rowman and Littlefield, 2003], 2), a discourse that occludes power imbalances under the name of racial progress. Ford argues that we are living in a postracist society where racial and identity politics have entered a gray area, such that just about anyone, minority or otherwise, can use the shadow of traditional racism for a personal or political edge (Richard Thompson Ford, *The Race Card*). This is the context in which Barack Obama could not name "race," even as efforts to racialize him were lodged subtextually, and relationally. For instance, his figure was racialized through his affinities with Bill Ayers, Jeremiah Wright, and his alleged collusion with "terrorists."

3. The term *transracial* draws on the deessentializing move of transgendered crossings to theorize the politics and practices associated with racial crossings. Michael Awkward reads Michael Jackson's optic whitening as "transraciality"—a "mode of masquerade" arising through "the radical revision of one's natural markings and the adoption of aspects of human surface (especially skin, hair, and facial features) generally associated with the racial other." Awkward, *Negotiating Difference*, 180; see also Giroux, *Border Crossings*; Gubar, *RaceChanges*. Andrea Newlyn deploys the transracial as a literary device that potentially displaces the "panoptical position" of the white male character, Neil, who "crosses into blackness" in *Kingsblood Royal* as he "becomes the object of the white male gaze" as the "authority of the signifying eye doubles back on itself, leaving whiteness—particularly its ability to racialize others." Newlyn, "Kingsblood Royal," 1047. Dorienne Kondo productively underscores the risks of "transcendence" associated with too easy manifestations of transracial crossing: the suspicion with which we should approach utopian "third space" politics within an era of racial violence. "Destabilizing the racial signifier is not enough." Kondo, "[Re]Visions of Race," 101; the work must attend to the movements of solidarity, empowerment, and accountability across multiple power lines. Thus, "transracial" has been deployed by cultural and literary critics to examine the risks and possibilities with various forms of movement across. *Power Lines* extends this work as both a critical reading practice through which to read ethnographic texts and as a theoretical frame to theorize coalitional subjectivity.

4. I draw on the work of Chela Sandoval to suggest that the hailings through which subjects are formed can be reimagined through a differential theory of power. If the subject is formed as she turns in response to being hailed—that she recognizes herself in the hailing—then it is useful to consider the multiple ways in which subjects turn, the multiple calls to which they turn, the multiple sites of power and resistance to which they recognize themselves as implicated.

5. Butler and Martin 1994, 3. If psychoanalysis understands identification as a psychological process in which subjects internalize and are transformed by aspects of the other, the concept also marks a conflicted relationship marked by simultaneous identification and counteridentification (Muñoz 1999), a process of negotiated reading through which audiences decode social cues with and against the grain of hegemony.

6. Indeed, my reading (2007) of *Monster's Ball* argues that the interracial relationship between Hank and Leticia is a tale of redemption that shores up white American supremacy and exceptionalism through the incorporation of the ambiguously racialized black female character into the white family/nation.

7. In my book, *Power Lines: On the Subject of Feminist Alliances,* I explore the political stakes in theorizing subjectivity as a function of belonging. I argue that who we love is who we are becoming; our loving, unlike our identities, is a political choice; our longings constitute our being. If who we love is political, then racial and sexual difference are not reducible to the facts of our bodies or too easy or essentialist categories of identity, but rather are manifest within our modes of belonging. So even while belonging is adjudicated, disciplined, and normalized through structures of sameness and difference, subjects might also transgress and remake these boundaries, thus remaking the very conditions that define the subject.

8. Even to argue that her "black identity" manifests and recedes seems to fix blackness in the ways I am trying to avoid. For instance, one could argue that her outspoken and opinionated qualities are those associated with aggressive black femininity (see Hill Collins; Hammonds), and yet these very attributes also enabled by her light-skinned and class privilege?

9. Here I argue that the audience is sutured to the action through Jenny's gaze in ways that dis/orient the viewer through the subsequent queering of her sexuality. However, the series also self-consciously figures the action through the white male gaze in subsequent episodes. For instance, one of the main story lines in the second season is when Jenny and Shane take on a male roommate, who is a filmmaker bent on making a documentary about lesbian sex. He secretly films the women, and the viewer is often positioned to view the lesbian erotics he sees through his camera. The effect of this story line is creepy and invasive, creating the white male spectator as an abject figure and cultivating identification with the women. I would suggest, then, that such gendered framings educate and position the viewer: in the case of Jenny, they invite the female viewer to indulge a queer erotic; in the case of the filmmaker, they discipline male viewers to refrain from voyeurism. And yet within these limits, the "trans" that I seek to develop invites male and female viewers to identify with and to feel through *queer female* desire.

10. Butler 2004b, 333.

11. This rhetorical uptake may be seen in the *L-Word* parties, in which viewers convene to collectively watch the show in homes and bars and, if the parties are in Los Angeles, the actresses will also be present.

12. Lorde 1984, 59.

13. Sternbergh 2005.

14. Butler 1993.

15. Elizabeth Freeman describes, in the context of cultivating a concept she calls "time binds," the role of queer world building in the formation of queer temporalities. "At the simplest level, 'binds' are predicaments," she explains. "Like Frankenstein's monster, we cannot reproduce little queers with sperm and eggs, even if we do choose to give birth or parent: making other queers is a social matter. In fact, sexual dissidents must create continuing queer lifeworlds while not being witness to this future or able to guarantee its form in advance, on the wager that there will be more queers to inhabit

such worlds: we are 'bound' to queer successors whom we might not recognize. 'Binds' also suggests the bonds of love, not only attachments in the here and now but also those forged across both spatial and temporal barriers: to be 'bound' is to be going somewhere" (2005, 61). It is the cultural work of queer world-building, with hopes of but without any guarantees for a future, that marks the departure between queer and straight time.

16. Muñoz 1999, 2.

17. Ibid., 55.

18. 1984, p. 54.

19. Sandoval 2000, 58.

20. Warn 2003.

21. Sternbergh 2005.

22. 1998, 340.

23. Bonilla-Silva; Lazarre.

24. See Carrillo Rowe 2008.

25. As Kaja Silverman (1983) explains, "suture" is the cinematic work of overcoming the anxiety the viewer experiences, upon encountering an image framed by the camera's reduced point of view, by stitching images together into a reliable series, structured through the narrative expectations of the viewer. This stitching provides a filmic technique through which the viewer apprehends her/his relationship to the image and, by extension, frames the point of view; subject position is constructed for the viewer. It works through the "180º rule," which limits the range of a shot to viewer's seeing capacity, even as it leaves unexplored the visual field that the camera itself occupies. "Thus it derives from the imperative that the camera deny its own existence as much as possible, fostering the illusion that what is shows has an autonomous existence, independent of any technological interference, or any coercive gaze" (201). The viewer will temporarily adhere to this imperative but soon will "demand to know whose gaze controls what it sees" (202). This demand is met through a series of shot/reverse shots, which orient the viewer to the gaze of the character or object from whose perspective she or he is invited to see. Thus the filmic strategies through which this identification is managed, produced, and crafted sutures the viewer into the film's movement and look—and hence its time-space qualities—sometimes through fairly straight-forward identifications and other times by generating multiple and even competing identifications.

26. Halperin, 52.

27. Freeman 2005, 59.

28. "Feminism" is a formation continually in process. Its production as an inclusive space is contingent upon the imaginary of those involved in struggles under its name. When feminists become blocked around issues of power, it is in large part a question of a blocking of the feminist imaginary—perhaps being too stuck in the head, too invested in hegemonic forms of power, or a lack of literacy in the realms of the heart. In the poetics of Lorde:

> We have chosen each other
> And the edge of each others battles
> The war is the same
> If we lose

6

Race and Feminist Standpoint Theory

Anika Maaza Mann

> A new Pew Research Center poll points to a surging tide of fury, especially among white women. . . . The women are angry at the ludicrous charges of racism leveled against Clinton by the Obama camp—amplified in the supposedly respectable media—and projected on themselves.
>
> —"White Women Take the Gloves Off," *Realclearpolitics.com*

> It is hard to relate what it feels like to see Mrs. Clinton . . . referred to as "a woman" while Barack Obama is always referred to as "a black man." One would think she is just any woman, colorless, race-less, past-less, but she is not. She carries all the history of white womanhood in America in her person; it would be a miracle if we, and the world, did not react to this fact. How dishonest it is to make her innocent of her racial inheritance.
>
> —Alice Walker, "Lest We Forget: An Open Letter to My Sisters Who Are Brave," *Theroot.com*

> Perhaps it is because feminists are still so busy cataloging past slights to Hillary that they have failed to mount a vivid defense of Michelle Obama, who has taken over from Hillary as the one conservatives like to paint as a harridan.
>
> —Maureen Dowd, "Mr. Darcy Comes Courting." *New York Times*

During the course of the historic 2008 Democratic primary contest between Senators Barack Obama and Hillary Clinton, a provocative schism developed between the allegiances of black and white women. Many white feminists offered fervent support of Clinton, while polls indicated that the majority of black women supported Obama. This marked divide among women along racial lines raises important questions concerning the significance of race within feminist standpoint theory. A central claim within feminist standpoint theory is that the particularity of the social situation of women in a sexist society affords women rich epistemic resources: women have a less distorted, less partial, view of the social world than men.[1] It is because of our social situation that women can develop a standpoint that necessitates political struggle. However, how do racial identification and stratification affect the production of knowledge and subsequent political struggles? Is there *a* standpoint that can account for the social situations faced by the diversity of American women? I think not. The notable split among African American and white women during the Democratic presidential primary highlights the need to reexamine the role of intersectionality, or interlocking forms of oppression, within feminist standpoint theory. In the following, I aim to show through revisiting the notion of intersectionality in relation to group formation that feminist standpoint theory may be better suited to describe the social situation of black women as a group as opposed to all women. Through an examination of Patricia Hill Collins' critique of contemporary interpretations of intersectionality and Jean-Paul Sartre's ontological account of group formation I will show the difficulties of developing a cohesive standpoint among women as a whole.

※ ※ ※

The treatment of the interlocking forms of race, gender, and class oppression has remained an enduring theme in the works of black feminists since the nineteenth century.[2] For instance, Anna Julia Cooper in her 1892 text *A Voice from the South* argued that the cause of black women cannot be subsumed under the quest for justice for blacks or women.[3] Cooper recognized the need for distinctive analysis concerning the multiple forms of oppression faced by black women that were missed by black men and white women.[4] Today, *intersectionality* is a term used frequently by black feminists when describing the particularity of their social location.[5] Employing intersectionality as a theoretical device allows one to account for the ways that race, gender, class, and sexuality mutually construct one another and impact the lives of black women. Such an account reveals a more nuanced portrayal than race-only and gender-only critiques, which often fail to capture the inequitable power relations that shape the experience of black women in the United States. Black women often face struggles at the crossroads of both race and gender, which renders race-, gender-only models of analysis insufficient to adequately examine multifarious layers of oppression. African American women constitute a group unto themselves and cannot simply be considered as subsets of African Americans or women.

While intersectionality has been particularly useful as an analytical tool, it is not without its problems. In *Fighting Words* Collins asserts that as a theory intersectionality is more valuable when applied at the level of the individual but becomes ineffectual at the group level.[6] According to Collins, it is simple to analyze how race, gender, and class intersect and mutually construct one another in the lives of individuals. As such, the comparison of the ways that varying forms of oppression operate in the lives of an individual black woman and an individual white woman is not that difficult. Complications arise, however, when trying to apply intersectionality at the level of women as a whole. The problematic stems in part because intersectionality has the potential to imbue individualism within group analyses. Collins maintains that intersectionality does not challenge the notion of individualism prevalent in American society as it is compatible with both "traditional liberalism" and "apolitical postmodernism."[7]

Given the significant differences between the formation and structure of individuals and groups, Collins states that intersectionality does not operate in the same way at the individual and group level. She thus questions the legitimacy of applying standpoint theory to gender relations. Reexamining the notion of the intersectionality of race, class, and gender, she comments that "race and class and gender may *all* be present in *all* social settings in the United States, yet groups will experience and 'see' them differently."[8] African American women and white women organize themselves differently along the axes of race, class, and gender. White women are less apt to view themselves as racialized, or as members of a racial group, while African American women, whose lived experience is shaped by institutionalized racism, are more likely to identify themselves as members of a racially marginalized group. To that end, Collins suggests examining the race-class axes separately from the axis of gender even though such an examination may be viewed as counterintuitive or intellectually conservative. A revisiting of the notion of intersectionality is necessary because it has contributed to the formation of a new myth of the equivalency of oppressions. She writes that "in a situation in which far too many privileged academics feel free to claim a bit of oppression for themselves—if all oppressions mutually construct one another, then we're all oppressed in some way by something—oppression talk obscures actual unjust powers."[9] While the intersectionality of race, class, and gender highlights the connections between forms of oppression, all forms of oppression should not be considered as equivalent. Within politics, Collins observes, "some groups benefit more from an assumed equivalency of oppressions than others."[10] We must be cognizant of the hierarchies internal to the group "women" in the United States, and black feminism can be a resource for unmasking racism within universalistic calls for sisterhood.

The segregating effects of race and class have created a stronger sense of unification among women of color than is shared between women of color and white women. Since women are not segregated from men in the same respect that blacks are systematically segregated from whites, for example, through housing, educational opportunities, and employment discrimination, it is difficult to create the same bond shared by many African American women and men across the racial divide. "Because structural power attached to race-class intersectionality in the United States can be recast within apolitical frameworks of differences among women," Collins explains, "White American feminist theories in particular maintain the illusion of gender solidarity while allowing hierarchy to be reformulated via actual practices."[11] The continued resistance that white feminists face in their call for solidarity with black women results, in part, from their underestimation of the primary importance of racial solidarity for black women. Black women are more apt to align themselves with the black race, or more specifically with black men, over and against the notion of a shared sisterhood with women of all races.[12] If a multiracial, multiethnic feminist standpoint is to be achieved at some future point, then racialized hierarchies must be addressed to a much greater extent than they are presently. Collins writes that African American women's social location within both race-class and gender collectivities could provide an "important lens for evaluating standpoint theory overall." She thinks standpoint theory is better suited to analyze the political issues facing black women because "women" as a group are less likely to even identify as a group given the segregating effects of race and class. My point is that black women are more apt to form a standpoint than women in general.

I believe that being-in-situation, or being-in-the-world is the ontological condition for achieving a standpoint. My account of the existential phenomenological notion of being-in-situation is influenced by Sartrean ontology, as developed from *Being and Nothingness* to the *Critique of Dialectical Reason*, volume 1.[13] We can be defined as beings who have freedom within the limits of our particular situation, though Sartre insists that we give meaning to our situation through the choices we make within it. Thus, our being-in-situation has epistemic consequences; it specifically shapes our knowledge of human relations or the social world. In *Anti-Semite and Jew* Sartre acknowledges that there is a universal human situation that involves certain abstract characteristics that are common to all of our situations, such as the fact that we are mortal, that we love or we hate, that we savor the joys of life and experience suffering.[14] I do not deny that as humans, all of us men and women, whites and blacks, gay and straight share certain aspects of a human situation. However, these abstract characteristics of the human situation reveal little of the particularity of the situation or the mode of being-in-the-world, for women and more specifically, for women of color. In the context of a discussion of anti-Semitism, Sartre recognizes that the aspects of the universal human situation will not reveal "the Jew." In the same respect, the common experiences of women in a society organized along a sexual hierarchy will not reveal the black woman.

The model of group constitution presented in both *Being and Nothingness* and the *Critique* offers a compelling resource to understand the differences in group formation between black women and women in general. In *Being and Nothingness* the situation is reflective of both my facticity and freedom, with facticity being the condition of my freedom as discovered by my freedom. Therefore the situation shapes our mode of being-in-the-world, and because we are situated in a human space and not by spatial, or temporal, locations, our identities are situated by others. Given the human experience of intersubjectivity, Sartre attempts to give a concrete description of our experience of being in community, or solidarity, with others by explaining the notion of the 'we,' or undifferentiated nous. In the experience of the 'we' (being-with or Mit-sein), the recognition of subjectivities is analogous to the self-recognition of the nonthetic consciousness, in which a plurality of subjects recognize others as subjectivities, or transcendences-transcending. Therefore, unlike the objectifying look of the Other, no one is an object in the 'we.' He says that the 'we' experience cannot ground our consciousness of the Other because being-for-others grounds the possibility of being-with-others; put differently, being-with is a particular experience that is founded upon being-for-others. Thus, the experience of the 'we' cannot comprise an ontological structure of human reality. Of particular significance is Sartre's identification of an existential difference between the situation of the Us-object and of the We-subject. As a consequence, oppressive groups "cannot be on the same ontological plane" as oppressed groups.[15] It is this existential difference in the situation of members of the Us-object, which remains consistent throughout his ethical writings.

According to Sartre, the Us-object is experienced as community alienation. There are institutionalized forms of the Us-object that must be distinguished from the everyday possible occurrences of the Us-object. In societies where economic and political structures sustain a marked disparity in the life conditions of the oppressed classes and oppressing classes, Sartre writes "the situation of the oppressing classes presents the oppressed classes with the image of a perpetual Third."[16] The appearance of the Third alters the situation between the Other and myself, and "I suddenly experience the existence of an objective situation-form in the world of the Third in which the Other and I shall figure as *equivalent* structures in *solidarity* with each other."[17] For example, I may be in a department store engaged in a heated disagreement concerning a transaction with a black salesclerk. As the white store manager approaches us, however, our dispute fades into the background as we present a united front of accord in the presence of the white Other. My sense of racial allegiance, which promotes my desire to prevent the salesclerk from the manager's possible scrutiny, superseded my need to settle the disagreement. The Us-object is made apparent for me through assuming my responsibility of this particular situation.[18]

The We-subject, on the other hand, is not an intersubjective consciousness but is rather experienced by a particular consciousness. The We-subject is solely psychological and does not found a concrete ontological relation with others in the 'we.' Since the We-subject has no metaphysical weight, the bourgeois "is described inwardly as a consciousness which does not recognize its belonging to a class."[19] Thus there is no corresponding form of solidarity among the members of the We-subject as is found among the Us-object. Instead, Sartre writes, "The member of the oppressing class sees the totality of the oppressed class confronting him as an objective ensemble of 'they-subjects' without his correlatively realizing his community of being with other members of the oppressing class."[20] There can be a blindness among the members of the We-subject and not simply a refusal to acknowledge the oppressive situation. In this respect, some whites experience difficulty engaging in a fruitful discussion regarding the implications of their white skin privilege because they fail to recognize themselves as members of a racial group. The impetus to break free of the antagonistic cycle of conflict and objectification must originate within the Us-object, whose members experience oppression.

The most unified communities in *Being and Nothingness* are those that are alienated, or oppressed, for it is by virtue of the gaze that the least favored form a collectivity. The We-subject is more disparate than the Us-object and the formation of a collectivity is dependent upon the reversal of the gaze.[21] So, for instance in this country, African Americans are more unified as a group because of the look we experience, and white Americans are only unified and experience themselves as an Us through instances of the reversal of the gaze.

In "Sartre and the Social Construction of Race" Donna Marcano explains that in the *Critique* the individual "is always the locus of a free constituting praxis, while the group is always constituted."[22] In American society, which is structured socially along a racial hierarchy, my individual experience of antiblack racism does not ensure in itself that I will feel unified with other African Americans who share in this experience as well. Racialized individuals are, according to Sartre, serial unities, or collectives. He illustrates seriality through the example of commuters waiting for the bus at a bus stop. Although the individuals are united by a common material field, each one remains in serial isolation from the others. Serial unities are, as William McBride writes, "agglomerations of human beings engaged in some enterprise to which a common name can be given but which, far from unifying them, reinforces their isolation and practico-inert impotence."[23] In racially stratified societies serial isolation among the racially marginalized is promoted. The activity of racism is "a *praxis* illuminated by 'theory' . . . aiming to keep the masses in a state of molecular aggregation" (italics in original text).[24] The constitution of oppressed *groups* arises as a response to the unlivability of their oppression and as a means to overcome it. The transformation of a collective into a group "is a complex event which takes place *simultaneously* at every level of materiality."[25] Just as the individual heiress believed her inheritance was threatened by her employees' acts of resistance, whites can become aware of themselves "as a unity of individuals *in solidarity*" through their efforts to dispel a perceived threat posed by people of color.[26] Through their individual interests, individual whites may act in concert to create, or sustain, institutions that protect their power and privilege.

Sustained attempts to suppress the freedom of the racially marginalized have the concomitant effect of showing the serialized individuals "their material being as collectives and as a point of departure for a constant effort to establish lived bonds of solidarity between its members."[27] The collective of the racially marginalized is defined by its impossibility, which can be experienced through racial profiling and police brutality, inadequate healthcare and educational opportunities, and discriminatory housing and employment practices. The collectivity transforms into a group when "impossibility itself becomes impossible, or" as Sartre explains, "the impossibility of change is an impossibility of life."[28] Revolutionary group praxis is not produced through the systematic questioning of an oppressive system but rather is generated as a response to the collective recognition of common need and common danger that is being imposed by the racially dominant Other. Sartre writes: "[T]he group constitutes itself on the basis of a need or common danger and defines itself by the common objective which determines its common *praxis*. Yet neither common need, nor common *praxis*, nor common objectives can define a community unless it makes itself a community by feeling individual need as common need, and by projecting itself, in the internal unification of a common integration, towards objectives which it produces as common."[29] Given the impossibility of life, or common danger, faced by blacks due to the continuation of racial segregation and antiblack racism, African American women are apt to develop a strong unifying bond. Such "common integration" is not often found among women in general, which lends credence to the belief that standpoint theory may be more aptly suited for black women and not women as a whole.

※ ※ ※

In this section, I identify some troubling interpretations and criticisms of the contributions of black feminism to standpoint theory. I argue that these white feminist critiques indicate that many white women do not yet fully comprehend the implications of their whiteness and make evident their limited understanding of their own situations as white women in a racially stratified society. By examining the work of Sonia Kruks and Sandra Harding, I will show the need for continued development of a black feminist standpoint.

Insisting that feminists need "to seek for non-exclusionary affirmations of difference and for forms of universalism that can accommodate particularity," Kruks denies that those engaged in identity politics, such as Collins, can accomplish this goal.[30] Kruks' concern is that identity politics advocates experience-based accounts of knowledge or what she terms an "epistemology of provenance." The call for political alliances is undermined by the presupposition that since knowledge is experience-based and thus group specific, those who are outside of the group cannot share that knowledge and are unable to evaluate the group's epistemic and political claims. She writes that "the unintended end point of an epistemology of provenance can be an acute and politically debilitating subjectivism" that prevents communicability between groups.[31] At worst identity politics lapses into solipsism as each individual's experience is different from everyone else's. Kruks' goal is to find "a way of acknowledging the claims to experiential knowledge of particular identity groups, without thereby wholly denying more general visions and projects of emancipation are possible."[32] However, such general "visions and projects" tend to replicate hierarchical power relations among women, for example, maintaining racism rather than challenging explicitly antiblack racism.

Kruks turns to feminist standpoint theory as a resource to overcome the shortcomings of identity politics. She heralds the work of Nancy Hartsock for insisting "on the epistemological validity of the knowledge of a particular oppressed group: women" while at the same time "concerning itself with a *general* human emancipatory project."[33] However, this position is not opposed to the arguments given by those whom Kruks has identified as engaging in identity politics, including Collins, who promotes an emancipatory general politics. Kruks also appreciates Hartsock's distinction between a standpoint and a perspective. According to Kruks, standpoint theory, unlike identity politics, involves more than the recognition of the experience of oppression; rather it also "involves a work of critical reflection on that experience and on the *social practices* out of which it is born. It aims to develop a critique of dominant knowledge claims and an alternative account of social reality on which a project of *general* human emancipation might be based."[34] Notwithstanding the fact Collins advocates such a distinction, Kruks must realize that white women in the United States do not have the experience of being racially marginalized from which to draw such critical reflection. The project of white feminists, who are committed to the creation of multiracial feminist coalitions, must be fully to realize the implications of their racialization and to develop critiques of their dominant knowledge claims. My concern with Kruks' analysis is twofold. First, the recognition of the saliency of race among black women and within standpoint theory evident in Collins' work should not lead to the hasty conclusion that Collins is engaged in identity politics. Kruks attributes to Collins' *Black Feminist Thought* the belief that "all black women share common culture, experience and ways of knowing."[35] In this work, however, Collins states, "Other factors such as ethnicity, region of the country, urbanization, and age combine to produce a web of experiences shaping diversity among African-American women. As a result, it is more accurate to discuss a Black *women's* standpoint than a Black *woman's* standpoint."[36] In *Fighting Words* Collins is at pains to show the differences among black women and offers several arguments denouncing the efficacy of identity politics.[37] Contrary to Kruks' reading, Collins' challenges black feminists to find ways to articulate a black feminist standpoint that addresses both our differences and shared location that will not replicate hierarchical power relations.

Second, it is curious that Kruks would turn to the work of Hartsock as a positive example of standpoint theory given Hartsock's problematic engagement with women of color. Hartsock, in her much heralded article "The Feminist Standpoint: Developing the Ground for a Specifically Feminist Historical Materialism," attempts to develop a feminist standpoint that is grounded on Marxist metatheory, namely, the ontological and epistemological consequences of Marxism.[38] She tries to establish that the institutionalized sexual division of labor found in every society has epistemological consequences, namely, the development of a feminist standpoint. She states a feminist standpoint arises from the contradiction found in the systematically different structures of female and male life activity in the West. Hartsock focuses on what she considers to be the dual aspects of women's "duties" within the division of labor: labor for subsistence and childbearing. Before making her case, Hartsock states, "In addressing the institutionalized sexual division of labor, I propose to lay aside the important differences among women across race and class boundaries and instead search for central commonalities."[39] Hartsock realizes the gravity of her exclusion noting, "I adopt this strategy with some reluctance, since it contains the danger of making invisible the experience of lesbians or women of color."[40] She tries to lessen this grave error by insisting that "the effort to uncover a feminist standpoint assumes that there are some things common to all women's lives in Western class societies."[41]

It is disturbing that Hartsock recognizes that her theoretical attempt to develop a feminist standpoint could render women of color invisible, and yet she still continues despite this omission. Further, it is difficult to understand how Hartsock believes that she can flesh out our commonalities in the absence of consulting any women of color. This absence is also evident in her acknowledgments and references in the text and footnotes. While I do not object to the search for commonalities shared among all women, I do question the fruitfulness of Hartsock's attempt to discover the characteristics of a universal woman's situation. By obscuring the differences among our concrete experiences within a capitalist system, Hartsock fails in her attempt to develop a feminist standpoint that will liberate all Western women, notwithstanding the rest of the world's women who are adversely affected by capitalism. The unreflective white feminist standpoint that Hartsock articulates does not provide the theoretical resources necessary to develop a political agenda that could combat the class oppression experienced by women of color.

Black feminist thought, as articulated by Collins, is not in danger of lapsing into solipsism as it is grounded upon the group experience of black women. Underlying Kruks' argument is her frustration with feminists of color that insist that the prevalence of racism obscures the ability of white feminists to fully understand the particularity of our experience as racially and sexually marginalized women. While Collins agrees that black feminist thought is derived from the lived experience of black women, she does not conclude that black feminist thought is incommunicable. Collins draws upon standpoint theory that Kruks embraces as a theoretical resource to analyze black women's collective experience. But Collins has a rich understanding of importance of race within feminism and epistemology. Collins is addressing the problematic of white skin privilege among white feminists and the complicating notion of intersectionality within standpoint theory.

Harding, a leading proponent of standpoint theory, offers a compelling argument for the existence of a feminist standpoint. The crux of my criticism, however, stems from her attempt to address the implications of incorporating the interlocking forms of oppression experienced by women of color into mainstream feminist discourses. The problem of intersectionality at group level discussed earlier can be seen in the trajectory of Harding's work. Although the discussion of race in her latest volume, *Science and Social Inequality,* is a vast improvement over her earlier works, the continued problematic concerning race in her work shows why a general feminist standpoint may not be sustainable in a racially stratified society. In the following I will focus upon Harding's early works to highlight my concern of the treatment of race within the arguments presented by white standpoint theorists.

Following the logic of her own arguments, as presented in her first major works—*The Science Question in Feminism, Whose Science? Whose Knowledge?* and *Is Science Multicultural?*—Harding should have been compelled to acknowledge that her situation as a white woman precludes her ability to generate the standpoint of feminists of color.[42] Instead of recognizing the instances where she needs to listen to feminists of color, Harding claims that she can, in fact, adopt our standpoint. She states that she can not only include the lives of racially marginalized women in her research projects but also start her research from the lives of these women. Through an examination of her argument, namely, her assertion that knowledge is socially situated and that one's social location within a hierarchical power structure creates systematic knowledge and systematic ignorance, I will show the improbability of her claims.

Harding further asserts that systems of knowledge and systems of ignorance are developed with respect to one's social location insofar as the distinct material conditions and life activities of men and women influence the production of different patterns of knowledge and ignorance. Power differences within societies also occasion the production of systematic knowledge and systematic ignorance. Harding argues that the social location of those dominant in society produces systematic ignorance because of "their inability to generate—indeed, their interests in avoiding, devaluing, silencing—the most critical questions about the dominant conceptual frameworks."[43] Put differently, marginalized groups have a vested interest in asking these kinds of questions, while dominant groups have an interest in ignoring them. Harding explains that investigating the relation between knowledge and politics is a principle aim of standpoint epistemology, which seeks to explain how various political arrangements effect the production of knowledge. Standpoint epistemologists maintain that those in oppressive positions have a more distorted view of the reality of the social world because in order to maintain unjust privileges and positions of authority, oppressors have a greater investment in obscuring the conditions that produce their privileges and authority. Conversely, it is to the benefit of the oppressed to identify and eradicate the mechanisms, which perpetuate their marginalization. It is through the struggle against oppression that those who are oppressed gain a less distorted vision of social reality. What is lost is an explicit discussion of systematic knowledge and systematic ignorance generated among racially stratified women.

It is when Harding begins to discuss the relationship between the political struggle of racially marginalized people and the production of knowledge that she departs from the logic of her own assertions concerning situated knowledge. This departure is indicative of the systematic ignorance of members of racially oppressive groups. Harding instructs white Western feminists to closely align themselves to all women and says that "doing so involves 'reinventing ourselves as Other."[44] The phrase itself is problematic and invites confusion. Harding states that such reinvention entails "the standpoint enterprise that produces agents of history and knowledge who use experience in their knowledge-seeking" in ways that differ from either those who advocate the Western tendency to view epistemology as an ahistorical 'view from nowhere,' also characterized by Donna Haraway as the "God-trick," or as experiential foundationalism, or the view that "spontaneous consciousness of individual experience is sufficient legitimating criterion for identifying true or false beliefs."[45] Harding's claim that she can reinvent herself as an African American woman and, subsequently, develop research questions and interpret data in the same manner as a black feminist is erroneous. There is a difference between participating in political struggle against oppression that one is actually experiencing and supporting the political struggle of those with whom one feels solidarity, which ultimately produces different kinds of knowledge. By her own admission, Harding states that men "can work to eliminate male supremacy, but no matter what they do, they will still be treated with the privilege (or suspicion!) accorded to men by students, sales people, coworkers, family members, and others."[46] It is precisely because of the different situations of men and whites in a racist and sexist society that renders their ability to either inhabit our social location or adopt our standpoint impossible. It is misguided, for Harding, to assert that by reading theoretical texts authored by feminists of color, having lengthy conversations with them, and participating in political struggles against racism that she can acquire the ability to start her research from our lives. As long as we live in a world of racial hierarchy, with pervasive institutional and individual acts of racism, Harding will not be able to have full knowledge of the concrete experiences that generate the standpoint of women of color.

White feminists should critically examine the ways in which their privileged whiteness in a racialized social hierarchy contributes to the oppression of other women; however, Harding misunderstands the boundaries of her social location when she states that African Americans cannot be the sole generators of African American knowledge. She maintains that while the work of a white Western philosopher, which critiques Western philosophy guided by analyses offered by African American philosophers, may not be called "African American" philosophy, "it must *be* African American thought if it is to become a maximally objective account of Western philosophy."[47] Taking responsibility for one's own race and supporting the political struggle of African Americans does not entail the generation of African American thought. The thought that is generated by Harding would not be African American thought, or knowledge, but new knowledge concerning the European self and one's own social location. Harding seems to acknowledge this at times as she states, "The self-understanding I seek is to emerge as a result of my locating myself as a European American person in the analyses originally generated by thinkers of Third World descent and then continuing in the analyses by thinking about my world with the help of the accounts they have provided—yet still out of my own different social location."[48] The tension between Harding's remarks is indicative of the difficulty of finding a common ground or unifying experience to generate a feminist standpoint as opposed to a black women's standpoint. Ultimately, Harding, in effect, renders the standpoint of feminists of color as articulated by feminists of color obsolete, because she informs us that she, herself, can produce original African American thought. She thereby ignores her own insight that her feminist analysis can only be based upon the concrete experiences shaped by her situation.

The emancipatory element within standpoint theory, as expressed by white Western feminists, is significantly flawed because the standpoint of racially marginalized women is consistently misappropriated. In light of the fact that one of the primary grounds of feminist standpoint theory is the belief that one's knowledge is attained through concrete experience, it is evident that the standpoint of white Western feminists cannot capture the interlocking oppression experienced by women of color in a world that is structured according to a racial hierarchy. This failing negates the efficacy of the liberatory element within standpoint theory. To that end, I have argued that race cannot simply be an addendum to an already formulated project of feminism set forth by white standpoint theorists. While I recognize that women, like men, experience forms of oppression other than sexism and racism, such as class oppression and homophobia, I do not believe that this recognition lessens the harm done when race is not at the forefront of discussions of a feminist standpoint. If feminist standpoint theory is to give rise to an ethical society, then the project of feminist standpoint theory must be transformed.

Notes

1. For background on feminist standpoint theory, see Donna Haraway, "Situated Knowledges: The Science Question in Feminism and the Privilege of Partial Perspective," *Simians, Cyborgs, and Women: The Reinvention of Nature* (New York: Routledge, 1991); Lorraine Code, "Taking Subjectivity into Account," *Feminist Epistemologies*, ed. Linda Alcoff and Elizabeth Potter (New York: Routledge, 1993); Sandra Harding, "How Social Disadvantage Creates Epistemic Advantage," *Social Theory and Sociology*, ed. Stephen Turner (New York: Blackwell, 1996).

2. For example, see Angela Davis, *Women, Race, and Class* (New York: Random House, 1983); *Words of Fire: An Anthology of African-American Feminist Thought*, ed. Beverly Guy-Sheftall (New York: New, 1995); bell hooks, *Ain't I a Woman: Black Women and Feminism* (Boston: South End, 1981).

3. Charles Lemert and Esme Bhan, eds., *The Voice of Anna Julia Cooper* (Lanham: Rowman and Littlefield, 1998). See also Vivian May, *Anna Julia Cooper, Visionary Black Feminist: A Critical Introduction* (New York: Routledge, 2007).

4. In a forthcoming article I argue that Cooper was a forerunner to contemporary versions of feminist standpoint theory. In so doing, I try to show that race has been and remains a salient feature of standpoint theory and that women of color are not to be "added" to accounts of standpoint theory as developed by mainstream white feminists.

5. The concept of 'intersectionality' is often attributed to Kimberle Williams Crenshaw "Mapping the Margins: Intersectionality, Identity, Politics, and Violence against Women of Color," *Stanford Law Review* 43, no. 6 (1991): 1241–99, though the idea of intersectionality had been articulated by many feminists of color. See Gloria T. Hull, Patricia Bell Scott, and Barbara Smith, eds., *But Some of Us Are Brave: All the Women Are White, All the Blacks Are Men: Black Women's Studies* (New York: Feminist Press at City University of New York, 1982). Judy Scales-Trent, "Black Women and the Constitution: Finding Our Place, Asserting Our Rights," *Harvard Civil Rights-Civil Liberties Law Review* 24, no. 1 (1989): 9–43.

6. Patricia Hill Collins, *Fighting Words* (Minneapolis: University of Minnesota Press, 1998); henceforth, FW.

7. Ibid., 207.

8. Ibid., 208.

9. Ibid., 211.

10. Ibid.

11. Ibid., 223.

12. See Bonnie Thornton Dill, "Race, Class, and Gender: Prospects for an All-Inclusive Sisterhood," *Feminist Studies* 9.1 (1983): 131–50; Collins, *Fighting Words*, 210.

13. Jean-Paul Sartre, *Being and Nothingness: An Essay on Phenomenological Ontology*, tr. Hazel Barnes (New York: Philosophical Library, 1956), henceforth BN; Jean-Paul Sartre, *Critique of Dialectical Reason*, vol. 1, trans. Alan Sheridan-Smith (London: NLB, 1976); henceforth CDR.

14. Jean-Paul Sartre, *Anti-Semite and Jew,* trans. George J. Becker (New York: Schocken Books, 1948); henceforth, ASJ.

15. BN, 414

16. Ibid., 410

17. Ibid., 418.

18. At this stage, in Sartre's early work it is only the gaze of the perpetual Third in the absence of an account of materiality, that unifies racially marginalized groups. The absence of an account of materiality does not detract from the saliency of the considerable ontological difference in the situation of oppressed groups and oppressing groups.

19. BN, 428

20. Ibid., 429

21. In *Being and Nothingness* Sartre writes that "it is only when the oppressed class by revolution or by a sudden increase of its power posits itself as 'they-who-look-at' in the face of members of the oppressing class, it is only then that the oppressors experience themselves as 'Us' " (BN, 429).

22. Marcano, "Sartre and the Social Construction of Race," 221.

23. William McBride, *Sartre's Political Theory* (Bloomington: Indiana University Press, 1991), 137.

24. CDR, 721.

25. Ibid., 349.

26. Ibid., 346.

27. Ibid.

28. Ibid., 350.

29. Ibid. Sartre has moved beyond the model of group constitution given in *Anti-Semite and Jew,* where the racially marginalized group was passively constituted through the look of the Other. In the *Critique* we discover that the unification of the group stems from both the repressive praxis of the Other *and* the free constituting praxis of the individual.

30. RE, 95.

31. Ibid., 109.

32. Ibid., 111.

33. Ibid.

34. Ibid., 112.

35. Ibid., 109.

36. BFT, 24.

37. See FW, 52–55 for an example of Collins' arguments against identity politics.

38. Nancy C. M. Hartsock, "The Feminist Standpoint: Developing the Ground for a Specifically Feminist Historical Materialism," *The Second Wave: A Reader in Feminist Theory*, ed. Linda Nicholson (New York: Routledge, 1997); henceforth, FS.

39. Ibid., 222.

40. Ibid.

41. Ibid.

42. Sandra Harding, *The Science Question in Feminism* (Ithaca: Cornell University Press, 1986); Sandra Harding, *Whose Science? Whose Knowledge? Thinking from Women's Lives* (Ithaca: Cornell University Press, 1991); henceforth, WS; Sandra Harding, *Is Science Multicultural?* (Bloomington: Indiana University Press, 1998); henceforth, IS.

43. IS, 151.

44. WS, 193.

45. Ibid., 270. Donna Haraway, "Situated Knowledges: The Science Question in Feminism and the Privilege of Partial Perspective," *Feminist Studies* 14, no. 3 (1988).

46. IS, 161.

47. WS, 288.

48. Ibid., 283.

7

Rethinking Black Feminist Subjectivity

Ann duCille and Gilles Deleuze

Maria del Guadalupe Davidson

The Occult of True Black Womanhood

Ann duCille's article "The Occult of True Black Womanhood: Critical Demeanor and Black Feminist Studies," offers a profound critique of the current popularity of the academic study of black women. "Within and around the modern academy," duCille aptly observes, "racial and gender alterity has become a hot commodity that has claimed black women as its principal signifier."[1] Concerning black women's current *en vogue* status as other, duCille states that she is "alternately pleased, puzzled, and perturbed—bewitched, bothered, and bewildered—by this alterity that is perpetually thrust upon African American women, by the production of black women as infinitely deconstructable 'othered' matter."[2] While duCille certainly believes that the condition of black women is a worthy topic of academic discussion and is pleased by the degree of recent interest in black women, duCille wonders why white men and women (and we might add black men as well) are so "interested in me and people who look like me (metaphorically speaking)? Why have we—black women—become the subjected subject of so much contemporary scholarly investigation, the peasants under the glass of intellectual inquiry in the 1990s"?[3] In response to this increased attention, duCille goes on to express a degree of suspicion: "It is not news that by virtue of our race and gender, black women are not only the "second sex"—*the Other*, in postmodern parlance—but we are also the last race, the most oppressed, the most marginalized, the most deviant, the quintessential site of difference. And through the inversionary properties of deconstruction, feminism, cultural studies, multiculturalism, and contemporary commodity culture, the last shall be first. Perhaps."[4] It is important to note duCille's use of "perhaps" in the above paragraph. While ranking "first" is usually positive, here duCille wonders whether it is a slight-of-hand that leads black women to be positioned as first. With her use of the qualifier "perhaps," duCille implores readers to ask whether being in the "first" position is really beneficial for black women. Although black women's position of other is celebrated within postmodern discourse, "perhaps" this celebration will not change her negative position in society.

The source of duCille's hesitation here is that the inversion of black females' status—from last to first—has occurred before.[5] The inversion to which she refers is the association of black female sexuality with the primitivism of the early twentieth century where the "black female functioned as an erotic icon in the racial and sexual ideology of Western civilization."[6] The exotic status of the black female led to a fixation of the black female body as ranking first in eroticism. The alternative to the erotic icon, the mammy figure, who ranks first in nurturing, was an equally damaging image for black women. In acquiescing to the mammy image, Patricia Hill Collins observes that black women do harm to themselves and their communities. In so doing, Collins believes that they "become effective conduits for perpetuating racial oppression."[7] Just as the early twentieth century inversion of black females' status was reductive and harmful, the same perils, duCille suspects, might recur with the postmodern *othering* of black women.[8]

To explore duCille's suspicion further, this chapter will critically evaluate postmodernism's project of defining the black woman as other. Steven Connor, in his analysis of postmodernism, writes that "from its beginning, postmodernism has always been more than a cartographic enterprise; it has also been a *project*, an effort of renewal and transformation. The questions raised by postmodernism were always questions of value."[9] If Connor is right, we must raise the question as to whose values are at stake in postmodernism. In examining this question of value, I will suggest that the projects of modernism and postmodernism, in spite of appearances to the contrary, are linked together. Just as the modern project has been shown to enact violence against all modes of otherness, a similar violence is likewise carried over into the postmodern exaltation of otherness, in spite of its best intentions. From this, I conclude that postmodern discourse has not brought about the liberation of black females, but to the contrary, has further solidified the status of black women as errant and marginalized.

The perils of postmodern discourse will be uncovered through a more detailed analysis of Ann duCille's article, "The Occult of True Black Womanhood: Critical Demeanor and Black Feminist Studies," where duCille sets forth a compelling critique of the association between black women and otherness in postmodern discourse. duCille has deep reservations about the positioning of black females as other. She rightly observes that, from her own perspective as a black woman, it is nonblack women who are the site of difference: "To myself, of course, I am not the Other; to me it is the white women and men so intent on theorizing my difference who are the Other."[10] As an alternative to the postmodern discourse of otherness, duCille calls for a rethinking of black female subjectivity, although she does not carry out this project in her essay. In order to take a first step in that direction, I will then bring duCille's work into dialogue with the work of Gilles Deleuze, specifically with his notion of the *fold.* The fold, I suggest, offers valuable resources for the effort within black feminist thought to develop a positive account of black female subjectivity, because it provides a means of conceiving an internally defined subjectivity, a notion to which duCille's work certainly alludes but is unable to articulate fully.

The Black Woman as Postmodern Other

One of the buzzwords of postmodern discourse is *alterity*, the notion of difference. Postmodernism reveals the underlying hostility, even the violence, of modernity toward all modes of difference.[11] The concepts of 'difference' and 'otherness,' by contrast, are embraced by postmodern thinkers such as Derrida, Levinas, and Lyotard. This prompts Costas Douzinas to conclude that in postmodern discourse, "The other comes first. He or she is the condition of existence of language, or self, of the law. In the philosophy of alterity, the other can never be reduced to the self or the different to the same. The demand of the other that obliges me is the 'essence' of the ethics of alterity."[12] While postmodernism's privileging of otherness and difference is readily apparent to even the most cursory glance at postmodern discourse, what needs to be considered is the deeper question as to whether this valorization of otherness really changes the status of the other. In other words, does the valorization of the other really establish the other on an equal footing with the subject? Or does it provide yet another means by which one group can retain its privilege over the so-called other? Here I am certainly not suggesting that postmodern thought is altogether negative for black feminism; quite the contrary, its deconstruction of metanarratives and unmasking of the transcendental ego as a male ego have important implications for black feminism.[13] However, I do want to suggest that black women should be wary of postmodernism's fascination with difference and its identification of black women as the site of difference.

One initial reason for caution here has to do with the center/margin model used in postmodern discourse. Concerning postmodern discourse, Steven Connor observes that "the romance of the marginal is to be found throughout postmodern cultural politics. . . . This form of subcultural study takes its place within a cultural/critical frame which explores the possibilities of inverting conventional mappings and distributions of power."[14] This inversion of conventional distributions of power has brought increased attention to those who have been marginalized. Inspired by the work of bell hooks, duCille writes, "Where gender and racial differences meet in the bodies of black women, the result is the invention of an other Otherness, a hyperstatic alterity."[15] By a "hyperstatic alterity," duCille means that black women, under the gaze of others, have come to be seen as the embodiment of racial, sexual, and economic difference. While duCille certainly does appreciate postmodern discourse's attention to the margins and the attention it has brought to the plight of black women, she wonders whether this romance of the marginal has really changed the status of black women. Indeed, even though postmodernism inverts the distribution of power between the center and the margin, bell hooks, for example, has drawn a negative conclusion about this inversion. hooks observes: "It is sadly ironic that the contemporary discourse which talks the most about heterogeneity, the decented subject, declaring breakthroughs that allows recognition of Otherness, still directs its critical voice primarily to a specialized audience that shares a common language rooted in the very master narratives it claims to challenge."[16] And duCille seems to concur with this conclusion when she notes that black women remain "exotic subjects" for postmodern discourse: "They are exotic this time out, however, not because they are rarely taught or seldom read, but because in the midst of the present, multicultural moment, they have become politically correct, intellectually popular, and commercially precious sites of literary subject . . . [B]lack women—that is, certain black women—and their texts have been taken up by and reconfigured within the academy, elevated and invoked by the intellectual elite as well as the scholarly marginal."[17] So the postmodern celebration of black females as other brings attention to the lives of black women, however this romanticism of the margins positions black women as "commercially precious," "politically correct," and "exotic."

The reason why many black feminists, including Alice Walker, Barbara Christian, Hortense Spillers, and Barbara Smith, have been wary of postmodern discourse—which is typically a discourse practiced by white men and women—is that they are keenly aware of the power of language. If language, as Heidegger writes, is the "master of man,"[18] then its creative power is undeniable. This implies that when black women are denied equal access to language, they become ensnared within a web of significations that they cannot steer or control. Postmodern discourse, in spite of its attention to black women, is not a discourse in which black women have a voice. They are spoken about but do not speak. The cost of otherness, *the* site of difference, is the loss of voice. Postmodern discourse's identification of black women as other, in turn, identifies white men and women as subjects and authors. So, in marking black females as tangible sites of difference, black women become a vehicle for whites to better understand their own experiences and establish their own authority. Minrose C. Gwin echoes this point, for example, when she insists that it is critically important for white women, in particular, not to regard black women and their texts as other, insisting that "if such a reading is to have any meaning at all, it must curve back upon itself to become a reflexive process which not only reads its own cultural assumptions . . . but which also turns back upon itself to read itself as *white* other in many black women's texts."[19]

To symbolize this condition in which the authority of others is established at the expense of black women, duCille evokes the image of bones—dry, whitened bones with no flesh left on them: "The griefs of African American women indeed seem to grieve on universal bones—'to concretize and make vivid a system of oppression.' But it also seems (and herein lies the rub) that in order to grieve 'universally,' to be 'concrete,' to have 'larger meaning,' the flesh on these bones ultimately always must be white or male."[20] Black women may symbolize what happens to a body that is tortured (physically, psychologically, and spiritually) by the forces of racism and sexism. To be sure, those bones that duCille refers to have their own way of communicating. But, since they do not have a voice that is recognized by the academy (so intent on theorizing them), it is left for others to claim their voice or to tell their story. Meat is put on their bones, when the stories of black women are articulated by others.[21] While duCille, like the black feminist scholars mentioned above, recognizes the power of language and regards it as an essential tool for black women, what she offers to this struggle is an interesting way of analyzing black female existence. The resistance to marginalizing discourse, according to duCille, can be developed through a consideration of black women not as other but as sacred texts.

The Black Woman as Sacred Text

To make sense of the metaphor of the sacred text, we must first address duCille's use of the term *sacred*. The sacred may refer to devotion to a deity, to something that should be approached with reverence, or to something that is protected or immune from violence. None of these definitions of the sacred, however, quite fit duCille's use of the sacred in relation to black female existence; instead the metaphor of the sacred seems to refer to the way in which black women transcend the myriad ways in which they are perceived. Her metaphor thus undoes the mythology that constructs black women as other by challenging those who suppose that *they can theorize* about black women. "As I have suggested," duCille writes, "the question of who speaks for me, who can write my sacred text, is emotionally and politically charged as it is enduring and controversial."[22] To further understand the issue at stake here, we should also consider the reference to black women as a "text." If black women are texts, within postmodernism their stories are already written and coopted by others who want to *tell* black women about their history and take credit for telling that history. The black woman is thus a *text* without ever being its author. In other words, the black woman is interpreted by someone looking from the outside who has not lived as a black woman but feels capable of speaking authoritatively about black women. To illustrate this reality, I will evoke two examples, among countless other possible ones.

In a rush to *give voice* to the black woman's story (as if black women have not told or were not capable of telling their own stories), duCille argues that black women stand, for so many critics, at the busy "intersection" of race, class, and gender; as such, black women are always in jeopardy of being "run over by oncoming traffic."[23] In support of her claim, duCille cites the relationship between white and black female scholars, pertaining to a conflict over the authoritative voice highlighted by Gloria Wade-Gayles that circled around Toni Cade Bambara and Gerda Lerner. duCille writes that although Gloria Wade-Gayles concludes that Toni Cade Bambara's book *Black Woman* was

> "the first book that pulled together black women's views on black womanhood" and Jeanne Noble's *Beautiful, Also, Are the Souls of My Black Sisters* was the "first history of black women in American written by a black woman." Yet despite the recovery and reconnaissance missions of Bambara, Noble, Joyce Ladner, and other black women intellectuals who did groundbreaking work in the seventies, it is white feminist historian Gerda Lerner whom the academy recognizes as the pioneer in reconstructing the history of African American women.[24]

And in many cases, the positioning of black women as marginal and outside the norm has allowed white male, white female, and black male scholars to construct successful academic careers, even though they might present their actions as altruistic. duCille highlights this point with respect to Lerner's approach to black female experience: "[H]er preface[] was to call attention to such 'unused sources' as black women's own records of their experiences and 'to bring another forgotten aspect of the black past to life.' In drawing on such first-person accounts as diaries, narratives, testimonies, and organizational records and reports, Lerner endeavored in her volume, she says, 'to let black women speak for themselves.' "[25] duCille takes issue with Lerner's obtuseness for several reasons, including the fact that Lerner's so-called unexplored sources had been explored "since the nineteenth century."[26] Lerner describes herself as offering a gift that brings voice to the voiceless black women, even though, as duCille notes, "black women had been speaking for themselves and on behalf of each other long before Gerda Lerner endeavored 'to let' them do so."[27] This issue of speaking for oneself is a pertinent one, because duCille rightly observes that numerous black women scholars have preserved the literary and scholarly creations of black women only to be forgotten, discredited, or ignored by the academy. This situation prompts duCille to ask the following question: "What does it mean for the future of black feminist studies that a large portion of the growing body of scholarship on black women is now being written by white feminists and by men whose work frequently achieves greater critical and commercial success than that of the black female scholar who carved out a field in which few 'others' were then interested?"[28] If we consider black women as sacred texts, then the controversy is rooted in the question over who has the right to write the text. The above examples suggest that this sacred text is interpreted primarily by those who do not occupy the space of black female existence.

While such examples are significant, I do not want to be taken to imply that only black women have the right to tell their own story. The point here is not that black women have the only voice but, more modestly, that they need to have *a* voice and to receive credit for their voices.[29] In a moment of bravery and vulnerability, duCille acknowledges that one must exercise caution in declaring (from within) that one's story is one's own to tell:

> Questions of turf, and territoriality, appropriation and co-option persist within my own black feminist consciousness, despite my best efforts to intellectualize them away. Again, this is not a new dilemma. The modern, academic version of the ageless argument over who owns the sacred text of me and mine is at least as old the work of white anthropologists Melville and Frances Herskovits dating back to the 1920s and reaching a controversial peak in 1941 with the publication of *The Myth of the Negro Past*, a study of African cultural retentions scorned by many black intellectuals.[30]

duCille's concern is an important one. She does not want to prevent others from theorizing black female subjectivity, because she is mindful of the pitfalls of essentialist thinking. Nevertheless, duCille believes that it is necessary for black women to have a voice, perhaps even the lead voice, in theorizing their own experience. This is especially important because black women have done much to preserve the gardens of their foremothers but have not received the "lion's share of the credit."[31]

While duCille avoids the lure of essentialism, her central point is that black women's voices should be an authority on their own text, that is, with respect to their lived experiences. This goes beyond issues of commodification and self-interest. More profoundly, it is an ethical claim that has to do with preserving one's own life. The right to speak for one-self, as Edward Said argues, is the "ethico-discursive principle" at the heart of "feminism and women's studies, black and ethnic studies, socialist and anti-imperialist studies." All of these disciplines "rest" on the "the right of formerly un- or misrepresented human groups to speak for and represent themselves in domains defined, politically and intellectually, as normally excluding them, usurping their signifying and representing functions, over-riding their historical reality."[32] While duCille's work leaves these matters of the ethics of voice and subjectivity open, I will now turn to the work of the French thinker Gilles Deleuze, whose thought provides potentially useful resources for thinking about black women, not as others but as subjects.

Deleuze: Subjectivity and the Fold

In turning to Deleuze, I do not intend to provide a systematic overview of Deleuze's work; instead my focus will be on the implications of Delueze's notion of the fold for black feminist thought. This choice of focus is not arbitrary because, as Tom Conley observes, the notion of the fold "counts among the most vital and resonate terms in [Delueze's] copious and varied writings."[33] Importantly, Deleuze develops his notion of the fold as a part of his analysis of power structures. In that analysis, Deleuze raises a question about the power of resistance that should be of central concern to all black feminists, including duCille. Deleuze writes: "What remains, then, except an anonymous life that shows up on when it clashes with power, argues with it, exchanges 'brief and strident words,' and then fades back into the night, what Foucault called 'the life of infamous men,' whom he asked us to admire by virtue of 'their misfortune, race or uncertain madness?' "[34] With this question, Deleuze wonders whether marginalized groups, such as black women, can produce any real change in speaking truth to power. What, in other words, is the point of struggling against the proverbial wall of racism, classism, gender discrimination, and economic oppression, if these struggles are destined to fade "back into the night"? This is certainly an understandable reaction on the part of many black women "who are daily beaten down, mentally, physically, and spiritually—women who are powerless to change their condition in life." One mark of their victimization, as hooks notes, is that they "accept their lot in life without visible question, without organized protest, without collective anger or rage."[35] In the face of such a reality, the question shared by both Deleuze and black feminists concerns whether there can be any source for resistance against power structures, and if so, what those resources are. Deleuze's notion of the fold, I want to suggest, is potentially significant in this regard. Like duCille and other black feminists, Deleuze is not so much concerned with alterity as with subjectivity, especially the becoming of subjects who are unable to self-define, to become themselves, or to create themselves anew due to the pressures of social forces. For this reason, Deleuze's notion of the fold can provide new and valuable resources for addressing questions of black female subjectivity raised by duCille and others.

The French term *pli*, as Conley explains, refers "both to a twist of fabric and to the origins of life, bears a lightness and density that marks many of the philosopher's reflection on questions of *being* and on the nature of *events*."[36] What is thought-provoking about Deleuze's notion of the fold is that, like a piece of fabric, it maintains its physical presence but at the same time can create new spaces within its formation of new crevices and pleats. This is why the fold is capable of "bearing almost infinite conceptual force."[37] Through its multiple *foldings*, the subject maintains access to the internal and external aspects of her being. This means that "[a] person's relation with his or her body becomes both an "archive" and a "diagram," a collection of subjectivations and a mental map charted on the basis of the past and drawn from the events and elements in the ambient world."[38] With this notion of the fold, then, I want to suggest that the folding of the subject provides an interesting model for thinking about the way in which black females can both inherit a historical condition and at the same time create new identities within that condition.

It bears noting that there is not an inside or outside prior to the fold, instead the *fold* creates the inside as well as the outside. The inside and outside of the fold are two sides of a single surface. Conley adds: "Thus the fold allows the body and the soul of the subject to be and to become in the world through "intensions" . . . felt about "extensions" in space. Because the inside and outside are conjoined by the point of view of the soul on the world, the apprehension of the condition of possibility of variation allows the subject to think about how it inflects and is inflected by the mental and geographical milieus it occupies."[39] That said we need to ask whether there can be an inside of thought for black women who are caught up in systems of power and trapped in the position of other forgotten. Has the internal been forgotten? If so, how can it be recovered? Echoing the insights of Fanon and hooks, duCille seeks a way for black women to escape the external gaze that fixes black women in the static, illusionary position of the other. This is accomplished through the recovery of a black female identity that is no longer a marker of alterity but is capable of speaking its own name. In this attempt, Deleuze is an important ally, because his notion of the fold signifies a way of producing an identity internally.

Like duCille, Deleuze rejects the idea of an ahistorical subjectivity whose identity would escape from the vicissitudes of history and the external world. Instead of being ahistorical and fixed, both thinkers would agree that subjectivity must be achieved, in other words, that there is a struggle for subjectivity. Conley explains that this struggle is a "battle to win the right to have access to difference, variation, and metamorphosis."[40] Similarly, duCille describes the nature of this struggle in terms of the struggle by black women to become the authors of their own text. Through this struggle, they seek to establish a space of their own, as something other than the other. The fact that this is a "struggle" suggests that the formation of positive subjectivity can only occur through resistance to existing systems of power. Subjectivity, according to Deleuze, is in a certain sense defined by its power to resist, because "diffuse centers of power do not exist without points of resistance that are in some way primary"[41]

What type of internal relation to oneself is established by *folds*? In *folding,* one is able to encounter another self, in a different way from the identity imposed by external, marginalizing forces. Deleuze explains the dual nature of this relation to oneself in the following terms: "On the one hand, there is a 'relation to oneself' that consciously derives from one's relation with others; on the other, there is equally a 'self constitution' that consciously derives from the moral code as a rule for knowledge."[42] In addition to the various forces that define the subject from the outside, Deleuze acknowledges the "moral code" to know thyself.[43] In this respect, his notion of the fold can be useful to black feminists who seek to counter the commodification and colonization of black women. This operation is at work in duCille's reference to the many women who have preserved counterhistories and countermemories of black women.

Importantly, Deleuze emphasizes that this counter-history need not be a mere reaction to a prior set of historical conditions. Instead, the relation to oneself has an independent status. As Deleuze explains: "It is as if the relation of the outside folded back to create a doubling, allowed a relation to oneself to emerge, and constitute an inside which is hollowed out and develops its own unique dimension. . . . [T]he relation to oneself that is self-mastery, 'is a power that one brought to bear on oneself *in* the power that one exercised over others.' "[44] Deleuze, like duCille, is interested in establishing a positive notion of difference. Instead of being a product of a relation to something else, positive difference is something like "the right to difference, variation and metamorphosis."[45] This means that the struggle for subjectivity is not just a reaction to a prior situation; instead it is a creative force and a source of change.

Along these lines, Deleuze's fold provides a space for black women to create a positive identity from a perspective and position internal to themselves. As Deleuze suggests, it is "a differentiation that leads to a folding, a reflection."[46] Folding is thus not merely about resisting the external; it is primarily about creating a "relation to oneself"[47] Since the process of folding functions "beneath the codes and rules of knowledge and power," what is also critical is that the folds are "apt to unfold and merge with them, but not without new folding being created in the process."[48] It is important to emphasize that Deleuze does not intend the fold as a retreat from the external world, since the outside and the inside are not distinct from one another.[49] Rather, while the fold provides a safe place for encountering oneself, what is as critical is that black feminist subjectivity also unfold. It is in unfolding that she may encounter the world in a newly constructed identity that can resist external constitution: "unfolding means becoming."[50]

Conclusion

This chapter is an attempt to challenge the postmodern identification of black women as other. Ann duCille, like a number of other black feminists, suggests that the postmodern identification of black women as a site of alterity and difference has at the best been ineffective and at the worst, harmful, to the liberation of black women. Instead of emphasizing their alterity, duCille is concerned with the subjectivity of black women and suggests that they be regarded as sacred texts. The problem with postmodern discourse and its predecessors is that they speak about black women without giving them authorship or voice. Instead of being objects of interpretation, duCille calls for black women to establish authorship. In carrying out this project, Deleuze's notion of the fold is useful, because it offers a site of creative resistance. The fold opens up a space in which black female identity can interact with itself and bring about a convergence between the outside and the inside of thought.

Notes

1. Ann duCille, "The Occult of True Black Womanhood: Critical Demeanor and Black Feminist Studies," in *Female Subjects in Black and White: Race, Psychoanalysis, Feminism*, ed. Elizabeth Abel, Barbara Christian, and Helene Moglen (Berkeley: University of California Press, 1997), 21.

2. Ibid.

3. Ibid.

4. Ibid., 22.

5. Ibid.

6. Ibid.

7. Patricia Hill Collins, *Black Feminist Thought: Knowledge, Consciousness, and the Politics of Empowerment* (New York: Routledge, 2000). 73.

8. For example, today black women rank first in the statistics concerning those likely to be unmarried and raising children without a husband or partner, that show black women as the most likely group of people to contract AIDS, and that show black women to rank first in poverty rates. While these statistics may well establish black women as outside of the norm and marginalized, they only position black women as a negative alterity.

9. Steven Connor, ed., *The Cambridge Companion to Postmodernism* (Cambridge: Cambridge University Press, 2004), 5.

10. duCille, "The Occult of True Womanhood," 21.

11. For an interesting discussion on the move from modern to postmodern thought see Martin Schiralli, *Constructive Postmodernism: Toward Renewal in Cultural and Literary Studies* (West Port, CT: Bergin and Garvey, 1999) 7–21.

12. Costa Douzinas, "Law and Justice in Postmodernism," in *The Cambridge Companion to Postmodernism*, ed. Steven Connor (Cambridge: Cambridge University Press, 2004), 196–223.

13. bell hooks, *Yearnings: Race, Gender, and Cultural Politics* (Boston: South End, 1990), 23.

14. Steven Connor, *Postmodern Culture* (Cambridge: Blackwell, 1989), 258–59.

15. duCille, "The Occult of True Womanhood," 22.

16. bell hooks, *Yearnings*, 25.

17. duCille, "The Occult of True Womanhood, 23–24.

18. Paul Sheehan, 23.

19. Minrose C. Gwin, "A Theory of Black Women's Texts and White Women's Readings or . . . the Necessity of Being Other."

20. duCille, "The Occult of True Womanhood," 49.

21. Another image evoked in this context by duCille is the image of black women as bridges: This, then, is the final paradox and the ultimate failure of the evidence of experience: to be valid—to be true—black womanhood must be legible as white or male; the texts of black womanhood must be readable as maps, indexes to someone else's experience, subject to seemingly endless process of translation and transference. . . . Under the cult of true black womanhood, the colored body, as Cherrie Moraga has argued, is "thrown over a river of tormented history to bridge the gap" . . . to make connections—connections that in this instance enable scholars working in exhausted fields to cross over into the promised land of the academy (duCille, 49). The image of the bridge is duCille's way of saying that black women get "walked on over and over again" precisely because, I would suggest, of their status as other.

22. duCille, "The Occult of True Womanhood," 29.

23. Ibid., 22.

24. Ibid., 27.

25. Ibid.

26. Ibid.

27. Ibid., 29.

28. Ibid., 26.

29. This middle ground is staked, for example, by Barbara Christian who writes, "For although the *idea* that there is a shared experience between African-American women's history and the reality of African-American women's lives is now being challenged, *my* experience is that we have both a collective life as well as individual variations that are ours and ours alone. That both these ideas are true does not mean that either is not true Barbara Christian." "Being the Subject and the Other: Reading African-American Women's Novels," in *New Black Feminist Criticism, 1985–2000*, ed. Gloria Bowles, M. Giulia Fabi, and Arlene R. Keizer (Urbana: University of Illinois Press, 2007), 123.

30. duCille, "The Occult of True Womanhood," 26.

31. Ibid., 24.

32. Connor, *Postmodern Culture*, 178.

33. Tom Conley, "Folds and Folding," in *Gilles Deleuze: Key Concepts*, ed. Charles J. Stivale (Montreal: McGill-Queen's University Press, 2005), 170.

34. Gilles Deleuze, *Foucault*, tr. Sean Hand (Minneapolis: University of Minnesota Press, 1988), 95.

35. bell hooks, *Feminist Theory from Margin to Center* (Cambridge: South End, 2000), 1.

36. Tom Conley, "Folds and Folding," in *Gilles Deleuze: Key Concepts,* ed. Charles J. Stivale, 170.

37. Ibid.

38. Ibid., 172.

39. Connor, *Postmodern Culture*, 178.

40. Ibid., 172.

41. Ibid.

42. Ibid., 100.

43. Ibid.

44. Ibid.

45. Ibid., 106.

46. Ibid., 100.

47. Ibid., 104.

48. Ibid., 105.

49. Ibid., 119.

50. Ibid., 175.

8

From Receptivity to Transformation

On the Intersection of Race, Gender, and the Aesthetic in Contemporary Continental Philosophy

Robin M. James

As many thinkers across numerous disciplines have noted, aesthetic agency and pleasure are, in the West, deeply racialized and gendered. From Catherine Clément's thesis that opera hinges on the "undoing" of (usually dark) women to Kodwo Eshun's critique of the "classic 60s myth" wherein white male rock musicians adopt the stereotypical attributes of working-class African American masculinity to heighten their sexual, and, by extension, artistic, prowess (just to list a few examples), it is evident that white Western culture grounds the ability to make and take pleasure in art in the white masculine subject's capacity to appropriate and "sublimate," as it were, traits stereotypically attributed to underprivileged bodies.[1] "Eating the other" (to borrow bell hooks' phrase) in this way, the white masculine subject metabolizes what, in stereotypically "weaker" beings, prevents genuine cultural achievement—for example, impulsiveness, irrationality, immediate embodiment, hypersexuality.[2]

In spite of their many merits, recent attempts to rethink the politics of aesthetic pleasure have not adequately addressed the intersection of race, gender, *and* the aesthetic. In her trilogy on female genius, particularly in the Colette volume, Kristeva's feminist reworking of traditional notions of narrative, embodiment, and sublimation relies upon the "eating" of the nonwhite other.[3] Her critique of phallogocentrism remains blind to whiteness. Kristeva's notion of female genius can access and rehabilitate the material, extrasymbolic aspects of experience only by appealing to and appropriating what Robert Gooding-Williams has described as the "receptivity" of nonhuman and subhuman—that is, nonwhite—others. However, Angela Davis's book on female blues singers is quite rigorous in its attention to the intersection of race and gender in the meaning and politics of Ma Rainey's, Bessie Smith's, and Billie Holiday's work.[4] Moreover, insofar as her analysis focuses primarily on the lyrical content of these women's songs and the historico-ideological issues surrounding them, Davis's work does not directly address the intersection of race and gender with the aesthetic, even though this issue of "the aesthetic" subtends, in a largely latent and unthematized way, her entire analysis. Thus I abstract from Davis's analysis of content and context the aesthetic theory which, I argue, is contained therein. In contrast to the aesthetics of receptivity, a paradigm of loss and appropriation grounded in white heteromasculine privilege, Davis's account develops what I call an "aesthetic of transformation." The aesthetics of transformation deploys tactics of complexity, contradiction, and irresolvable tension to produce works that are uniquely apt and canny expressions of working-class black women's experience/consciousness. Pleasure is then found in a sense of canniness, of finding something that (finally) "fits" or "works," of recognizing the shared character of one's seemingly isolated experiences. Davis's aesthetic of transformation works with and against the traditional aesthetic of receptivity to reconfigure the race-gender politics of aesthetic pleasure.

Since the notion of "receptivity" that Gooding-Williams articulates is helpful in thinking about the role of race in Kristeva's reading of Colette, I begin with his discussion of gender, race, and aesthetic pleasure.

Gooding-Williams on Race and Receptivity

Reading Nietzsche's *Thus Spoke Zarathustra* alongside Vincent Minnelli's 1953 film *The Band Wagon*, Robert Gooding-Williams focuses on the tendency, within Western culture, to consider aesthetic experience as a process wherein the normatively white masculine subject appropriates traits stereotypically attributed to women and black men—that is, their "receptivity" to corporeal and emotional life—in order to overcome the skeptical melancholy that characterizes white identity. Gooding-Williams compares the function of femininity in *Zarathustra* to the function of blackness in *The Band Wagon*, claiming that their status, in white Western patriarchy, as symbols of nature, immediacy, embodiment, and emotion, situates them as both outside civilization proper, and as the remedy for the alienation endemic to its (white, masculine) subjects.

Gooding-Williams argues that Zarathustra "genders the truth-willing, heroic subject of knowledge as male and his body's power of receptivity as female."[5] Further attention to Gooding-Williams's descriptions of Nietzsche's knower reveals that the masculine comportment exhibited by said knower is a specifically white form of masculine embodiment. Because Zarathustra's knower "withdraw[s] into himself," the subject of knowledge "projects the image of a deathly and otherworldly life, appearing to be a shadowy phantom whose essence is surpasensible."[6] Insofar as he aspires to death/disembodiedness, the knower engages in what Richard Dyer identifies as a key component of white identity/white embodiment: "the soul, the mind, and also emptiness, nonexistence and death" are "part of what makes white people socially white."[7] Because he experiences his body as a lack, as a state of dis-embodiedness, then, Zarathustra's melancholic knower exhibits a specifically white form of masculinity—knowledge is defined in such a way that only those exhibiting white, masculine comportments (distance, disinterestedness, objectivity) can be considered epistemically credible.

In Zarathustra's story, the knower *may* long to be redeemed by a white femininity, a "passivity, expectancy, receptivity, a kind of sacred readiness"[8] best exemplified by the Virgin Mary. In *The Band Wagon*, however, the protagonist seeks rehabilitation via cross-racial identification, appropriating not femininity but a specific stereotype of African American masculinity. The film's protagonist, Fred Astaire's Tony Hunter, longs to regain *receptivity*, that is, "intimacy with existence."[9] Like Zarathustra's knower, Hunter has lost touch with his corporeal capacities, and exists (as a mind) in the mode of (physical) nonexistence. "Unable to transmute his singing into a dancing that finds and feels the ground," in the beginning of the film, "Astaire seems a soul in suspension above the earth, a man uncertain and doubtful that he exists as a man with feet—to wit, as a dancer."[10] Hunter's whiteness is, in Gooding-Williams's account, a relation not only to one's body but also to expressive culture—to dancing, to song. Because of his white comportment, Hunter cannot dance, and can't really sing a catchy hook; as Gooding-Williams notes, the first routine's song is somewhat stilted and awkward in its rhythmic structure. By alienating him from his body, Hunter's whiteness also prohibits from compelling or being compelled by artistic performance.

In the film's second musical number, Astaire finally connects to a song and, in learning how to use syncopation, regains his ability to sing and dance. While the first number is characterized by Hunter's "Wagnerian musical syllabification,"[11] the second number "shows [Hunter] acquiring that blackness through the agency of a 'shine' who, by shining his shoes, works a sorcery that disseminates his blackness"[12] and thereby "teaches Astaire to 'swing.' "[13] Absorbing, appropriating, and neutralizing some of the shoeshine's "blackness," Hunter/Astaire is put back in touch with his body, his ability to dance and to feel a "groove." It is significant that Hunter learns to "swing" (especially in the big-band sense used in this part of the routine), because swing is/was the most commercial of all midcentury jazz forms and the one most heavily marketed to and associated with white mass consumption. Indeed, as soon as Hunter joins in the music making in this scene, there is an abrupt shift from a dirty N'awlins jazz to a distinctly swing style. Swing is smooth and sophisticated, rounding out many of the rough, brash, and bright edges of some other jazz styles. This stylistic shift accomplishes musically what, according to Gooding-Williams, Minnelli's direction accomplishes visually: "by mocking a white woman's terror of a white man suddenly become a 'White Negro' (Norman Mailer's notorious phrase), the arcade routine discredits that fear. It attributes a blackened masculinity to Astaire, but denies that a blackened masculinity endangers white women" (59). What is key here, and what Gooding-Williams misses, is that it is precisely Astaire's whiteness that neutralizes the threats posed by black masculinity.[14] This second routine establishes that aesthetic pleasure is possible (only) when white masculinity appropriates, exploits, but nonetheless neutralizes the excesses of black masculine embodiment—when jazz becomes swing (or when the blues become classic rock, and so on).

Gooding-Williams leaves us with the question of how to experience pleasure. If aesthetic pleasure is so politically problematic, how do we account for the pleasure we take in art?[15] This question is especially important since, as we know, pleasure is not automatically negated by problematic content—for example, some Jews like Wagner, and some feminists like the Rolling Stones.[16] In her reading of Colette, Kristeva attempts such a reimagining of aesthetic pleasure. However, even though Kristeva tries to rehabilitate what aesthetics has traditionally devalued as "feminine"/feminized, she does this by employing the same colonial logic of "receptivity" that Gooding-Williams describes above. Colette can "write the world's flesh," can render the sensory in language only by calling upon the perspective of nonhuman others.

Kristeva and the "Receptive" Female Genius

In her article "Whiteness Feminizes," Rey Chow argues that "feminization in its avant-garde form becomes racial power."[17] Developed in an interpretation of *Jayne Eyre* and *Hiroshima, Mon Amour*, Chow's principle indicates that these novels rework the traditional gender politics of narrative—that is, a masculine protagonist who conquers all the feminized elements of the text—by displacing gender oppression onto racial oppression.[18] The female protagonists of these novels assume their role by appropriating and metabolizing the nonwhite elements/characters in the respective works.[19] Chow emphasizes that the functioning of race as an ersatz femininity is particularly characteristic of avant-garde works. Toying with conventional forms, techniques, and values, avant-garde works often, in Chow's account, reinstitute in a different guise many of the same political problems present in traditional/classical forms. Thus, while Gooding-Williams's analysis focuses on the commutability of femininity and blackness in American *popular* culture, I argue that Kristeva's assessment of Colette's *avant-garde* "writing of the world's flesh" hinges on precisely this same capacity for race to assume, within a text, functions that are traditionally articulated in terms of gender.[20]

The psychoanalytic notion of castration describes the repression and alienation that characterize white culture generally. Insofar as Freud holds that civilization is fundamentally and necessarily repressive, that it requires one to alienate oneself from one's drives and desires, then traditional psychoanalytic models generally represent, in Kristeva's argument, a mode of subjectivity grounded in alienation and a loss of bodily immediacy. This is what Kristeva means when she claims that "psychoanalysis . . . rely[ies] on a subject conscious of 'castration.' "[21] Arguing that oedipalization and "civilization" assume, in traditional psychoanalysis, a normatively masculine subject, Kristeva uses feminine sexuality and a normatively female/bisexual subject to explore possible remedies to such masculine alienation.

By appropriating/expressing a specific form of femininity, Colette's writing rehabilitates the Western subject's receptivity to pleasure. Consistent with Kristeva's longstanding association of preoedipal processes with femininity, the "other [girl's] jouissance"[22] that is elicited in Colette's writing is not strictly bound to the constraints of oedipalized subjectivity (civilization). For Kristeva, Colette's writing taps this "other jouissance" and thus gives us access to the "archaic repressed, with the prepsychic that inhabits our drives and sensibilities . . . [H]er writing has the genius to keep in contact with it, to rehabilitate and transmit it.[23] Just as Hunter's encounters with blackness in *The Band Wagon* renews his access to sensory pleasure, embodied performance, and cultural production, Colette's use of "femininity" produces a style of writing that reunites language with the sensuousness and bodily intimacy that oedipalization forces one to renounce. Writing in the West is usually thought to rely upon distance and abstraction and is seen as part of the "intellectual" domain that is often opposed to physical, corporeal experiences; consequently, oedipalization and repression are seen as necessary steps in the subject's ascension to language. Modeled after a girl's socialization, Colette's writing "diverges from that path" described in the boy's oedipalization.[24] If patriarchal civilization makes us discontent by forcing us to adhere to a number of suspiciously clean distinctions between mind and body, language and desire, culture and nature, and individual and community, then Colette's "feminine" writing "assures . . . a perpetual rebirth" of literature, culture, and the individual by "stir[ring]" readers "to their very—inadmissible—core" and helping them to "perceive[e] more profoundly."[25] It is in this sense that this "other jouissance" is "a pleasure that is also a deliverance."[26]

"Deliverance" is conditioned upon the subject's mastery of this pleasure, of his or her ability to regulate potentially dangerous indulgence. Because it undoes much of the discipline introduced by and maintained in traditional oedipalization, this "other jouissance" could, in fact, sabotage rather than liberate the subject's ability to think, act, and create. The "infinite sensuality" experienced by the subject reunited with the world's flesh "can be experienced as a threatening, unfathomable excitement" and "is also feared, like a routine that allows mental laziness to set in, and runs the risk of abolishing . . . creative capacities."[27] The newly receptive subject could be completely overstimulated or completely understimulated, hyperactive or passive. Kristeva describes the sensory experience written in/by Colette as a "body at once wildly excitable and scrupulously submissive."[28] This over/under dichotomy plays all too easily into the racialized bad girl/good girl dynamic at work in American culture generally: black femininity threatens white patriarchal culture because it represents uncontrollable sexuality, just as white femininity threatens white patriarchal culture because it in turn represents passivity and domesticity. Since stereotypical femininity (white or black) remains an impediment to cultural achievement, this "feminine" jouissance is beneficial (to the subject, to dominant culture generally) only when it appears as a form of "bisexuality" (and not, indeed, in "women" per se). Contrasting "femininity," a superficial "masquerade . . . amusing and seductive"[29] with "the feminine," a "hypersensitive receptivity of . . . psychic depth,"[30] Kristeva argues that Collette's writing is successful because it "make[s] the feminine coexist with femininity, a receptivity with seduction . . . [A] 'mental hermaphrodite' is how Colette diagnosed it."[31] Kristeva thus privileges "the feminine" over "femininity." In her theory of genius, "femininity" is pathological when found in women; however, when "the feminine" appears as part of the subject's preoedipal psychic bisexuality, or in the writer's "mental hermaphrodism," it is evidence of genius. The feminine is a "monstrosity" that can be "livable and invigorating" when "tamed."[32]

Engaging with the "monstrous" and thereby restoring the body and sensuousness to alienated, hyper-intellectualized, disinterested patriarchal language, the "feminine" becomes, in Colette's avant-garde literature, racial power. Kristeva suggests that, in the case of Colette's own life and works, "femininity" becomes "the feminine" when Colette opens herself to nonhuman animals. Kristeva writes that "it is a cat, Kiki-la-Doucette, to whom, in 1908, Colette entrusts the task of articulating a new version of objectless love, the incommensurable love of an ecstatic ego that, because it is free of its objects, can remake the world to fit its excitement."[33]

To imagine a nonoedipalized relation to language and to one's sensing body, to experience an ego "free of its objects," Colette needed to abandon the domain of the properly human. Not coincidentally, nonwhites/non-Europeans also occupy and have occupied this position of the nonhuman or subhuman animal; closer to nature, "savage," hypersexual, emotional, nonwhites are/were excluded from the category of the "human" precisely because they had no "civilization" to make them "discontent." It is, however, precisely this supposed lack of civilization that endows nonwhites with the power of "receptivity" and the ability to rehabilitate all the overly oedipalized melancholics[34] like Hunter (or Clapton, or Cobain . . . or Colette). Colette gains the receptivity necessary to write the world's flesh in the same way that Hunter learns to swing: "Faced with the untenable strangeness of self and other, the writer tames extreme perceptions and desires as if they were those of a beast—both a formidable stranger and a beloved companion. Hence, through the 'Four-legged Ones' . . . the other is not only my enemy, his beastly jouissance is inside me: I am that beast."[35]

Colette can, in Kristeva's reading, successfully render the sensory in words because she has "tamed" savage impulses and incorporated them into otherwise "civilized" language and subjects. Although Kristeva never frames her reading of Colette in overtly racial terms, it is, insofar as it calls upon the "monsters" and the "beasts," full of racial overtones and racialized mind/body and culture/nature hierarchies.

Careful attention to Kristeva's word choice reveals that her discussion of Colette's sensory "genius" is framed in obvious and objectionable colonial tropes. For example, Colette's rehabilitation of the sensuous within writing poses "a challenge to the universe of *civilized mastery attributed to humans*"[36] because it "can be read as *exquisite or troubling dehumanization.*"[37] Colette appropriates the corporeality, sensuousness, and sensuality of "primitives"[38] and not-fully-human animals in order to rebel against and rehabilitate human civilization.[39] Indeed, Kristeva suggests that Colette's genius comes from her willingness to, as it were, "slum it." Kristeva argues that "Colette wants to describe the extreme destitution of her own sensibility, pushed to the limits of animality. *Savage* intuitions and brutalities dwell within her. She immerses herself in that universe, unknown or repressed by most of us, in that archaic dimension of the psyche of us 'Two-legged Ones.' . . . *Thanks to these beasts, Colette succeeds in taming and excusing the paroxysms of the psyche that, in other people, dig hells and promise paradises.*"[40] Just as it is able to master "femininity," feminine genius is the "strength" that overcomes what in most people is a downfall—savage animality that "digs hell" in "other people," particularly actual "savages" and "animals" (i.e., nonwhites and non-Europeans).[41] If Colette were not considered white, her "savageness" would have been expected, not exceptional. When tamed by writing or other properly sublimatory activities, nonhuman animals, savages, and monsters become the means for accessing desires and pleasures.[42]

The racially marked other's instrumentality is not isolated, in Kristeva's work, to her reading of Colette. As Sam Haigh notes, Kristeva's meditation on "National Depression" views immigrants (particularly those of African descent from the Caribbean)[43] as key to the rehabilitation of France's national melancholy.[44] According to Haigh, Kristeva claims that "openness to the other, the foreigner, the immigrant, is one way in which France can rescue itself from depression . . . What is striking, of course, is that the immigrant him- or herself disappears as a subject, and instead remains simply a means through which the

French subject may be healed."[45] Suffering from a deep melancholia wherein it is unable to properly mourn the loss of its identity as a world-important imperial power and as a nation unified with a clear (and racially homogeneous) sense of self, France looks to its supposedly "happily assimilated immigrants" to regain and reconnect with its lost sense of self and self-esteem. Accordingly, Haigh concludes that, for Kristeva, "national melancholia is thus, more specifically, 'racial melancholia': a desire both to introject the racial other, to welcome it and hold it within, yet also to devour and destroy it."[46] Just as the black shoeshine was the means for Astaire's Hunter to overcome his white melancholy, black Caribbean immigrants are the mere means for France to rehabilitate its (white) national melancholy; in neither instance are the nonwhite figures considered as ends in themselves, as fully human subjects.

The instrumentality and ultimate disposability of the nonwhite other is confirmed in Kristeva's discussion of Colette's "voracity" and "cannibalism." What hooks calls "eating the other"—the metabolism of exotic, racially marked individuals as a means for the self-improvement and education of the white subject—is, in Kristeva's reading of Colette, the very basis of aesthetic pleasure.[47] Traditionally, aesthetic taste is based on gustatory taste yet distinguished from it by the former's attempt at intellectual distance (e.g., disinterestedness), which is opposed to the latter's connotations of bodily immediacy.[48] Throughout her female genius trilogy, Kristeva rethinks aesthetic taste's relationship to gustatory taste in order to reconnect words and sense, meaning and desire. However, in *Colette*, Kristeva argues that "rehabilitation" of taste is possible only through the absorption and assimilation of others (just as France will overcome its melancholy through the "melting-pot" type of assimilationism).[49] Thus Kristeva argues that taste is "*a cannibalistic pleasure. Through taste I appropriate the other, assimilate it.*"[50]

Kristeva suggests that the particular genius of Colette's writing is that it offers the key to white melancholia insofar as "cannibalism" initiates "proper" mourning by re-framing pleasure as something that culture produces and not something that it has repressed or lost.[51] For Freud, melancholia was a sort of failure of mourning, the refusal or disavowal of an object's loss (usually via an attempted introjection of said object or of a substitute).[52] Colette's writing diverts melancholia into proper mourning because it does not seek to "liberate" what civilization/Oedipalization supposedly "represses," but instead creates *new* forms of sensuous bodily intimacy. As Kristeva explains, "Cannibalistic mourning of the other thus leads Colette to a conception of love that disassociates itself from happiness to become a pure quest for the *mot juste* and to culminate in extreme voluptuousness, which is nothing other than the voluptuousness of naming" (260). Writing reinvigorated by the metabolism of the nonhuman/nonwhite "animal" other is the cure for cultural melancholia, for it recognizes that traditional paradigms of pleasure (in this instance, "happiness") are impossible to realize, and thus refocuses the aim of art/writing/sublimation onto an attainable pleasure, "the voluptuousness of naming."

Kristeva is clearly invested in deconstructing traditional mind/body hierarchies (which are oftentimes implicated in racist stereotypes about nonwhites) and reimagining the possibilities of a meaning that is firmly connected to desire, intellect that is not severed from corporeality. In her attempt to frame this attempt in terms of a "voluptuous naming," however, Kristeva's avant-garde theory/theory of Colette's avant-garde writing participates in white culture's longstanding habit of cannibalistically appropriating nonwhite bodies and vernacular expressive traditions as a way to compensate for the various things white culture thinks it is missing. So, insofar as Kristeva tries to rehabilitate a "melancholic" language alienated from desire and sense, she does so in exactly the same way that Hunter's melancholic performance is "cured" in Minnelli's film—by "eating" the clearly racialized other. Colette's particular "female genius" is the ability to "cannibalize" the receptivity and rebelliousness of nonhuman animals and metabolize/sublimate this into a new form of sensuous writing. In this sense, then, the "other jouissance" Kristeva identifies as the source of Colette's female genius is, in the end, the same old racialized (normatively white) pleasure at work in *The Band Wagon*. Feminization, in Colette's avant-garde writing, becomes racial power.

Both Minnelli's film and Kristeva's reading of Colette posit notions of aesthetic pleasure grounded in the historical and political coordinates of European colonialism. In contrast to Minelli and Kristeva, Angela Davis's *Blues Legacies and Black Feminism* offers a theory of aesthetic pleasure grounded in the real-world experiences of African American women. Although her study of black female blues singers has not received sustained attention in the scholarly literature on philosophical aesthetics, Davis's analysis of the political import of the works of Ma Rainey, Bessie Smith, and Billie Holiday does in fact offer, if latently, claims about aesthetics—about what art is, what it does, and why and how it is pleasurable.[53] In what follows, then, I demonstrate how Davis's text elaborates a black feminist blues aesthetic, one that normalizes the experiences of the working-class black women who sang and listened to the blues. This aesthetic, I argue, identifies an experience of pleasure in art that results not from appropriation, but from complexity, contradiction, and transformation.

Davis and an Aesthetics of Transformation

In *Blues Legacies and Black Feminism*, Davis's interest in the works of Ma Rainey, Bessie Smith, and Billie Holiday is focused on the content and political implications of their lyrics. According to Davis, the collective oeuvres of Rainey, Smith, and Holiday offer rich accounts of working-class black female experience in early to midtwentieth-century America. The book, then, "is an inquiry into the ways their recorded performances divulge unacknowledged traditions of feminist consciousness in working-class black communities."[54] Davis analyzes the meaning of these singers' lyrics in order to make an argument about the political import of the content of their songs. In a sense, Davis is not analyzing Rainey's, Smith's, and Holiday's songs *as art*, but *as politics* or political speech that "addressed urgent social issues and helped to shape collective modes of black consciousness."[55] While Davis privileges the political import of working-class black feminist consciousness, I am interested in teasing out its aesthetic import. Describing how the ideas and feelings represented in these artists' songs both overlap with and diverge from dominant norms governing gender, race, sexuality, and class, Davis's text offers an implicit theory of aesthetics, which I call an "aesthetics of transformation." In contrast to the aesthetics of receptivity, which is grounded in a notion of white masculine embodiment, the aesthetics of transformity begins from Rainey's, Smith's, and Holiday's experiences as working-class black women.

As I discussed earlier, traditional Western aesthetic paradigms frame aesthetic pleasure as the resolution of a problem, the return of/to a supposedly lost bodily immediacy. In Davis's text, aesthetic pleasure is also framed as a way of working through a problem of sorts: the problem of oppression and dehumanization, of being out of place or "abnormal" within a normatively white, masculine, bourgeois world, of relating to the world as simultaneously object of oppression and subjective agent. Instead of an aesthetics of receptivity, where pleasure is not the result of regaining something lost, Davis offers us an aesthetics of transformation, one where pleasure is produced by reworking the limitations of what one already has (or, more accurately, what one is stuck with). Just as "hints of feminist attitudes emerge from their music *through fissures of patriarchal discourse,*"[56] hints of a black feminist blues aesthetic emerge through fissures in traditional musical practices and aesthetic norms.

Davis identifies the situation of being "located both outside and inside" (54) groups and traditions as a common and characteristic feature of blues singer's lives; thus, their experience of the world is structured by contradiction, complexity, and irresolvable tension.[57] Davis writes, "Historically, the blues person has been an outsider on three accounts. Belittled and misconstrued by the dominant culture that has been incapable of deciphering the secrets of her art, she has been ignored and denounced in African-American middle-class circles and repudiated by the most authoritative institution in her own community, the church. Yet at the same time, she has been loved, praised, and emulated by the masses of black people as her community's most intimate insider."[58] The fact that working-class black women are multiply marginalized creates a situation in which they may feel both included in and excluded from the identity groups of which they are members. This tension between inclusion and exclusion is just one example of the ways, in Davis's analysis, working-class black women's lives are characterized by contradiction and complexity.[59]

In their songs, Rainey, Smith, and particularly Holiday cultivated contradiction and complexity both in their musical technique and, as a consequence, in their musical representations of working-class black female sexuality. According to Davis, these singers all delivered their lyrics in ways that set "the literal, semantic level" of meaning against the metaphorical, nonliteral level of meaning.[60] This tactic creates meaning by bringing the two apparent opposites into a very close relationship and then "working" them with and against one another. Claiming that "beneath the apparent simplicity and straightforwardness of the blues, complex visions—reflecting the complexity with which reality is perceived—can always be uncovered,"[61] Davis sees "simplicity" or "superficiality" as inherently complex. Similarly, these singers often use silence or understatement in combination with verbose hyperbole to "say" something that neither tactic could on its own. "Blues discourse," as Davis explains, "is always complicated, contextualized, and informed by that which is unspoken as well as by that which is named."[62] Further examples of this tactic include deploying multiple rhetorical strategies within the same song—"a sophisticated combination of realism, humor, and irony"[63]—and adopting multiple narrative perspectives.[64] Utilizing the consonant and dissonant resonances that arise when differences work with and against one another, Rainey, Smith, and Holiday were able to transform meanings in an almost dialectical fashion, where the "new" meaning contains within it, as its condition of possibility, the trace of the "old." In their songs, limitations are vehicles for emancipation[65] regression is progress,[66] and dejection is mirth.[67]

Adopting musical techniques that cultivate multiple resonances, these female blues musicians sing lyrics whose political message is complex, contradictory, and often seemingly at odds with itself. Since working-class black women exist on the margins of American feminist, antiracist, and class struggles, the available political discourses are individually and collectively inadequate to capture such women's experiences and desires; thus, it makes sense that Rainey, Smith, and Holiday make political claims that work with and against accepted feminist, antiracist, and working-class positions. Discussing subjects such as domestic violence and gender roles, "the blues provided a space where women could express themselves in new ways, a space in which they sometimes affirmed the dominant middle-class ideology but also could deviate from it."[68] An example of this ambivalence toward dominant norms is Smith's "Yes, Indeed He Do," which is about a woman's experience of domestic violence. On the one hand, the lyrics could be seen to romanticize domestic violence and reassert male dominance; the fact that many women would identify with this song would serve only to normalize this horrific phenomenon and reinforce negative stereotypes about black men and women. On the other hand, Smith's delivery encourages the listener to sympathize with the victim, who is often faced with an untenable choice: stay and be beaten, or leave and face economic uncertainty and still perhaps be subject to physical and psychological harassment from one's former partner. In this light, Smith's song gives voice to the oftentimes taboo subject of domestic violence, and thus allows victims of domestic violence to feel some sort of recognition, solidarity, and perhaps even empowerment.[69] In the same way that these female blues singers often narrated their songs from multiple perspectives, they do not adopt a single, unified, or traditionally coherent ideologico-political position on gender, race, and class. The song works with and against both dominant norms and the standard feminist, antiracist, and socialist critiques of these norms. Drawing on, but never fully identifying with any group or discourse, Rainey, Smith, and Holiday developed a lyrical content and musical technique that reflect and express the complex, contradictory situation[70] of working-class black women in twentieth-century America.

These features, then, become the foundation for Davis's notion of a black feminist blues aesthetics. On the one hand, there is pleasure in expressing oneself and in recognizing oneself in others' descriptions of their real or imagined experiences. In representing—both in content and in formal/technical aspects of a piece—contradiction and complexity, the blues suddenly becomes a "canny" manifestation of working-class black women's social and political uncanniness. Because they so accurately depict their experience of being simultaneously in- and excluded, blues strategies "fit" working-class black women in ways that other discourses do not. Transforming the uncanny into the unexpectedly canny, Rainey, Smith, and Holiday develop an aesthetics of transformation. Not only do they use technical musical strategies to make the lyrical content of a song mean something other than its literal content, but they more importantly transform the very idea of aesthetic pleasure itself. As I will discuss later, in claiming this concept/category, whose sense and consistency has relied on their exclusion from it, these working-class black female artists fundamentally alter its logic. By including within it the condition of its impossibility (working-class black female experience), black female blues singers do not merely "expand" the traditional notion of aesthetic pleasure to include them; instead, they reconfigure the very foundations of Western aesthetic pleasure.

According to Davis, Holiday's genius lies in her ability to work with and against dominant cultural norms. Because Holiday creates "complex works of art that *work with and against* the platitudinous ideological content of undistinguished contemporary love songs,"[71] her songs "simultaneous[ly] . . . confirm and subvert racist and sexist representations of women in love."[72] As a black artist, Holiday was more often than not given second-rate songs that white artists would not/did not sing, songs that Davis describes as Tin Pan Alley cast-offs. Because Holiday wanted popular success, and because she was contractually obligated to record labels and club owners, "the very prospect of producing her music was contingent on her acceptance of a kind of song . . . that was imposed upon her repressively by the popular culture market. Had she rejected the often insipid Tin Pan Alley material, she would have denied herself the possibility of song and thus of offering her musical originality to the black community, to the dominant culture, and to the world."[73] Since her continued career as a musician relied on her ability to appeal to popular tastes (and thus to sell records and draw patrons to clubs), Holiday had to work with "the words and concepts of the songs imposed upon her,"[74] with the musical traditions, tastes, and political norms she was stuck with.

Although she did not get to choose the terms of the debate, as it were, Holiday employed transformative strategies, working with and against the limits of the material she was given, using these very limitations as the means of their own transformation. Emphasizing the banality and/or absurdity of a particular statement, Holiday develops, from the literal meaning of the lyrics, a more reflective, complex statement. For example, "the way Billie Holiday sings 'My Man'—now playfully, now mournfully, now emphatically, and now frivolously—highlights the contradictions and ambiguities of women's location in love relationships and creates a space within which female subjectivity can move toward self-consciousness."[75] Holiday uses a song's limitations—banal lyrics, formulaic or uninspired composition—as resources; she works with these limitations as a means of working against them. Transformation is the result of *emphasizing,* not resolving, contradiction, complexity, and tension: it is only by maintaining the tension between the literal and aesthetic dimensions of a piece that it is possible for Holiday to make something apt and incisive out of something awkward and vacuous.

This aesthetics of transformation characterizes art that, precisely because it is so "uncanny," is a uniquely canny expression of working-class black women's experience. It is the affirmation and canniness of the "uncanny" (*unheimlich,* feeling not at home) that is the source of pleasure in these artworks. As Maria Lugones has explained, women of color can feel "out of place" in predominantly patriarchal and/or white spaces.[76] People admire Holiday's songs because, according to Davis, the songs affirm and examine the contradictions and complexities of our everyday lives, especially the ways in which one's experiences are inconsistent with dominant norms.[77] Holiday's work, like Rainey's and Smith's, is crafted in a way that uniquely expresses—both in its form and in its content—the experience of not feeling quite at ease or at home. In so doing, it "fits" the experience of not "fitting in." Refusing to collapse complexity into resolution, "these songs construct a women's community in which individual women are able to locate themselves on a jagged continuum of group experience,"[78] a space where working-class black female identity is the model and the norm. Affirming the "abnormality" of working-class black femininity within white bourgeois patriarchy, Holiday, Smith, and Rainey's work transforms the "abnormal" into the "normal" and offers the pleasure of feeling at ease, of fitting in, of finding a tool that finally works, of being in a community of more or less sympathetic individuals.

Even though Holiday's music spoke from and to a specifically working-class black female perspective, it should not be forgotten that she was and is, above all, a mainstream figure—a legend of American *popular* song. As Davis explains, Holiday's "music proved that she was capable of negotiating an entrance into the dominant culture that did not disconnect her from her people. She was able to recast for her own ends the very elements of that culture that might have devoured her talents and her identity."[79] Holiday's transformative work cultivates a niche while remaining well within the mainstream and, indeed, transforms the very notion of the mainstream itself. Working with and against both Tin Pan Alley and the classic blues, Holiday transforms each without abandoning either one. Like Hunter and Kristeva's Colette, who take up black vernacular practices and styles, Holiday takes up mainstream music and dominant aesthetic norms—precisely the aesthetics of receptivity that "might have devoured her talents and her identity." Since the aesthetics of receptivity is grounded precisely in such voraciousness, and, indeed, would necessitate her being "devoured," Holiday's appropriation is in and of itself a transformative act—because she represents and expresses all that is excluded from and devalued by the aesthetics of receptivity, the fact of her working "with" it is immediately also a working "against" it. As Judith Butler argues, when "those deemed illegible, unrecognizable, or impossible nevertheless speak in the terms of" the discourse/category that excludes them, they are "in and through the utterance opening up the category to a different future."[80] Via her performance of mainstream songs, Holiday deploys the aesthetics of receptivity in a way that subverts their drive toward resolution, voraciousness, and "eating the other," positing a productive but irresolvable tension in its place. Holiday's work embodies the contradiction and complexity that informs both working-class black female experience and the aesthetics of transformation that Davis develops in her reading of Ma Rainey, Bessie Smith, and Holiday's own oeuvres.

Conclusion

Both Gooding-Williams and Kristeva look to race-gender politics to critique or rework notions of aesthetic receptivity, while Davis, uses race-gender politics to imagine an alternative aesthetic, one of transformation. My work here fleshes out Gooding-Williams's account by more thoroughly addressing the intersection of race and gender in traditional notions of aesthetic receptivity. With respect to Kristeva's reading of Colette, my project brings to light the way in which Kristeva's allegiance to an aesthetic of receptivity leads to questionable racial politics in her notion of female genius. Attending to the underexamined aesthetics that accompanies Angela Davis's thesis on the political import of Ma Rainey, Bessie Smith, and Billie Holiday's music, I argue that Davis develops an alternative to the aesthetics of receptivity, namely, an aesthetics of transformation. While the former is grounded in white hetero masculine identity, which is itself based in/on the value of dominance, conquest, and appropriation, the latter is grounded in what Davis identifies as working-class black female identities, which are unified by their common situation on the margins of dominant culture, feminism, and antiracist discourses. Valuing complexity and contradiction above resolution and the voracious metabolism of difference, the aesthetics of transformation is characterized by the strategy of "working with and against," that is, of productively deploying contrast, tension, dissonance, and disagreement. While the aesthetics of receptivity frames pleasure in terms of white embodiment (i.e., as regaining a supposedly lost bodily immediacy), the aesthetics of transformation looks to the complex, contradictory character of working-class black women's experiences to fashion a notion of pleasure grounded in the tension between the canny and the uncanny, inclusion and exclusion, heteronomy and autonomy.

Notes

1. See Catherine Clement *Opera: The Undoing of Women* (Minneapolis: University of Minnesota Press); Kodwo Eshun, *More Brilliant Than the Sun: Adventures in Sonic Fiction* (London: Quartet Books).

2. Christine Battersby makes this point—quite elegantly and rigorously—with reference to the gendering of traditional Western notions of genius: the "genius" is conventionally the masculine figure whose virile self-mastery allows him to appropriate stereotypically feminine/feminized traits (e.g., intuitiveness or closeness to nature) which, in actual women, are supposedly evidence of their inability to be "geniuses." See Christine Battersby, *Gender and Genius: Towards a Feminist Aesthetic* (Bloomington: Indiana University Press, 1989). For bell hooks reference, see "Eating the Other," in *Black Looks: Race and Representation* (Boston: South End).

3. Julia Kristeva, *Colette*, tr. Jean Marie Todd. (New York: Columbia University Press).

4. Angela Davis, *Blues Legacies and Black Feminism* (New York: Vintage Books, 1998).

5. Robert Gooding-Williams, *Look, a Negro!* (New York: Routledge, 2006), 48.

6. Ibid., 47.

7. Richard Dyer, *White* (London: Routledge, 1997), 45.

8. Ibid., 17.

9. Gooding-Williams, 55.

10. Ibid., 50.

11. Ibid., 58.

12. Ibid., 57.

13. Ibid., 151.

14. While Gooding-Williams follows Stanley Cavell's reading of the second number's dance routine to the (limited) extent that they both see Astaire and Charlie Daniels, the black shoeshine, as "equally standing, equally kneeling . . . each equally manifesting the black masculinity that joins them" (Gooding-Williams, 61), they are in no way "equally" dancing or "equally manifesting" some performance of black masculinity. Astaire can perform a version of black masculine embodiment, but he is still ultimately and will always be read as white; he never becomes black but remains a white man acting black, just as a deeply-tanned white person retains his or her white identity in spite and because of his or her dark skin color. Dyer explains: "[T]he point about tanning is that the white person never does become black . . . [N]ot only does he or she retain the signs of whiteness . . . not only does tanning bespeak a wealth an life style largely at white people's disposition, but it also displays white people's right to be various, literally to incorporate into themselves features of other peoples" (49).

15. "The problem is a difficult one: How, within American culture, pervaded as it is with white counterfeits and caricatures of black cultural productivity, can 'white praise of black culture whose very terms of praise it has appropriated'—in Cavell's words—persuade that it is not false praise? Or, to borrow one of Cavell's key critical concepts: How can white praise of a black culture whose terms of praise it has appropriated defeat its perhaps inevitable tendency to a sort of theatricality that is pitched to white fantasies and ideologies about African Americans?" (62)

16. Norma Coates writes: "The Rolling Stones trouble me. As much as I love their music, it periodically grates against my sensibilities and produces spasms of feminist guilt. 'What am I doing,' my inner voice inquires, 'dancing around and getting crazy to such blatant misogyny?" Norma Coates, "(R)evolution Now? Rock and the Political Potential of Gender," in *Sexing the Groove: Popular Music and Gender,* ed. Sheila Whiteley (London: Routledge, 1997),. 50.

17. Rey Chow, "When Whiteness Feminizes," *Differences: A Journal of Feminist Cultural Studies* 11, no. 3 (2000): 155.

18. Importantly, for Chow, "the term 'feminization' " refers not to women or femininity per se, but to "the historical—that is, mutating—relationships among various parts of culture as they have been socially institutionalized" (142). The "feminized" elements in an art object or an aesthetic theory are those that function analogously to the political role "femininity" plays in a patriarchal culture, that is, the "Other" which, to use Beauvoir's terms, establishes the "Absolute" as such.

19. In *Hiroshima, Mon Amour*, for example, "the ascendance of the cosmopolitan woman as text . . . goes hand in hand with the minimalization, if not a disappearance [of] . . . the Japanese architect, whose presence . . . is mainly for the purpose of serving as a screen on which the woman can recall and project her past." Chow, 155. As in *The Band Wagon*, the conflict that drives the plot is the protagonist's alienation (from self, from one's body, from society), which she ultimately finds in the body of a nonwhite man or woman.

20. Sidonie-Gabrielle Colette, better known simply as Colette, was an early twentieth-century French novelist well known for her strong female characters and her stories of their coming-of-age.

21. Kristeva, *Colette*, 389.
22. Ibid., 139.
23. Ibid., 223.
24. Ibid., 389.
25. Ibid., 167.
26. Ibid., 174.
27. Ibid., 259.
28. Ibid., 243.
29. Ibid., 419.
30. Ibid.
31. Ibid.
32. Ibid., 246. On this point black Barbadian singer Rihanna's 2008 song "Disturbia" is particularly interesting insofar as it suggests that, in a society that privileges white masculinity, black women are made to "feel like a monster."
33. Ibid., 255.
34. Following Gooding-Williams, I see receptivity and melancholy (in the Freudian sense) as closely intertwined. Whites such as Hunter cannot mourn or "get over" their perceived loss of receptivity, affectivity, and felt bodily immediacy, thus rendering them melancholic.
35. Kristeva, *Colette,* 85; emphasis mine.
36. Ibid., 12; emphasis mine.
37. Ibid., 105; emphasis again mine.
38. Kristeva chooses to highlight critic Paul Morand's characterization of Colette: "Her art, '*meticulous like [that of] a primitive*' (Paul Morand), imposes and demonstrates the idea that pleasure itself is possible if and only if it understands voluptuousness and at the same time its prolongation in an alphabet written as part of the world's flesh." Kristeva, *Colette,* 105; emphasis mine.
39. "To belong to the beasts is, in the first place, to rebel against humans, an innocent version of the anarchism cultivated by a Colette disgusted with society." Kristeva, *Colette,* 214.
40. Kristeva, *Colette,* 85; emphasis mine.
41. "Animality, installed in the hearts of men and women, is truly a monstrosity . . . [y]et, without avoiding contradiction, since she considers monstrosity a fascinating human singularity." Kristeva, *Colette,* 215.
42. Colette's writing "shows a glimpse, precisely through the door of the impure, of the paradises of childhood now inaccessible to the pragmatic postwar society and to any society?" Kristeva, *Colette,* 313. Kristeva's discussion of the figure and function of "childhood" can be included in her overarching theme of the animal/savage/monster, for it is through childhood (specifically, the renewed access to childhood memory) that, according to Kristeva, Colette's writing accesses the corporeal and sensual experiences unavailable to oedipalized/civilized adults. "The psychosexual polymorphism characteristic of childhood, the abnormal sensuality that constitutes us at a profound level and that the childhood memory in fact crystallizes" (312) is opened by Colette's invocation of Sido and childhood in general.
43. As Kathryn Gines has helpfully pointed out, "immigrant" is used to refer to even the children and grandchildren of the actual black migrants to France, suggesting that "immigrant" itself is a term used to indicate not one's national origins (a native

or a migrant/naturalized citizen) but one's race and/or ethnicity. Also, I want to clarify that, while there are most certainly black migrants to France from Africa and other non-Caribbean locales, the focus of Haigh's text is on black Caribbean immigrants to France. Since I do not have the sociological or demographic expertise required to expand on Haigh's focus, I stick within his parameters.

44. Sam Haigh, "Migration and Melancholia," *French Studies: A Quarterly Review* 60, no. 2 (2006): 232–50.

45. Ibid., 232.

46. Ibid., 238.

47. "Taste, a cannibalistic dependence, is, according to Kristeva "the true embryo of judgment" (Kristeva 203). hooks (1992) uses this phrase "eating the other" to describe the phenomenon wherein whites "claim the body of the colored Other instrumentally, as unexplored terrain, a symbolic frontier that will be fertile ground for their reconstruction of the [dominant] norm, for asserting themselves as transgressive desiring subjects" (24). hooks continues, concluding that this neocolonial appropriation "establishes a contemporary narrative where the suffering imposed by structures of domination on those designated Other is deflected by an emphasis on seduction and ongoing where the desire is not to make the other over in one's image but to become the Other" (25). This desire to become the racialized other as a means of asserting oneself as a transgressive subject is precisely what I think Kristeva finds valuable in Colette's work—which, I argue, is problematic.

48. See especially the second chapter of Carolyn Korsmeyer's book on gender and aesthetics, *Gender and Aesthetics: An Introduction* (New York: Routledge, 2004).

49. Perhaps the most disturbing aspect of Kristeva's discussion of Colette's creativity is that she emphasizes artistic and authorial "sublimation" as a way to "forget" past violence. For example, in response to her question, "Might sublimation therefore be the maximum, ideal protection against aggressive violence, its supreme absolution?" (96), Kristeva claims "that appropriation of the other, of the external, of the outsider, compensates for the pain of loving and suspends vengeful cruelty into appeasement" (96). Here she seems to be claiming that by assimilating the "other"—in blues-rock, in a melting pot, if you wish, or perhaps in the Academy Francaise—past violence toward this "other" is, indeed, "absolved" (and supremely at that!). For example, black vernacular traditions dominate nearly every genre and form of contemporary American popular culture, so we can forget about slavery, Jim Crow, and the overrepresentation of African Americans in the prison population. (I think the "I'm not a racist, I have a black/Hispanic/Asian/etc. friend!" fits here, too). Kristeva argues that the "forgetting" of "skirmishes" is key to social life: "[S]ocial life is an ordeal among Narcissuses who pit their singular tastes against each other in long hard battles before extracting a 'general spirit' supposed to calm them. The community that results is in fact only an accord of tastes, and people prefer to forget the skirmishes that led to it, in order to celebrate only the shared pleasure, now supposed to be universal" Kristeva, *Colette,* 203. If "taste," the shared pleasure of the sensus communis is grounded in a gendered colonial violence, then why call this struggle a mere "skirmish"? Who can and/or would want to forget or overlook this violent past in the first place? It would seem that only privileged whites would be invested in forgetting Western civilization's colonial past and neocolonial present. Forget about slavery and colonialism; we all love hip-hop!

50. Kristeva 203; all emphasis mine. Kristeva continues: "If I write taste, that of my mouth or of my aesthetic preferences, I push its devouring logic to its extreme: I appropriate the shared object that I claim to sample with the reader, I capture it through the creation of a language of my own. Fed on my sensations, this language contaminates the object, *assimilates it by confining it in my own sensory experience*, before I bind the reader himself with the range of my pleasures, the rhythm of my words, a sovereign trap which I force my two preys to brew—the world I eat and the reader I devour." Kristeva, *Colette,* 203/4; emphasis mine.

51. When non-Europeans/non-whites practice "cannibalism" they are seen as savage (e.g., 1980s media representations of inner-city black-on-black violence, current portrayals of sectarian violence in Iraq), but when privileged whites engage in cultural cannibalism, it is offered as evidence of their artistic genius or spectatorial taste. Because Colette's "cannibalistic" writing challenges the norms and limits of "civilization," it can, when not practiced by an appropriately disciplined and masterful writer, "pass from alphabet play in enchanted gardens to alphabet chaos." Kristeva, *Colette,* 226. Chaos seems to happen when the other gazes back, when I realize that the gazing is not just a reflection of me back to myself, when what I consume is not a mere means to my own development, but an agent/end in him or herself: "When the writer stops seeing clearly, when the vigilant eye dominating her object (in this case, a snake) is replaced by imaginary eyes supposedly belonging to that object itself, then writing takes its leave from the civilized surface of appearances. . . . Representation becomes blurred, the watcher, watched, is 'terror-stricken' to observe the uncanniness at the site of the other facing her: 'we are not of the same country or the same belly.' It is only when she understands that those eyes that watched her were not those of the others but the effect of a blurring of her own sight . . . that the author can come to her senses. . . . The strangeness is over. It stemmed from a scopic inversion of watcher/watched, subject/object, of a projection of my eyes onto the skin of the other with its unfamiliar monograms." Kristeva, *Colette,* 226. Notably, what Kristeva describes here is an "uncanniness" or, we might say, a form of nausea induced by attention to racial-epidermal features ("the skin of the other"). Like an inversion of Fanon's experience of being "fixed" or objectified by a racial-epidermal schema that shatters and replaces his sense of himself as a human, Colette's account of an encounter with a snake works, in Kristeva's reading, to demonstrate the dis-ease of a writer who finds herself in a world that writes on its own, that refuses to be written in terms any other than its own. When the writer is not skilled or strong enough to "come to her senses" and see that this apparent agency and human-ness of the "other" one would cannibalize is nothing but a misinterpretation/misperception, power hierarchies are inverted, and chaos ensues. Indeed, insofar as Kristeva praises Colette's writing for the way it produces the feeling that "there is no longer any 'subject' or 'object,' and the 'ego' is disseminated, incorporated, into the writing of Being" (Kristeva, *Colette,* 15), she could be read as claiming that, for a privileged person, a shattered corporeal schema is a sign of genius. This shattering, when experienced by underprivileged individuals (like colonial subjects) is radically disempowering; however, when manifested in privileged bodies, it is a sign of heightened mastery, of one's ability to "sublimate" the various of civilization's repressions that keep one's (white) corporeal schema integrated.

52. Sigmund Freud, "Mourning and Melancholia."

53. Monique Roelofs does briefly discuss Davis's text in her article "Racialization as an Aesthetic Production." I agree with Roelofs's reading of Davis and think the article does an excellent job in examining the ways in which aesthetic value and racial identity work in and through one another. However, because Roelofs's purposes in this article are not to tease out the aesthetic theory developed in Davis's book, and, as a consequence, her analysis of Davis is brief and limited to the overarching purposes of Roelofs's article, I do not think that Roelofs has given an exhaustive analysis of the "aesthetic dimension," as it were, of Davis's text. See Monique Roelofs, "Racialization as an Aesthetic Production," in *White on White: Black on Black*, ed. George Yancy (Oxford: Rowman and Littlefield, 2005).

54. Davis, *Blues Legacies and Black Feminism*, xi.

55. Ibid., xiv.

56. Ibid., xi; emphasis mine.

57. Davis finds an example of the multiple marginalization of working-class black women in Rainey's "Hustlin Blues": "The woman in this song is not only subject to the abusive and exploitative behavior of her pimp and to the general hazards of her trade. When she stands before the white judge as a black woman, she is already hypersexualized within a context of power relations defined by race. There is thus a tragic incongruity to this woman's plea, for she stands between a white male symbol of power and repression and a black male purveyor of abuse and exploitation . . . This song invites audiences to fashion their own critique of the impact of racism on black life." Davis, *Blues Legacies and Black Feminism,* 108. For a discussion of intersectionality, see Kimberlé Williams Crenshaw, "Mapping the Margins: Intersectionality, Identity Politics, and Violence against Women of Color," *Stanford Law Review* 43, no. 6 (July, 1991): 1241–99.

58. Davis, *Blues Legacies and Black Feminism*, 124/5.

59. In her analysis of Linda Gibson's 1989 work *Flag*, Amy Mullen identifies the same sort of complexity as characteristic of black women's experiences as represented in their artwork. "Her work, especially in a scene where images of first Marilyn Monroe and then Angela Davis are superimposed on the photograph of a teenaged and smiling Gibson, suggests the pain and inner complexity involved when one's girlhood was spent admiring both Marilyn Monroe, an icon of passive white femininity, and Angela Davis, a Black radical. Throughout *Flag*, Gibson's diverse and shifting socio-identities as a loyal American, woman, Black, radical, and feminist are traced and explored, as well as the emotions aroused by her sense of both belonging to and being alienated by U.S. society." Amy Mullin, "Art, Understanding, and Political Change," *Hypatia* 15, no. 3 (Summer 2000): 114–15.

60. Davis, *Blues Legacies and Black Feminism*, 100.

61. Ibid., 49.

62. Ibid., 61.

63. Ibid., 97.

64. "The blues never remain fixed on one perspective, but rather different songs—sometimes the same song—explore experiences from various vantage points" (49).

65. "When Ma Rainey sings, 'I got a trunk too big to be botherin with on the road,' the matchbox emerges as a metaphor for the protagonist's conscious decision to strip herself down to the bare essentials, leaving behind everything that may have defined her place under former conditions. What once served as a sign of impoverishment and want becomes for Rainey an emancipatory vehicle" (78).

66. The work of female blues singers "encourages a spiritual identification with black southern culture, which produced a standard of womanhood based on self-reliance and independence. The song appeals to women to summon up within themselves the courage and independence of their foremothers. Movement backward into the African-American historical past becomes movement forward" (81).

67. "If Bessie Smith was the 'world's greatest blues singer,' it was at least in part because, like John the Conqueror, she brought song and laughter as she evoked the harshest and cruelest experiences of black people in America" (157).

68. Davis, *Blues Legacies and Black Feminism*, 47.

69. "But when Bessie Smith sings 'Because I love him, 'cause there's no one can beat me like he do,' it is clear from her performance that far from relishing the beatings she has received, she is expressing utter desperation about her predicament." Davis, *Blues Legacies and Black Feminism,* 30.

70. I use "situation" here in Simone de Beauvoir's sense of the term, to describe the socially constructed material reality of one's everyday lifeworld. See Simone.de Beauvoir, *The Second Sex*. tr. H. M. Parshley (New York: Vintage Books, 1952).

71. Davis, *Blues Legacies and Black Feminism*, 163; emphasis mine.

72. Ibid., 164.

73. Ibid., 166.

74. Ibid.

75. Ibid., 179.

76. María Lugones, "Playfulness, 'World'-Travelling, and Loving Perception," *Hyptatia* 2, no. 2 (Summer 1987).

77. Davis claims that "people are touched so profoundly" by Holiday's work because of the "complexity" and "emotional range" of a "perspective . . . [that] summons a critical examination of the social relationships taken so for granted by the very nature of the popular song" (177).

78. Davis, *Blues Legacies and Black Feminism*, 62.

79. Ibid., 172.

80. Judith Butler, *Undoing Gender* (New York: Routledge, 2004), 13–14.

9

Extending Black Feminist Sisterhood in the Face of Violence

Fanon, White Women, and Veiled Muslim Women

Traci C. West

An ideal vision of feminist global sisterhood is concerned with supporting political freedoms, moral agency, and well-being for women of diverse cultural backgrounds who face a myriad of assaults on their bodies, minds, and spirits. To fully participate in the work of realizing this vision, United States–based, black feminist theorists in religion and philosophy would need to address the freedom-seeking interests of other women besides African American women. But how? I want to consider what it means, methodologically, for a black feminist approach to conceptualize a notion of sisterhood that extends to women whose social status is distinctively other than that of African American women, such as sexually objectified white women and veiled Muslim women in a foreign nation.[1] In response to issues surrounding sexual violence against women, for instance, there ought to be common interests that foster such inclusivity. There are also tensions and sometimes even conflicting interests related to differences in social identity, privileges, and status. Ignoring these problems undermines any feminist claim that in response to male sexual violence there is an overarching, shared solidarity among women that mitigates racial and national differences.

Frantz Fanon is one of few widely utilized, antiracist global theorists whose work enables a specific focus on the conflicts and tensions when considering such inclusiveness.[2] His approach allows close scrutiny of some troubling, related issues of race/nation, sexuality, and religion that can arise. Fanon's work explores gendered, psychopolitical relationships and how they have been pathologically distorted by oppressive structural realities with consequences across continents.

The reflection on black feminist method that I invite below takes place in conversation with Fanon's writings.[3] This endeavor resembles the process one might engage in while sitting on the psychotherapist's couch. It presumes that only by probing pathology-ridden and anxiety-provoking sites of inquiry can there be a chance of discovering more constructive forms of human relatedness.

Fanon has been a valuable resource for my work in ethics. In his method and ideas, I have found innovative tools for an antiracist, black Diaspora approach to addressing intimate violence against black women.[4] Utilizing Fanon's thought as a resource for crafting a black Diaspora framework destabilizes the Eurocentric continental emphasis that dominates Western religious studies and philosophy, especially in the subfields of Christian studies. Moreover, the consciousness of continental cultural geographies in Fanon's work connects cultural dynamics in Africa, (Caribbean) North America, and Europe with a decidedly anti-imperialist trajectory. Fanon offers a uniquely provocative and political analysis of incendiary issues of violence, including interracial sexual violence and nationalist violence linked to religious identity. In the latter case, his views have a timely resonance with certain aspects of current global politics, as in his assertion that "not enough attention has been given to the reasons that lead a revolutionary movement to choose the weapon that is called terrorism."[5] Fanon's theoretical work is explicitly shaped by his life experiences, such as his psychiatric clinical practice that included soldiers from French colonial wars and colonized North Africans, his political involvement in the Algerian struggle for independence, and his interaction with Caribbean and African students in Paris. Fanon's method maintains an interlocked connection between individual mind/body experience and the politically adaptable, systemic apparatus of subjugation.

Although his work concentrates on the cultural conditions of European colonialism, his insights about the dynamics of antiblack racism are usefully applied to the United States context. Interpreting his thought for my consideration of U.S.-based black feminism offers creative possibilities for exploring U.S. racism and its colonizing invasion of mind, body, and spirit. In addition, Fanon's approach supports a much needed version of "postcolonial" studies, which takes white supremacy within the United States as seriously as the imprint of European global racisms.

Admittedly, there are several obstacles that I must confront as I seek his insights for constructing a black feminist perspective in Christian religious ethics that repudiates violence. Fanon's exploration of the psychosocial impact of racism on the black psyche is much more centrally concerned with black males and their interactions with white women than with black women's lives.[6] And when he celebrates anti-imperialist revolutionary efforts such as the participatory role that Algerian Muslim women played in their struggle for national freedom, he seems to condone, perhaps even valorize violence. He also holds a thoroughly antagonistic view of Christianity—the colonizer's religion. Finally, some of Fanon's reflections on race, gender, and sexual violence include disturbing depictions of women's culpability that I reject. It is in my direct confrontation of these problem areas, however, that possibilities emerge for a more expansive black feminist ethic.

I have no interest in defending Fanon by dismissing feminist critiques of his androcentrism and homophobia.[7] Nor do I excuse these prejudices by silencing them in a reading of Fanon that offers gender-neutral analysis of antiblack racism or nationalist revolution. I want to experiment with claiming Fanon as my principal conversation partner in a feminist project where black feminism occupies the space of normative paradigm, and women's relatedness to one another is the driving concern. Androcentric representations of racial realities can be decentered by a black feminist agenda[8] focused upon the nuances of developing its own methodological expansiveness.

First, I consider Fanon's view of the convoluted, psychosocial constraints of race and colonization in the daily interactions he depicts in *Black Skin, White Masks*.[9] In conversation with these ideas from *Black Skin, White Masks*, I explore some of the methodological complications for black feminist inclusiveness that extend to white women sexually linked to black men. Second, I consider Fanon's examination of the resistance strategies of the colonized in *A Dying Colonialism* and focus on methodological concerns that arise when the liberation of veiled Muslim women abroad is at issue. Collectively, these details contribute guidance for identifying impediments to the conceptualization of an inclusive black feminist ethic that critically addresses sexual objectification of women and sexual violence against them.

Testing the Limits of Inclusion: White Heterosexual Women

White women are foregrounded as a major subject of interest throughout Fanon's *White Skin, Black Masks.* He analytically reflects upon their breasts, their role as racist mother-figure, and their desires for and fear of black men's violence. These examples, as well as other references to white women, are woven into the fabric of this treatise on the psychosexual entrapment of the colonized Negro. Black feminist critical attention to this major text of Fanon's cannot avoid this perspective on gender relations. When engaging Fanon's ideas here, how should a black feminist approach interpret the significance given to white womanhood?

For example, Fanon explains that for the black man who is loved by a white woman, her breasts represent inclusion in white civilization: "When my restless hands caress those white breasts, they grasp white civilization and dignity and make them mine."[10] He shows how, under the distorting conditions of colonialism, white women's breasts are a prized possession, indeed, a forbidden possession for the black man. In Fanon's depiction of the black man's response to these distorting conditions, the white woman's breasts are, as feminist cultural theorist Anne McClintock describes, seized and appropriated.[11] Seizing them represents a crucial form of license: this act offers liberation to the black male psyche in the midst of a pathologized struggle with his belief in his own innate black inferiority that white colonialist dominance has instilled. By seizing them he gains access to privileges he has previously been denied. Yet it is a morally demeaning interaction that takes place as these white female breasts are instrumentalized, and their worth is located in their utility to their black male possessor. Precisely at the moment that they are caressed by the black male she loves, sexual objectification of the white woman's body parts occurs, and those body parts become a commodified symbol of liberation. In that crucial moment, apparently without her conscious consent to it, the seizing of her breasts releases the civilizing cultural forces of whiteness and implicitly, of heterosexuality as well. If subjectivity must include, at a minimum, recognition of one another's unique, embodied consciousness,[12] as I believe it does, this white woman is denied certain aspects of her gendered subjectivity at the same time as her body parts confer a raced, heteronormative subjectivity.

When positioning the moral status of white womanhood conveyed in Fanon's project in relation to black feminism, do I experience the desire to somehow write myself (read: black womanhood) into the text? Do I, for instance, feel a sense of longing as I am introduced to those white female breasts with the black male fingers caressing them? Could it be that I long for my own breasts to supplant hers and get the exaltation hers receive from the black male lover? Or perhaps my longing is a desire to caress those breasts myself, wanting the freeing/dignity-granting power they bestow to revert to me instead of him. Alternatively, do I forge a relationship to the conscious being/white woman by acknowledging her as true possessor of those breasts and condemn any appropriation of them/her?

It could be strongly argued that for black feminism, concern with representing the subjectivity of the normally overprivileged white woman should always be superseded by concern for black women's subjectivity. For, in other interactions Fanon describes in *Black Skin, White Masks* white women are not treated as disparate body parts, though their centrality is maintained. A white mother is seen with her boy child in one of the most frequently quoted passages of Fanon's writings. In an encounter with the narrator (Fanon), the white child expresses his fear: "Mama, See the Negro! I'm frightened. Now they were beginning to be afraid of me."[13] This scene epitomizes Fanon's conceptualization of Negrophobia and its impact on the person who has become the phobic object of the white gaze.[14] The mother joins the white boy in a shared Negrophobia ("they" were becoming fearful). Sharply contrasting with the white woman's role mentioned above that confers dignity, in this encounter with a black man, the white woman is part of a classic scenario of racist assault on black personhood. Here she participates in delivering the dehumanizing white gaze that reduces the black male to an object of phobia.

In her essay "Missing Persons: Fantasizing Black Women in *Black Skin, White Masks*,"[15] feminist cultural theorist Lola Young comments on this scene. She notes the silence in Fanon's analysis about what black woman-centered white racist phobia would entail. Young interrupts this silence by imagining the possibilities if a black woman were written into the scene with the following inquiry.

> How might this sequence work with a different cast of characters? What if the scene were of a white father and daughter, with the child gazing back at a black woman? Would the little girl speak out in the same startling manner as the little boy? . . . Since the power implicated in the act of looking and being looked at is asymmetrically allocated to white and black, to male and female, in racially stratified patriarchal societies, changing the sex of the participants in this ritualized version of the encounter between black and white to one which focuses on a black woman as the object of the look, serves to foreground a different set of relations and experiences: a set of relations to which Fanon does not turn his own critical gaze.[16]

As Young points out above, there is a conceptual void created by the fact that Fanon's focus in this experiential exploration of the dynamics of antiblack racism does not include black women. And if he had done so, a description of the black woman's encounter with a white father, not a white mother, would be in keeping with his pattern of "allocating" race and gender. Under these patriarchal constraints, analysis of a Negrophobic reaction by the white mother to a black woman would not be considered of critical concern.

However, imagining and interrogating a white mother/black woman version of this scene would not only disobey a fixed patriarchal ordering of social relations but perhaps also hold some ingredients for helping to build black resistance to white Negrophobia. It could still fully account for the harmful impact of the white mother/white son phobic response. Couldn't it? Or perhaps a white mother/black woman script could never be a worthwhile supplemental version of the phobia Fanon describes. His construction of Negrophobia may require a patriarchal context. In my scenario, the black woman's shared womanness with the white mother might too forcefully mitigate the sexual dangers at issue in Negrophobia. In the original text when the white mother-son gaze is directed at a black man, there are white woman/black man heterosexual sexual tensions lurking there, and if the boy is understood to be representative of white manhood, black male/white male homosexual sexual tensions as well. I wonder if it is possible to identify lurking, possibly explosive, raced antagonisms in the potential for same-gender sexual contact between white and black women. If such tensions could be identified, could they validate the importance of also imagining a white mother/black woman scene for interrogating antiblack racist phobias?

In any case, the white female is seen as a potent societal actor. Even in Young's re-write, the white girl-child presumably plays a role in delivering a dehumanizing phobic gaze. Fanon's inclusion of this scene does helpfully illustrate the poisonous diminishment of moral worth and the blow to the black psyche brought about by an ordinary, everyday encounter with white objectification. This experiential reminder raises a fundamental, underlying question about what kind of black feminist theoretical consideration white women deserve. Does their participation in systemically supported, everyday black devaluation make white females intrinsically undeserving of a humanizing critical assessment within black feminist thought?

Trying to make herself "appear in the text" because of the way that "Fanon makes the black female disappear," bell hooks articulates an approach to the work of political resistance in black feminism that leaves whites out altogether.[17] For hooks, the necessary healing process in the wake of damaging psychosocial assaults by whites will involve black self-love. This self-love or ethic of care[18] gives primacy to the relationship between black females and males. Her explanation of this ethic seems to contain transgendered elements (or at least hold that potential) when she asks, "What does it mean if Fanon is unable to embrace the black female—what part of himself remains unembraced?"[19] But mostly, the vision she offers appears to be one of heterosexually sex/gendered healing.[20] Hooks argues that Fanon ignores the liberating potential in relationships between black males and black females.[21] She asserts that "the sado-masochistic crux of the Hegelian master/slave dialectic is ruptured when the black female is recognized as an 'other' with whom the black male may, in acts of solidarity, engage in various states of ontological resistance."[22] It is a hopeful perspective. Resistance can be achieved when the toxic presence of white racism is eclipsed by an "ontological" blackness that black males and females can produce in their solidarity.

This conceptual strategy by hooks of making whites disappear (albeit temporarily) creatively responds to the way that "Fanon makes the black female disappear." In the process of righting conceptual wrongs of erasure, there is a constructive redeployment of that very tactic. Her approach constitutes an exercise of human agency: "the insistence that we must determine how we will be" instead of allowing colonizing responses to be determinative of the legitimacy of black identity[23] However, further exploration is needed of how this remedy addresses the problems of fear and violence that Fanon raises with regard to black men's relationships with white women. One would still need to clarify exactly how this ontological, black male/black female united front might, for instance, diminish the psychosexual perils of black male/white female encounters.

Differentiating Myths from Truths: White Women and the Black Male Rapist

Fanon's discussion of white women's fear of rape by black men and their corollary fantasy desires to be raped by black men deserve black feminist attention. How should a black feminist argument that is concerned with eradicating violence against women interpret Fanon's description of the fantasy desires of white women to be raped by black men? Do I minimize the importance of these contentions about white women's sexuality in Fanon's work? Characterizations of black women's sexuality in Fanon's writings and in other global theorists urgently need critical attention, and black feminist interests are unambiguously served by offering that attention. This point raises yet another fundamental method question: how are black feminist interests served by giving attention to problematic views of white women's sexuality?

When they are not expending intellectual energy on combating black women's erasure from standard conceptual frameworks and texts, black feminists are often analyzing the distorted representations of black women that do appear in scholarly texts, including perverse depictions of black women's sexuality. Such distorted depictions are often coupled with comparisons depicting white women as normative. As literature scholar Hazel Carby's 1980s black British feminist article "White Woman Listen! Black Feminism and the Boundaries of Sisterhood" explains, "*his*tory has constructed our sexuality and our femininity as deviating from those qualities with which white women, as the prize objects of the Western world, have been endowed."[24] Or, in her 2004 *Black Sexual Politics*, black feminist sociologist Patricia Hill Collins describes how depictions of black women as "icons of hypersexuality" help to reinforce ideas of pure white womanhood.[25]

Schooled in the necessity of this approach, I think: perhaps black feminist discussions of black women's sexual agency and personhood as sexual beings can influence white members of my audience to shed some of the historically rooted misrepresentations of black women they may have learned. Analyzing Fanon's decoding of antiblack racism and even his silences about the lives of black women may contribute to this goal. With the hope of preventing their unwitting participation in future assaults, I can try to teach my white audience members how antiblack racism by whites is enfolded into sociopolitical assaults on black womanhood. Yet Fanon's theoretical perspective has been useful to my formulation of antiracist feminist concepts, in part, because of his indictment of the psychosocial destructiveness of black preoccupation with how whites see them. If for no other reason than the liberation of my own psyche, I must broaden my black feminist concerns beyond a focus on how black women might be more authentically seen and known by whites. I hope that I also have other reasons for broadening my black feminist concerns beyond a focus on my own clear self-interests. In the terminology of hooks, the "ethic of care" to which I subscribe promotes the necessity to honor the worth and dignity of all persons. It should therefore include recognition of white women's subjectivity with a repudiation of Fanon's warped sexualized images of them, should it not?

There are several core assumptions that form an underlying premise for Fanon's claims about white women having "the fantasy of rape by a Negro"[26] and even beyond fantasy, they underlie his query: "just as there are faces that ask to be slapped, can one not speak about women who ask to be raped?"[27] Fanon illustrates how racism is linked to sexual desire, phobia, and violence in a range of settings (across continents).[28] First, for both white males and females, rape is inextricably associated with black maleness: "Whoever says rape, says Negro."[29] Second, white women's phobic response to black men is always sexually charged. As she sees him/fears him: "He *is* a penis."[30] Third, for Fanon, violence and sexual desire are merged in white women's expression of sexuality. This is true for psychiatric patients with varying degrees of neurotic disorders as well as for ordinary women for whom "it is commonplace . . . during the sexual act to cry to their partners: 'Hurt me!' "[31]

Fanon describes all Negrophobic white women patients who have lost their husbands through death or divorce as having "abnormal sex lives."[32] According to him, in their perverted fantasies about black men, the women experience a conjoined form of both terror and fascination with how black men make love.[33] And in more ordinary women's lives, the "extra-fragile" white woman, for example, fearfully shudders at the thought of being touched by a black man but actually wants "to have the powerful Negro bruise her frail shoulders."[34] Fanon situates a range of these exaggerated images throughout *Black Skin, White Masks* in order to articulate a distinct form of antiblack racism manifested in white women's self-expression. For Fanon, to understand white women's authentic response to black men that belies their stated revulsion requires that one "interpret by opposites."[35] There is an almost pornographic construal of white woman's terror as indistinguishable from her sense of desire and pleasure. In this portrayal, the psychic and physical fragility of white womanhood adheres to violence. This racialized process of adhesion—between white female fragility and black male violence—constitutes a heterosexual version of white racism that supposedly feels good to a white woman.

The notion of masochism is key for how sexual desire and violence are linked in the psychosocial process Fanon identifies here. Mere desire for sexual contact with a black man can literally drive a white woman mad "because what she wanted was the destruction, the dissolution, of her being on a sexual level."[36] It is not only white women who have been "driven mad" that have such fantasies and desires. Fanon's vivid descriptions of white women's violent masochistic desires below are part of his argument about the "commonplace" occurrence of women telling their sexual partners to hurt them that I mentioned earlier. He explains: "If we go farther into the labyrinth, we discover that when a woman lives the fantasy of rape by a Negro, it is in some way the fulfillment of a private dream, an inner wish. Accomplishing the phenomena of turning against the self, it is the woman who rapes herself. . . . The fantasy of rape by a Negro is a variation of this emotion: "I wish the Negro would rip me open as I would have ripped a woman open."[37] As the white woman's wish to be victimized by heterosexual black male violence evolves into sexually violating acts upon herself, and then merges with a reference to a lesbian urge to sexually violate another woman, one cannot help but wonder if it is more likely that Fanon has been captured by a voyeuristic male sexual fantasy than a psychosocial theory."[38]

Nevertheless, one way to make sense of this troubling passage is to try to place it within its broader context, such as its broader textual context and its colonial historical context. Young, for instance, notes how this rape fantasy by white women is analogous to Fanon's portrayal of a white male repressed desire for a homosexual relationship with a black male.[39] For Young, white women's supposed masochism fits with a broader problematic pattern of fear and hatred of the "feminine" in Fanon that encompasses male homosexuality together with white female heterosexuality.

But Young's arguments also help to maintain a competitive relationship between black and white women. Unlike Fanon's inattention to black women, Young points out that at least in this account of white women's sexual fantasies and desires Fanon recognizes the "inner world of white women's psyche."[40] Similarly, after discussing Fanon's problematic interracial rape theories, even white feminist Diana Fuss declares that what is "most worrisome . . . is not what Fanon says about white women and black men but what he does *not* say about black women and white men."[41]

Thus for some antiracist feminist critics of Fanon, it seems that the privileged whiteness of white women negates or certainly trumps the gross unfairness of asserting that white women take pleasure in being victimized by black rapists.[42] At best, their white feminine selves are defensible (a la Young), but when competitively compared to the treatment of black women, distorted depictions of white women constitute lesser concerns. In contrast to these views, hooks offers the equalizing assertion that in Fanon, "the female body, black or white," is not only always sexualized and one that does not think, "but it also appears to be a body that never longs for freedom."[43]

Few if any black feminist scholars have devoted more attention to studying Fanon's relationship to feminism than T. Denean Sharpley-Whiting. She defends Fanon's claims about white women and rape with a differing appeal for contextualization. In her black feminist perspective, these claims about rape make sense when placed within his broader psychosocial schema. Sharpley-Whiting explains that "we are speaking here of white women whose psychosexualities have been corroded, abnormalized, which in turn incite the cultural mythology of the black male rapist."[44] The context for white women's rape desires is a "structurally ill" culture where their psyches assimilate the culture's misogyny and antiblack racism. For some white women, not all, their expression of this kind of "duped" masochism is a form of culturally induced psychosis.[45] Thus for Sharpley-Whiting, white women's desire to be raped by black men fits within the logic of the pathologizing white racist culture, but with the caveat that not all white women are affected in this way.[46]

I think that Fanon may generalize white women's violent sexual masochism more broadly than the interpretation Sharpley-Whiting posits. However, she helpfully draws attention to the underlying point of his argument about white women and rape—perhaps his most compelling insight here—about the capacity of racism to thoroughly distort white human personhood. But couldn't Fanon's ingenious ability to capture the convoluted, distorting imprint of racism in our psychosocial relationships itself be distorted by his own sexism, in this case, a sexist view of male-perpetrated sexual violence against women? Moreover, it may be possible for white racism to become an overly determining paradigm where any claim about the potency of white depravity and its behavioral manifestations becomes plausible. There is a problem with heeding that latter caution on this topic of interracial rape. Some white women have played a pivotal role in unconscionable, depraved treatment of black men accused of sexually assaulting them, making it more difficult to place limits on white women's capacity for racist irrationality.

Arguing for the historical contextualization of Fanon's argument about white women and rape, Fuss reminds us that the writing of this text takes place "during a period when fabricated charges of rape were used as powerful colonial instruments of fear and intimidation against black men."[47] White women's historical complicity in the terrorizing and lynching of black men by fabricating the charge of rape may create hesitancy when criticizing a black male intellectual for perpetuating a harmful, stereotypical depiction of white women. One may be tempted to vengefully suggest that the historical, devastating impact of one harmful myth about black males as inherently rapists of white women excuses another harmful myth about white women as inherently desiring to be raped by black males found in Fanon's writings, especially since Fanon's theorizing is unlikely to have any direct impact on the everyday lives of actual white women.

U.S.-based black feminism, in particular, cannot escape the echoes of the ugly history of lynching when engaging Fanon's analysis. As womanist theologian Kelly Brown Douglas describes, during the late nineteenth and early twentieth century, "while lynchings were justified by the claim that the man hanged had violated a white woman, it was more often simply 'rumors of rape' that led to such lynchings."[48] Douglas then points out that the real threat to "white male supremacy" could be found in the actual attraction of some white women to black men and their voluntary sexual relations with them. During this period of U.S. history, both white women's consensual relations with black men and white women's (usually) false cries of rape held the possibility of lethal consequences for black men. When focused upon such consequences for black males that resulted from their supposed defilement of white womanhood, the difference between white women's consent and lack of consent to sexual relations with them did not matter as much as it should have. Since the purity of white women has historically been defended at such great cost to black men, it would be understandable if the idea of mounting a black feminist defense of white women as innocent of the Fanonian charge of fantasy desires to be raped by black men is seen as an unpopular endeavor.

But a black feminist "rape-analysis" reading of Fanon shifts the framing of these concerns. One of the most entrenched myths about heterosexual male rape upholds women's blameworthiness for the sexual violence against them. Many women victim-survivors of rape struggle with varying degrees of self-blame, as they repeatedly ask themselves, for example: did I send the wrong "signals" to him to make him think that I wanted it? This is especially true for the most common cases of sexual assault where the perpetrator is not a stranger. He is usually the first one to tell her that she wanted the assault. Questions about how she may be at least partially responsible for the rape are too often echoed by her family members and friends and criminal justice authorities.[49] In addition, consensual, erotic, sexual playfulness is seen as indistinguishable from nonconsensual sexual assault because women are allegedly confused about the difference. Therefore, it is never clear when rape is really rape because women are supposedly confused about what they want. This cultural climate fosters the conclusion that women are the problem; they are the ones to blame.

Fanon's construction of white womanhood as physically fragile and psychically unstable nicely sets up the conditions for perpetuating the myth of white women's partial culpability when raped. As noted above, it is as if their very constitution invites the overpowering perpetrator to take control. Nonconsensual and consensual relations are confused and overlapping in some of Fanon's illustrations. A white woman's breasts represent the availability of sociopolitical power when seized and appropriated by her black male lover. In the black male lover's view, which has been twisted by white subjugation, the consensual availability of the white woman's body means that an elevated social status is there for the taking.

Most important, in his conceptualization of the merger of white women's fear with their sexual desire, Fanon does not account for the peculiar form of violence that rape inflicts. Its soul-shattering impact attested to by so many victim-survivors could never have been desired by them, not even as a fantasy desire. In short, his assertions about white women's desires for rape provide a conceptual vehicle for reinforcing a classic rape myth. Black feminist interests are, however, always served by unequivocally disputing cultural support for myths that perpetuate women's blameworthiness for sexual violence committed against them. This construction of innate blameworthiness cements in place conditions that breed multiple forms of racial, economic, and sexual identity subjugation, alongside of the gender violence, which are core concerns black feminism has consistently sought to address.

In relation to the act of rape, it is more plausible to assume that white women instinctively "long for freedom" (as hooks puts it) rather than the unfreedom of intimate, violent victimization. There might be a possibility for a black woman/white woman kinship in that common longing, as well as in women's shared vulnerability to male sexual violence, violation, and harassment. But when Fanon's harsh reminders about phobically racist white women are recalled, they help to challenge the idea that white women deserve to be seen as kin to black women. His distillation of white women's ongoing, active contribution to racist realities makes a retreat from concern about rape myths about white women more comfortable than acknowledgment of kinship to them.

The distinction between deserving and undeserving victims represents another crucial component of myths about a woman's responsibility for her own rape. When this cultural logic about the need to make such distinctions is enfolded into the recognition of white women's culpability in perpetuating racism, it enhances the legitimacy of supporting Fanon's claims about white women and rape. The historical complicity of white women in the lynching of black men; the ways in which white women are hardly ever disregarded to the same extent that black women are in the ideas of renown global theorists such as Fanon; and of course white women's everyday, dehumanizing Negrophobic gaze all prove that they are certainly not innocent. These sociohistorical realities support a view of white women as noninnocents who seem to be "asking for it." Especially in the U.S. cultural context, white women are already tainted by their willing participation and silent complicity in varying degrees of ongoing racist assaults on blacks. This compromised moral identity helps to make the idea that rape fantasies could adhere to white women's volition more credible. Even if, in the face of all the evidence of their social culpability, one maintains the improbability of their desire to be raped, one could still be influenced by the cumulative effect of this evidence. It may begin to seem reasonable to conclude that these noninnocent foes do not deserve black feminist, empathetic concern when they are accused of having such a desire. But the rape-tolerating logic of the broader culture has to be actively fended off to keep it from seeping into black feminist hermeneutics.

Besides, friends and foes are not always easy to sort out. They can coexist in the same person and identity groups. I will never forget an incident that took place during my first year as a college student (during the late 1970s). I was railing about the racism of my white student peers to a young white female professor at my elite, majority white university.[50] She had become a trusted mentor for me. As I calmed down and entered into more of a dialogue with her, she told me about her traumatic experience of having been raped by a black man several years previously. She spoke of her confusion and anger about the rape. In part, because of her extensive commitment to antiracist "movement" work helping poor urban blacks, she felt uncertain about her right to have such strong anger and revulsion toward her black male attacker.

I remember my feelings of inadequacy as she started to cry. I was unable to find the right words to offer her the counsel she was so obviously seeking from me. I mumbled something sympathetic and soon left her office. I was struck by her deep emotional scars from the brutal attack she had endured and by my own discomfort with her unstated request. She seemed to be asking me, an eighteen-year-old mentee, to suddenly become both peer-confidante and redeemer of her faith in blacks. I angrily felt like I was being reduced to some kind of black mammy/redeemer object. But at the same time, I felt guilty about having been so disappointingly useless to this white ally who was in such pain.

There are many reasons why it should be unacceptable to include conformity to any notion that certain raped women are undeserving of the effort to create a more humanizing, less sexually objectifying cultural gaze in a black feminist approach. But the experiences of devalued black womanhood that peculiarly mark the interests of black feminist struggle should be one of the major reasons. Black feminist political scientist Cathy Cohen describes a unique version of transformational queer politics that I would apply to the issue of sexual violence. It illustrates an inclusive approach to conceiving black feminist interests. Cohen's proposal suggests cutting across identity-group cleavages to cultivate "radical politicalization" and an agenda that seeks to change "values, definitions, and laws" that generate oppressive conditions.[51] Cohen's visionary approach is based upon the premise that "in the roots of a lived 'queer' existence are experiences of domination, and in particular heteronormativity, that form the basis for genuine transformational politics."[52] She also deliberately includes examples of the conditions of certain socioeconomically subordinated heterosexual women in that vision of transformation.

By adapting Cohen's model, there are possibilities for the "radical politicalization" of black female social identities that could provide an impetus for pursuing a transformative agenda related to sexual violence. For instance, stereotypes of black women, such as their supposed sexual promiscuousness, sometimes contribute to a cultural perception of them as noninnocent victim-survivors of sexual harassment or violence.[53] This cultural experience of being sexually stereotyped could be a catalyst for an analysis of Fanon that is guided by a transformational political goal. "Politicalization" of such experiences of cultural devaluation would lead to the realization that even a Negrophobic white woman racist does not deserve to be imaged as having an inner desire to be sexually ripped open by a black man. But more important, it demands that one recognize as invalid any questions about which women are deserving innocents or undeserving noninnocents. The needed and more disruptive conceptual move involves a critical engagement of Fanon's antiracist theories that will aid the struggle to transform our rape-tolerating culture.

In its own way, Fanon's method is thoroughly preoccupied with radical politicalization of identity. One of the best examples of this preoccupation can be found in his discussions of Algerian Muslim women in his text *A Dying Colonialism.* In his treatment of the Algerian struggle against colonialism Fanon does, in certain instances, portray women's bodies as longing for freedom. He offers a detailed description of women who not only longed for freedom but actively participated in a liberation struggle for national independence. The ways in which their bodies are linked to violence (metaphorically and literally) have direct relevance to the methodological concerns of an antiviolence black feminist ethic. The incorporation, within this ethic, of a sense of African American women's kinship, perhaps even feminist sisterhood, with women who are as culturally distant as the Algerian women described in Fanon's analysis may be easier to conceptualize than kinship with white women. The discussion of the rape of white women by black men is loaded with explosive and interlocking white/black racial history. When exploring Fanon's depictions of the Algerian women there are, however, new pitfalls to avoid attached to religion and national identity that can generate mistaken perceptions and warped terms for relatedness.

Opposing the Use of Women's Bodies: Veiled Muslim Women

To effectively transform our rape-tolerating culture, the habit of treating women's bodies as useful sites for contesting political interests has to be eliminated. One of the initial steps for undermining the legitimacy of this predatory approach to women's bodies is to consider and discern alternative views. Yet even strategies of resistance can reproduce the very objectifying treatment of women that they oppose. The inclusive black feminist ethic that I seek will require ferreting out moral assumptions that support sexually objectifying and assaultive, colonizing practices toward women abroad, in tandem with scrutiny of alternatives represented as resistance to this subjugating treatment.

A Dying Colonialism describes Fanon's view of the 1950s Algerian struggle for liberation from French colonial rule. In this historically rooted reflection on revolutionary social change, women's bodies are linked to violence through a variety of illustrations. Fanon demonstrates a connection, too often severed in discussions of violence in society, between individually perpetrated and collectively organized violence, or more precisely, between intimate sexual violence and state-sponsored violent repression by a colonial power. In *A Dying Colonialism*, the treatment of Muslim Algerian women's bodies as available for varying political uses includes metaphorical references to nationalist political struggle, actual, covert acts of carrying weapons for the liberation movement, and sexual violence and violation by colonial authorities. The theme of sexual violence can be found in all of these cases.

In his "Algeria Unveiled" chapter, Fanon describes Algerian resistance to the decision by the colonial administration to ban "the wearing of the veil."[54] Because women are seen as the bearers of national and cultural identity, their bodies are literally targeted as a tool for colonialist appropriation of that identity. According to Fanon, the colonial government understood that to "destroy the structure of Algerian society, its capacity for resistance, we must first of all conquer the women."[55] Thus his title "Algeria Unveiled" recalls the colonial project in Algeria where women's bodies represent Algerian society in the minds of the colonizers. Insofar as "the veil" refers to clothing that conceals the body and protects Muslim women from sexual objectification, this title metaphorically depicts sexual assault. "Every veil that fell," Fanon explains, was evidence "that Algeria was beginning to deny herself and was accepting the rape of the colonizer."[56] Thus, Algeria is also symbolically imaged as a woman's body in Fanon's prose about colonization and revolution.

The moral grounding of this struggle for freedom from colonialism is intertwined with religious grounding. With an eerie prescience of global conflicts of the twenty-first century, Fanon describes the (Christian) Western obsession with battling Islam. He points to the colonizer's bitter exasperation with the extent to which "Islam holds its prey" in Algeria.[57] In *Wretched of the Earth*, Fanon identifies the religious stakes of this colonial context as one in which the Christian religion, manifested through the actions of the church, implants foreign influences in colonized people.[58] He explains that "the Church in the colonies is the white people's Church," and calls the native to "the ways of the white man, of the master, of the oppressor."[59] Therefore, for this project of colonization in North Africa, one has to consider the ways in which "unveiling" was a Christian concern for the colonists, and give religion as much attention as their antipathy toward Algerian nationalism.

When the subject of "the veil" arises in Western feminist discourse on revolutionary movements in countries such as Algeria (with a majority Muslim population), it is all too easy to veer off into an analysis of veiling practices in the context of fundamentalist Islam or Islamic nationalism and neglect a feminist discussion of the role of Christianity in shaping Western views of Islam. Feminist social scientist Homa Hoodfar responds to the failure of Western feminists to interrogate colonial and racist constructions of Muslim women and veiling practices. She queries: "[A]s Muslim feminists have often asked, must racism be used to fight sexism?"[60] Her challenge is applicable here. The kind of Western feminist racism she points out can be manifested in an identification of cultural impediments to Muslim women's autonomy that leaves out the broader global and colonial contexts, particularly, European (and Euro-American), *Christian* cultural perspectives and influence. Hoodfar's critique reminds us that conceptualization of racism should not neglect the role of religion. In this instance, black feminist, radical politicalization of my identity that is aimed at building a notion of sisterhood across political and historical divides poses very different challenges than in the case of the rape myths and African American women's experiences of cultural devaluation discussed above. Here, it requires a critique of religious identity and related cultural experiences that I value, specifically, a critique of what I and most other Christian African American women have experienced as salvific.

Colonialist violence in North Africa should be understood as consistent with certain foundational Christian religious values, such as Christian theology's fusion of state violence by the Roman Empire with Divine redemptive action. This fusion is found in the theological meaning of Christianity's quintessential symbol: the cross. Acceptance of state violence as wrongful, but sometimes necessary for the triumph of God, is a fundamental component of traditional Christian theology. Christianity interprets the Roman state's execution of Jesus as a deliberate act of God the Father to redeem the whole world.[61] In violence-affirming theology, the "breaking of his body" ritually celebrated by all Christians is seen as necessary to bring about God's kingdom. The establishment of Christian dominance/redemption throughout the whole world is a fundamental goal of Christian kingdom building evident in Christian complicity (through missionaries) in European colonization of Africa.

Violence-legitimating Christian theology and its negative impacts have taken varied forms. Church leaders have too often dismissed the harm of intimate male violence against Christian women with spiritual guidance for those who have been victimized that reinforces the virtue of "picking up your cross and suffering like Jesus." Violence-legitimating Christian theology has also been useful for justifying Christianity's extensive genocidal history of crusades and pogroms. This Christian worldview that includes historical and theological endorsements of certain forms of supposedly obligatory violence and suffering fully inhabits the cultural context of the French colonizer's religious worldview. And it is within this religious worldview, a predominantly Christian worldview, that the sexually violating practice of unveiling Muslim women was hatched.

This practice involves a spiritual assault, as well as a physical, emotional, and political one.

In short, fundamental moral and religious values of the European colonizers informed their actions in Africa. In *A Dying Colonialism*, Fanon claims that unveiling the Algerian woman became a central focus of the colonialist program in order to win "her over to foreign values."[62] The colonizers tried to achieve "real power over the man" through this campaign, thereby "destructuring Algerian culture."[63] To Fanon, women's bodies were a weapon used by the French to subdue Algerian men. Fanon's patriarchal lens views the "unveiling" of women more as an instrumental event aimed at men than as an evil in itself. Alternatively, when Algerian feminist Marie-Aimée Helie-Lucas recounts how the French army forced Algerian women "to unveil publicly, thereby proving the renunciation of outworn traditions," she also asserts that "both Algerian men and women resented this symbolic public rape."[64] Unlike Fanon, Helie-Lucas's description of the women's victimization includes recognition of their own consciousness (subjectivity) in response to their violation.

In seeking an analytical perspective that recognizes the subjectivity of the assaulted Algerian Muslim women who wore those veils, there is a temptation to hide in the authorial privilege of obscuring my own national identity. As I stress the ways in which my black feminist identification with Algerian women that crosses historical and nation-state boundaries is rooted in recognition of their subjugated personhood, my own location is obscured. The political implications of their national and cultural identity related to gender are named and probed in this emphasis, while my cultural and national identity remains unmarked. This omission relieves me of the burden of examining my complicity in contemporary colonizing violence as a tax-paying citizen of a nation that aggressively claims to "liberate" veiled Muslim women through making war, especially in Afghanistan (though "liberation" was also a central goal claimed by the United States as justification for its preemptive military attack on Iraq).[65] These recent, neocolonialist U.S. efforts labeled as "liberation campaigns" have contributed much suffering, death, destruction, and overall hardship for the conditions of women's lives, in addition to the loss of autonomy that foreign occupation brings. But as television news reporter Charles Gibson so excitedly exclaimed in 2001 during the initial U.S. bombing strikes against Afghanistan, a marker of our success was that "women walked the streets without veils for the first time in more than two years."[66] Similar to the revelations in Fanon's critique of French colonial battles against Algerians, in this contemporary media coverage, the public presence of unveiled Muslim women signals a U.S. victory over the people the United States is trying to defeat through the violence of war.

Furthermore, for my methodological inclination to merge the freedom-seeking interests of women of color across the world, it would be more comfortable to ignore the leadership of Condoleezza Rice than to acknowledge it. As U.S.

national security adviser, and later as the secretary of state, Rice played a key leadership role in the U.S. policy of waging imperialist wars with justifying propaganda about liberating oppressed peoples. Recognition of her leadership role provides a sharp corrective for any black feminist construction of African American womanhood as synonymous with political victimization. Because of the power she held during those "liberation" campaigns, one does not have to merely imagine the ominous global implications when, as she expressed to a group of Muslim women from North Africa, Central Asia, and the Middle East, she intended "to send a clear message to the women of the world who are not yet free: As you stand for your rights and your liberty, America stands with you."[67]

A trustworthy, African American feminist conceptualization of common interests with North African Muslim women's autonomy rights has to critically interrogate its own cultural positioning and any automatic assumptions about women's shared, similar, victim status. False narratives of freedom embedded within shrewd, neocolonial manipulations like those employed by Rice are now commonplace in the U.S. and the cultural biases they carry remain largely unexamined in public discourse. These narratives actively work against the possibility of authentically recognizing the subjectivity, autonomy, and agency of veiled Muslim women.

One of the major strengths of Fanon's discussion of resistance to colonization can be found in his commitment to enhancing recognition of the multiple forms of agency in the efforts of the colonized. Controversially, he viewed the violent resistance of the colonized as emancipatory for their minds as well as their bodies. For women, he gives details on the use of their bodies and "the veil" for this process. He attributes a degree of agency to Algerian women when celebrating their participation in the revolution, specifically, their use of "the veil" to hide weapons. Fanon writes about the accommodating shape of veiled women's bodies in *A Dying Colonialism* with the following imagery: "The Algerian woman's body, which in an initial phase was pared down, now swelled. Whereas in the previous period the body had to be made slim and disciplined to make it attractive and seductive, it now had to be squashed, made shapeless, even ridiculous. This, as we have seen, is the phase during which she undertook to carry bombs, grenades, machine-gun clips."[68]

In this framing, the woman's body has two forms of availability. Her body invites sexual attention in the first phase, and it bears the tools of war in the second phase. In both cases, the woman's body carries hidden dangers: seductive power in one and lethal power in the other. The lethal power that the weaponry represents is subtly linked to sexuality because of its shared moorings with her sexual power. Said differently, her sexuality and the tools of war share the utility and prowess of the woman's body. In this image, there is an almost erotic conflation of ideas about the use of women's bodies, women's sexual seductiveness, and women's openness to participating in acts of violence. This conflation invites fascination with subject matter that contains the exact same ingredients as rape myths.

Anne McClintock points out a different reference to weaponry and Algerian women's symbolic power that contains a less subtle eroticized illustration. Fanon describes the male resistance fighters' urge to immediately recover their pistols, guns, and grenades from the girl who carries them under her clothing. In this moment, the men are aware of their vulnerability and their fear of "being caught short" and unable to defend themselves.[69] Fanon interprets this "phase" as an indication that "the Algerian woman penetrates a little further into the flesh of the Revolution."[70] McClintock responds: "Here, the Algerian woman is not a victim of rape but a masculinized rapist."[71] She notes that it is odd how the women are imaged as penetrating the revolution rather than the colonial opposition. Fanon presents the instability of gender power in this perspective where women are "masculinized and the male revolution is penetrated."[72] Although I agree with McClintock that women's sexuality is oddly masculinized here, the image is consistent with how any degree of power/agency exercised by women is frequently sexualized in Fanon. This reference to penetration is also consistent with the fertile source of meanings and currency Fanon finds in rape imagery, repeatedly utilized throughout his texts.

In contrast to this assessment of Fanon's rape imagery, Sharpley-Whiting emphasizes Fanon's insights on the subject of rape and "the veil," underscoring his revelations about the colonial perpetrators. For her, Fanon "unveils" the male colonizer's supposed desire to "unveil/liberate the woman" that, in fact, only imprisons her in stereotypes "that render her more violable, more ripe for rape."[73] Sharpley-Whiting uses the suggestive language of "unveiling" to convey Fanon's ability to analytically strip the colonizer. In her view, Fanon's "unveiling" of the colonizer seems to be justifiable self-defense. For he exposes their perversity and hypocrisy with a critique of the colonizer's rape fantasies about Algerian women that "taps into the European male unconsciousness."[74] However, I think that the usefulness of rape metaphors in Fanon as well as black feminist thought needs reconsideration. It seems too much as if the usefulness of women's bodies by rapists becomes useful to the scholarly critic to make a point and then that utility is taught to the critic's readership. Also Fanon's discussion of the colonizer's rape fantasies seems almost pornographic in its level of detail about how "the woman-victim screams, struggles like a doe, and as she weakens and faints, is penetrated, martyrized, ripped apart."[75]

This history is, of course, far more brutal than fantasies by the European colonizer about raping Algerian women. Fanon also reminds his readers that it is a history of French conquest that includes "the confiscation of property and the raping of women, the pillaging of a country."[76] Unfortunately, his phrasing alludes to an unstated assumption that in the taking of property and raping of women, this pillaging victimizes the (male) owners of both.[77] Nonetheless, as

Fanon stresses, rape was an important part of the European strategy of colonization in Africa. It was used to quell resistance and combined with the "unveiling" campaigns of the French. Feminist historian Joan Wallach Scott reports that during this period in Algeria "so potent an instrument did the veil become that French soldiers patrolling the countryside violated women first by forcibly removing their veils and then raping them."[78] Fanon also indicates that sexual assault was a rampant practice by soldiers when women were imprisoned.[79]

Because of the colonizer's campaign against it, the practice of wearing the veil became an important symbol of resistance within the struggle for independence. Helie-Lucas articulates the problem that resulted for Algerian feminists who wanted to criticize this practice: "how, therefore, could we take up the veil as oppressive to women without betraying the *nation* and the *revolution*?"[80] Of course, in the postrevolution incidents of violent repression of women in Algeria, the dynamics she describes intensified. Fanon turned out to be wrong in his optimism about the extent to which women's participation in revolutionary violence would result in equality and new freedoms in society for women.[81] It should also be added that, as Algerian feminist scholar of gender and religion Marnia Lazreg points out, "Fanon was aware that anticolonial violence was a necessary but not a sufficient step toward psychological decolonization."[82] But the benefits of anticolonial violence for feminist aims in psychological decolonization remain dubious.

In conceiving of freedom that brings gender equality, one should never assume that violence has any currency to contribute. Even the conceptual goal of revealing new insights about anticolonial resistance is eroded by symbolically imaging violence as part of that conceptualization, especially when sexually violating forms of violence are referenced. If the utility of this imaging is tested by the actual, unfreeing conditions of rape that are symbolically represented in our texts, the serviceability of this symbolism for furthering resistance to subjugation is at the very least brought into question. The repetition of metaphorical, rhetorical references to sexual violence dull one's cognizance of its pain, creating the illusion that the pain of sexual violation is not really painful, which perpetuates a dangerous form of deception.

To form a common freedom struggle that women jointly share—one that directly attends to the racist realities in the politics of their histories—is to embark on a truth-telling mission. Applying the terms that Caribbean feminist M. Jacqui Alexander employs in her mapping of Pan-African feminism to the interracial, interreligious contexts discussed here, we must seek "the unborrowed truths that lie at the junction of the particularity of our experiences and confrontation of history."[83] Ultimately, my antiviolence ethic demands a notion of sisterhood that is built, not one that is spawned by matching elements in the cultural histories of women. It is an ethic that is built by embracing the truths of how certain forms of complicity in dehumanizing practices and histories of subjugation divide us and hide the means for supporting one another's self-determining spiritual, bodily, political, and socioeconomic well-being. In truthful encounters with the particularities of these differences and oppositions comes the chance for kinship in the longing for freedom and the work of resistance.

Notes

1. I want to thank Sally N. MacNichol and Jerry G. Watts for their invaluable feedback on early drafts of this chapter.

2. "Global theorist," used to describe Fanon, was used by Henry Louis Gates in "Critical Fanonism," *Critical Inquiry* 17, no. 3 (1992): 457–70.

3. My discussion of Fanon focuses on sexual violence against women. For a comprehensive study of Fanon's work and its relationship to feminism, see T. Denean Sharpley-Whiting, *Frantz Fanon: Conflicts and Feminisms* (Lanham, MD: Rowman and Littlefield, 1998).

4. Examples of my references to use of Fanon can be found in *Wounds of the Spirit: Black Women, Violence, and Resistance Ethics* (New York: New York University Press, 1999), especially 72–73, and in "Spirit-Colonizing Violations: Racism, Sexual Violence and Black American Women," in *Remembering Conquest: Feminist/Womanist Perspectives on Religion, Colonization and Sexual Violence,* ed. Nantawan Boonprasat Lewis and Marie Fortune (Binghamton, NY: Haworth Pastoral, 1999), 19–30.

5. Frantz Fanon, *A Dying Colonialism,* trans. Haakon Chevalier (New York: Grove, 1967), 55.

6. Gwen Bergner aptly summarizes his androcentrism by explaining that although "his description of colonial psychodynamics as a relationship between white men and black men" is sometimes "mediated through women's bodies . . . feminine subjectivity is removed from the center of his analysis," but even this omission signals "women's role as objects of exchange in the homosocial, heterosexual economy." *Taboo Subjects: Race, Sex and Psychoanalysis* (Minneapolis: University of Minnesota Press, 2005), 17.

7. On his homophobia, see, for example, the discussion by Diana Fuss's conclusion that "[t]he most serious problem with Fanon's theory of sexual perversions is the pivotal role assigned to homosexuality in the cultural construction of racism. . . . Fanon's theory of sexuality offers little to anyone committed to both an anti-imperialist and an antihomophobic politics." "Interior Colonies: Frantz Fanon and the Politics of Identification," in *Rethinking Fanon: The Continuing Dialogue,* ed. Nigel C. Gibson (New York: Humanity Books, 1999), 313, 314. Offering a differing perspective, Kobena Mercer affirms the usefulness of Fanon for lesbian and gay critics by allowing "his analysis of negrophobia to open up the issue of homophobia both in Fanon's own text and broader narratives of nationalism as a whole." "Decolonisation and Disappointment: Reading Fanon's Sexual Politics," in *The Fact of Blackness: Frantz Fanon and Visual Representation,* ed. Alan Read (Seattle: Bay, 1996), 128; also see Terry Goldie, "Saint Fanon and 'Homosexual Territory,' " in *Frantz Fanon: Critical Perspectives,* ed. Anthony C. Alessandrini (New York: Routledge, 1999).

8. bell hooks offers a model for this approach of naming her "own agency in claiming a relationship with Fanon, a fact that enabled me to be nurtured to grow through work despite sexism." "Dialogue," *The Fact of Blackness: Frantz Fanon and Visual Representation*, 104.

9. Frantz Fanon, *Black Skin, White Masks*, trans. Charles Lam Markmann (New York: Grove, 1967).

10. Ibid., 63.

11. Anne McClintock, "Fanon and Gender Agency," in *Rethinking Fanon: The Continuing Dialogue*, 286.

12. I am borrowing "embodied consciousness" from Christian feminist ethicist Margaret Farley, *A Framework for Christian Sexual Ethics* (New York: Continuum, 2006), 130.

13. Fanon, *Black Skin, White Masks*, 112.

14. Also see discussion of this scene in Vicky Lebeau, "Children of Violence," *Frantz Fanon's Black Skin, White Masks: New Interdisciplinary Essays*, Maxim Silverman (Manchester and New York: Manchester University Press, 2005; distributed in the United States by Palgrave).

15. Lola Young, "Missing Persons: Fantasizing Black Women in *Black Skin, White Masks*," in *The Fact of Blackness: Frantz Fanon and Visual Representation.*

16. Ibid., 93.

17. bell hooks, "Dialogue," in *The Fact of Blackness: Frantz Fanon and Visual Representation*, 104.

18. hooks uses these terms to represent mutually reinforcing notions of normative moral behavior. For other versions of a feminist ethic of care, see Nel Noddings, *Educating Moral People: A Caring Alternative to Character Education* (New York: Teachers College, 2002); Joan Tronto, *Moral Boundaries: A Political Argument for an Ethic of Care* (New York: Routledge, 1993); Emilie Townes, *Breaking the Fine Rain of Death: African American Health Issues and a Womanist Ethic of Care* (New York: Continuum, 1989).

19. Ibid., 106

20. This perspective is also evident in her other writings; see bell hooks, "Loving Blackness as Political Resistance," in *Black Looks: Race and Representation* (Boston: South End, 1992).

21. However, Fanon represents the Algerian heterosexual couple as "the fertile nucleus of the nation" from which an "*effervescent emergence*" of citizen and patriot comes forth. Frantz Fanon, *A Dying Colonialism*, 114.

22. hooks, "Feminism as a Persistent Critique of History: What's Love Got to Do With It?" in *The Fact of Blackness: Frantz Fanon and Visual Representation*, 84.

23. bell hooks, *Yearning: Race, Gender and Cultural Politics* (Boston: South End, 1990), 22.

24. Hazel Carby, "White Woman Listen! Black Feminism and the Boundaries of Sisterhood," in *Theories of Race and Racism*, ed. John Solomos (New York: Routledge, 2000), 389.

25. Patricia Hill Collins, *Black Sexual Politics: Africans, Gender, and the New Racism* (New York: Routledge, 2004), 30.

26. Fanon, *Black Skin, White Masks*, 179.

27. Ibid., 156.

28. In his discussion of Fanon's references to the United States on this topic, David Macey claims that Fanon illustrates his thesis about white women and their desire for rape with a misreading of U.S. literature, particularly of Chester Himes's novel *If He Hollers Let Him Go* (New York: New American Library, 1945). *Frantz Fanon: A Biography* (New York: Picador, United States, 2000), 193–94. For a more general discussion that sociohistorically contextualizes the locations Fanon references in *Black Skin, White Masks*, see Jim House, "Colonial Racisms in the 'Métropole': Reading *Peau Noire, Masques Blancs* in Context," in Silverman, *Frantz Fanon's Black Skin, White Masks*, 46–73.

29. Fanon, *Black Skin, White Masks*, 166.

30. Ibid., 170.

31. Ibid., 179.

32. Ibid., 158.

33. Ibid. Similarly, for white men, issues of sexuality and racist phobia merge in their response to black men. Fanon explains that "the Negrophobic man is a repressed homosexual." *Black Skin, White Masks*, 156.

34. Ibid., 167.

35. Ibid.

36. Ibid., 171.

37. Ibid., 179.

38. For an example of a sympathetic psychoanalytic reading of this rape fantasy idea, see Vicky Lebeau's explanation of his use of the oedipus complex and how his discussion of masochism draws upon the psychoanalysis of female sexuality by Helene Deutsch and Marie Bonaparte. "Children of Violence," 134.

39. Young, "Missing Persons," 96.

40. Ibid., 95.

41. Fuss, "Interior Colonies," 312.

42. See Susan Brownmiller's critique of Fanon in her landmark study *Against Our Will: Men, Women, and Rape* (New York: Simon and Schuster, 1975), 249–50. Also see Sharpley-Whiting's critique of Brownmiller, *Frantz Fanon: Conflicts and Feminisms*, 14–16.

43. hooks, "Feminism as a Persistent Critique of History," 84.

44. Sharpley-Whiting, *Frantz Fanon: Conflicts and Feminisms*, 13.

45. Ibid., 14.

46. Sharpley-Whiting explains that "many white women will not find themselves here." Ibid.

47. Fuss, "Interior Colonies," *Rethinking Fanon: The Continuing Dialogue*, 311.

48. Kelly Brown Douglas, *Sexuality and the Black Church: A Womanist Perspective* (Maryknoll, NY: Orbis, 1999), 48.

49. See Catherine A. McKinnon, "Rape: On Coercion and Consent," in *Toward a Feminist Theory of the State* (Cambridge: Harvard University Press, 1989), 171–83; Peggy Reeves Sanday, *Fraternity Gang Rape: Sex, Brotherhood, and Privilege on Campus*, 2nd ed. (New York: New York University Press, 2007).

50. I have altered a minor detail in this description to protect this woman's anonymity.

51. Cathy J. Cohen, "Punks, Bulldaggers, and Welfare Queens: The Radical Potential of Queer Politics?" in *Black Queer Studies: A Critical Anthology*, ed. E. Patrick

Johnson and Mae Henderson (Durham: Duke University Press, 2005), 29.

52. Ibid.

53. See examples in Darlene Clark Hine, "For Pleasure, Profit, and Power: The Sexual Exploitation of Black Women," in Geneva Smitherman, ed., *African American Women Speak Out on Anita Hill-Clarence Thomas* (Detroit: Wayne State University Press, 1995): 168–77; Charlotte Pierce-Baker, *Surviving the Silence: Black Women's Stories of Rape* (New York: Norton, 1998), especially Yvonne's Story, 122–39; *Wounds of the Spirit,* especially 32, 147.

54. Frantz, Fanon, *A Dying Colonialism,* 37.

55. Ibid., 37–38.

56. Ibid., 42. For a thoughtful feminist reading that differs from mine on this point and argues in favor of emancipatory possibilities in Fanon's depiction of Algerian women, see Drucilla Cornell, "The Secret Behind the Veil: A Reinterpretation of 'Algeria Unveiled' *Philosophia Africana* 4, no. 2 (August 2001): 27–35.

57. Fanon, *A Dying Colonialism,* 41.

58. Frantz Fanon, *Wretched of the Earth,* trans. Constance Farrington (New York: Grove, 1963), 42.

59. Ibid., 42. Also, Marnia Lazreg gives examples of how Algerian girls were taught to love God and love France in Christian schools during the nineteenth and twentieth centuries. *The Eloquence of Silence: Algerian Women in Question* (New York: Routledge, 1994), 68–79. Also see Leila Ahmed, *Women and Gender in Islam: Historical Roots of a Modern Debate* (New Haven: Yale University Press, 1992), 151–68.

60. Homa Hoodfar, "The Veil in Their Minds and on Our Heads: Veiling Practices and Muslim Women," in *Women, Gender, Religion: A Reader,* ed. Elizabeth A. Castelli (New York: Palgrave, 2001), 422. Also see *The Muslim Veil in North America: Issues and Debates,* ed. Sajida Sultana Alvi, Homa Hoodfar, Sheila McDonough (Toronto, ON: Women's, 2003).

61. See Rita Nakashima Brock and Rebecca Ann Parker, *Proverbs of Ashes: Violence, Redemptive Suffering, and the Search for What Saves Us* (Boston: Beacon, 2002); Rita Nakashima Brock and Rebecca Ann Parker, *Saving Paradise: How Christianity Traded Love of This World for Crucifixion and Empire* (Boston: Beacon, 2008); Delores S. Williams, *Sisters in the Wilderness: The Challenge of Womanist God-Talk* (Maryknoll, NY: Orbis, 1993), especially 161–70.

62. Fanon, *A Dying Colonialism,* 39.

63. Ibid.

64. Marie-Aimée Helie-Lucas, "Women, Nationalism, and Religion in the Algerian Liberation Struggle," in *Rethinking Fanon: The Continuing Dialogue,* 275.

65. See Kevin Ayotte and Mary E. Husain, "Securing Afghan Women: Neocolonialism, Epistemic Violence, and the Rhetoric of the Veil," *NWSA Journal* 17, no. 3 (Fall 2005): 112–33.

66. Charles Gibson, *Good Morning America,* ABC News (7 am) November 12, 2001.

67. Serena Parker, "Women/Muslim World," *Voice of America News,* March 9, 2005.

68. Fanon, *A Dying Colonialism,* 62.

69. Ibid., 54.

70. Ibid.

71. Anne McClintock, *Imperial Leather: Race, Gender and Sexuality in the Colonial Contest* (New York: Routledge, 1995), 366.

72. Ibid., 367.

73. Sharpley-Whiting, *Frantz Fanon: Conflicts and Feminisms*, 68.

74. Ibid.

75. Fanon, *A Dying Colonialism*, 46.

76. Ibid., 45.

77. For examples of similar, androcentric language referring to rape, see *Wretched of the Earth*, 92, 254.

78. Joan Wallach Scott, *The Politics of the Veil* (Princeton: Princeton University Press, 2007), 65.

79. Fanon, *A Dying Colonialism*, 119. Also see Joan Wallach Scott, *The Politics of the Veil*, 65–66.

80. Helie-Lucas, "Women, Nationalism, and Religion in the Algerian Liberation Struggle," 275.

81. For a fuller discussion of these issues of violence, see Aaronette White, "All the Men Are Fighting for Freedom, All the Women Are Mourning Their Men, but Some of Us Carried Guns: A Raced-Gendered Analysis of Fanon's Psychological Perspectives on War," *Signs: Journal of Women in Culture and Society* 32, no. 4 (Summer, 2007): 857–84.

82. Marnia Lazreg, *Torture and the Twilight of Empire: From Algiers to Baghdad* (Princeton: Princeton University Press, 2008), 219.

83. Jacqui Alexander, *Pedagogies of Crossing: Meditations on Feminism, Sexual Politics, Memory, and the Sacred* (Chapel Hill, NC: Duke University Press, 2005), 275.

10

Madness and Judiciousness

A Phenomenological Reading of a Black Woman's Encounter with a Saleschild

Emily S. Lee

Introduction

> Buzzers are big in New York City. Favored particularly by smaller stores and boutiques, merchants throughout the city have installed them as screening devices to reduce the incidence of robbery: if the face at the door looks desirable, the buzzer is pressed and the door is unlocked. If the face is that of an undesirable, the door stays locked. . . . The installation of these buzzers happened swiftly in New York . . . I discovered them and their meaning one Saturday in 1986. I was shopping in Soho and saw in a store window a sweater that I wanted to buy for my mother. I pressed my round brown face to the window and my finger to the buzzer, seeking admittance. A narrow-eyed, white teenager wearing running shoes and feasting on bubble gum glared out, evaluating me for signs that would pit me against the limits of his social understanding. After about five seconds, he mouthed "We're closed," and blew pink rubber at me. It was two Saturdays before Christmas, at one o'clock in the afternoon; there were several white people in the store who appeared to be shopping for things for *their* mothers.[1]

Patricia Williams, a black, female law professor, relays the above account in *The Alchemy of Race and Right.* Since so much of phenomenological work is preoccupied with describing phenomenology, it has become common to jokingly wonder when phenomenologists will actually *do* phenomenology. Drawing primarily from Maurice Merleau-Ponty's *Phenomenology of Perception* this chapter attempts to actually *do* phenomenology in exploring Williams's encounter with the saleschild.[2]

I chose this particular interaction between Williams and the saleschild because this encounter brings to stark focus an important moment in phenomenological analysis: a contestatory moment of the meanings in the horizon or, perhaps alternatively, a moment when a meaning becomes more solidly embedded into the horizon. I read this particular encounter between Williams and the saleschild as a moment when, in regards to a racial meaning in our social world, that which defines reason is contested. As a contestation over reason, society awards the winner as reasonable and deems the other as unreasonable, perhaps even mad.

This contested moment demonstrates a limit condition in regards to the phenomenological concept of the 'horizon.' The concept of the horizon helpfully illustrates the sedimented, prevailing meanings in the world and how these meanings originate always as products of negotiations among members of society. But phenomenology and the conception of the horizon do not illustrate how individuals can change these meanings. Considering the weight of history and the shared quality of the meanings, Merleau-Ponty's elucidation that individuals change the meanings in the horizon through isolated actions appears far from satisfying and seems almost futile. Yet Merleau-Ponty posits such individual contestations as the only means to influence the meanings of the horizon. Hence, although this chapter attempts to do phenomenology, it concludes with a critique of the limits of phenomenological analysis.

The three goals of this chapter are to do phenomenology, to illustrate a moment of racial meaning contestation on the horizon, and to present a limit in phenomenological analysis. Let us return to Williams's account of her experience.

The Given World, the Lived World

A phenomenological understanding of the interaction between Williams and the saleschild must begin with the given world, a notion made familiar by the works of Edmund Husserl and Martin Heidegger. Williams's description of the world in Soho, New York City, during the Christmas season of 1986—a world where boutiques install buzzers to prevent theft—illustrates that one enters into a particular place, into a specific time and into certain fixed scenarios. One experiences the world within a concrete situation; the world is given to me. As Merleau-Ponty states, "I am given, that is, I find myself already situated and involved in a physical and social world."[3]

The given world is experienced phenomenally. Drawing from Husserl's work, Merleau-Ponty defines phenomena as a "layer of living experience through which other people and things are first given to us."[4] Husserl and Merleau-Ponty argue that all of our initial contact with the world occurs phenomenally, rather than already, clearly, distinguishable as subjective or objective. Husserl's lived world steers through the unnecessary setup of stark contrast between the naturalism of empiricism and the psychologism of intellectualism, where one reduces the world either to its materiality or to the projections of consciousness. Husserl explains that one experiences the world phenomenally; one experiences both contrasts ambiguously. In describing Husserl's understanding of phenomena, Ronald Bruzina states that "consciousness is now a pure field of experience-in-the-living (lived experience, *Erlebnis*), in which various objects [and features] are found as appearings-in-the-field."[5] Such an understanding of our phenomenal relations within the world acknowledges not only the influence of the world but also that of the subject. Phenomenology recognizes that experiences of the world are negotiations between the subject and the world, between the intentions of the subject and the givens of the world.

Merleau-Ponty's phenomenology posits a gestaltian contact with the world. Gestalt theory advances that the "most basic unit of experience is that of figure-on-a-background," anything simpler reflects mere mental constructions.[6] Human experience of the world cannot reduce the smallest unit of experience to solely the figure. Rather, one always experiences the figure with its background. The Gestalt *principle of contextual relevancy* holds that "the meaning of a theme is co-determined (a) by the unity formed by the internal coherence of [the theme's] parts, and (b) by the relation between the theme and the horizon that provides its context."[7] Empiricism and intellectualism recognize only the first condition of unity within the theme and fail to recognize the second condition of balance between the theme and the horizon. This second condition is gestalt theory's unique contribution. Gestalt theory explains that one experiences and perceives the theme because of and with the horizon. One cannot perceive the theme without its horizon; one cannot recognize the theme within a different horizon—not without much encouragement. Rather, an optimal relation must exist between the theme and the horizon for perception of the theme.[8]

Merleau-Ponty develops the notion of the theme and the horizon with the gestaltian framework. He advocates against reducing the gestaltian framework to solely a spatial sense. With the new vernacular, Merleau-Ponty elaborates the meanings—the significations already functioning in the world. The horizon represents the sense of possibilities in the world because the world is "an open and indefinite multiplicity of relationships which are of reciprocal implication."[9] In this sense of the irreducibility of the world to any one aspect, Merleau-Ponty repeats over and over again that human beings are in the world.[10] Human beings are always subject to the influences of the world; we are always situated.

Within the *Phenomenology of Perception*, however, Merleau-Ponty fails to significantly deemphasize the role of consciousness in the structure of the horizon. As such, even in his insightful idea of sedimentation, Merleau-Ponty mistakenly prioritizes the domain of thought. To explain sedimentation, he writes that, "there is a 'world of thought,' or a sediment left by our mental processes, which enables us to rely on our concepts and acquired judgments as we might on things there in front of us, presented globally, without there being any need for us to resynthesize them."[11] Although the notion of sedimentation beautifully depicts the meaning complexes in the world, it mistakenly attributes them solely to the mind.

In his last text, *The Visible and the Invisible,* Merleau-Ponty more successfully moves away from privileging consciousness. In his working notes, he credits the horizon as the source of all concepts, of a certain style of being, and of being itself.[12] The notion of the horizon functions both in relation to space as exterior to the theme and to time as interior to the theme. In its earlier instantiations, Husserl held forth the possibility of infinity in knowing the theme. Here Merleau-Ponty parts ways with Husserl, for he gives up this possibility of infinity in the sense of absolutely knowing the theme and instead relies upon and evokes historicity in the horizon.[13] The horizon refers to the history surrounding and circumscribing the theme.

For theorists concerned with feminist or race theory, the horizon must be reminiscent of the idea of social or cultural construction. Postmodernism has made the notion of social construction common parlance, and Judith Butler's work is especially important for feminist concerns, with the idea that gender and sex are social constructs. Critical race theorists have made a similar claim in regards to race. Although the horizon and social construction appear similar, the horizon does not conceptualize everything as social constructions. Within the *Phenomenology*, culture plays a central configuration in the notion of the horizon, yet Merleau-Ponty is not explicit about his use of the word *culture*. Merleau-Ponty simply contrasts culture with nature, where, for him, culture serves as the overlay upon nature. He does not explore the possibility that more than one culture may exist, and consequently he does not explore the ramifications of several distinctive cultures. Merleau-Ponty recognized different cultures as demonstrated in his interests in anthropology and Levi-Strauss's work. But by the time of *The Visible and the Invisible*, Merleau-Ponty demands the dissolution of such distinctions of culture and nature, insisting any such distinctions are merely abstract.[14] He uses the term *abstract* in all its Hegelian negative connotations. To specifically speak of social or cultural construction, as the poststructuralists do, requires distinguishing between culture and nature, a discernment Merleau-Ponty believes impossible.[15] Instead, suffice it to note that culture, in a form indistinguishable from nature, functions within his understanding of the horizon.

Through all of the changing conceptions of the horizon, Merleau-Ponty consistently promotes two central ideas: first, the phenomenological basis that the horizon cannot be removed or eliminated; and second, the horizon, although constantly changing, functions as the meaning framework for our society. In this sense, the horizon functions as a motivating force that guides the experience and perception of the theme. The horizon depicts the sense in which we live in the given world, as beings-in-the-world.

Patricia Williams's Embodiment

In the given world, Williams sees the desirable sweater, presses her round brown face to the window, and places her finger on the buzzer. Members of our world recognize the behavior patterns; the ringing of the bell communicates to the saleschild that Williams desires admittance to the store. The communicated meaning of the body movement indicates that Williams and the saleschild share a culture and a world. As Merleau-Ponty describes, "behavior patterns settle into . . . nature, being deposited in the form of a cultural world."[16] The actions of the body simultaneously draw attention to the implements, the buzzer, the window, and the locked door, which also serve as symbols of culture. "No sooner has my gaze fallen upon a living body in the process of acting," writes Merleau-Ponty, "than the objects surrounding it immediately take on a fresh layer of significance: they are no longer simply what I myself could make of them."[17] Merleau-Ponty astutely recognizes the interplay between body movement, implements, and culture. The three mutually validate each other and facilitate communication among the members of society.

Merleau-Ponty's focus on body movement lies at the center of his challenge of the belief in the divide between the body and the mind in the tradition of Plato, Descartes, Hume, and even Husserl. These traditions leave us with "the living body bec[o]me an exterior without interior, subjectivity bec[o]me an interior without exterior."[18] Such traditions have left us with the problem of intersubjectivity. In perhaps his most radical proposal, Merleau-Ponty locates subjectivity not in something interior to the body, such as a consciousness or a soul, but as the body. To understand how he comes to this conclusion, we must appreciate his early work in child psychology.

Beginning with the discovery of the infant's initial experience of the body as intrinsically reflexive, Merleau-Ponty explains that this initial experience of the body precedes distinctions of subject or object.[19] In this indistinguishable state, the corporeal schema is intrinsically reflexive. From this reflexivity, Merleau-Ponty proposes that the body is experienced as the body image. Body image is "the thematization of the corporeal reflexivity underlying the corporeal schema."[20] Martin Dillon explains, "My body-image is my image of myself: as image, it is object; as myself, it is the subject I am."[21] The body's reflexivity defies the law of noncontradiction. Merleau-Ponty suggests the following definition of body image: "The word 'here' applied to my body does not refer to a determinate position in relation to other positions or to external co-ordinates, but the laying down of the first co-ordinates, the anchoring of the active body in an object, the situation of the body in face of its tasks."[22] The body serves as the measure of all of our contact with the world. The body image represents the body's spatiality and temporality. The body image evokes how the body in action, the body in movement, acts in the world.

Without a subject interior to the body guiding body movement and without a reductive conception of the body as mechanistic, Merleau-Ponty must explain how the body comes to move. Merleau-Ponty offers the idea of body motility, his third conception of the body. With the idea of body motility, he proposes that the body retains its own intentionality.[23] To appreciate the idea of body intentionality, one must understand the difference between act intentionality and operative intentionality. Act intentionality refers to the common understanding of intentionality, the intentionality of conscious judgments culminating in individual actions, an intentionality familiar to liberal theory.[24] Operative intentionality, first introduced by Husserl, refers to an intentionality functioning within the world.[25] Distinct from the act intentionality of isolated, conscious individuals, operative intentionality depicts an intentionality always already present in the world because of the historical and social meaning influencing all beings-in-the-world.[26]

In between act and operative intentionality, the body's movements project beyond the immediate. For in the relationship between act and operative intentionality, body motility defines the relation between the significance of an individual act and the meanings operating in the world. Merleau-Ponty introduces the concept of 'body motility' to capture this relationship between single acts and the meanings enveloping the world. He writes, " 'Already motility, in its pure state, possesses the basic power of giving a meaning.' "[27] With an elaboration of body motility, Merleau-Ponty's body image captures precisely the body in movement as a movement from the individual, immediate and actual to the community, the world, the future and the ideal. The two moments form a unique totality.[28]

The movement from the immediate to the surrounding world is a movement from the space of the concrete to the space of the abstract. The immediate vicinity of the body in action establishes the setting for the possibility of body movement that extends toward abstract, creative space. In more existential language, Dillon explains that "by virtue of the possibilities opened to it by thematization of the 'I can,' consciousness is liberated from the immediacy of the bodily projects made in response to the concrete and given context, and may now undertake movements in the human space of potentiality (as opposed to the physical space of actuality)."[29] Our body image retains an intentionality of its very own, which motivates movement toward possible space. The body's abstract movement arises from the accumulation of learned, habitual body movements.[30] Merleau-Ponty describes the movement from the lived to the abstract space as a spiraling centrifugal movement.[31] The body in movement, the body facing its projects is a projective being.[32] The body projects outside itself.

With the body subject, this world remains "undivided between my perception and his . . . both are not cogitations shut up in their own immanence, but beings which are outrun by their world, and which consequently may well be outrun by each other."[33] Perception of the other is possible; intersubjectivity is not impossible.[34] In the given world, when Williams rings the bell, her body movements project her desire of moving from the actual sphere outside the store on the street to the possible sphere of the store. The saleschild in turn perceives her body and her consciousness simultaneously; the saleschild perceives a subject. The saleschild perceives her body movements and surmises her intentions to enter the store because they share a horizon where her body movements convey intentions understood by both of them.

The saleschild does not perceive Williams in her entirety; he sees an anonymous black woman. Merleau-Ponty writes, "In the cultural object, I feel the close presence of others beneath a veil of anonymity."[35] Merleau-Ponty's analysis foregoes the philosophical problem of perceiving the body with its consciousness, yet his analysis leaves us with the perception of an anonymous other.[36] Perception of a particular person does not occur. The saleschild does not recognize Williams as a thinker who contemplates her personal interactions, a person who publicizes seemingly ordinary interactions does not come to pass.

The Saleschild's Perception

In just five seconds, the saleschild mouths the words "we're closed" and "blows pink rubber" at Williams. The saleschild refuses entrance to Williams. Williams leads us to believe that the saleschild must be lying; after all it is one o'clock in the afternoon, a Saturday, two weeks before Christmas. The saleschild lies to deny entry to Williams and avoids telling her directly that she is undesirable, that she appears likely to commit theft. The saleschild only understands Williams's intention to enter the store. The saleschild misunderstands her intentions subsequent to entrance of the store.

As beings-in-the-world, perception occurs phenomenally; perception opens us to the world. Merleau-Ponty's understanding of perception emphasizes an ongoing contact with the world. Perception occurs continuously; one cannot simply turn perception on and off.[37] But perception is a lacuna; it never finishes;[38] as a result, it can be deceiving because it is partial and full of gaps and holes.[39] Perception occurs through a horizon, through an atmosphere of generality and anonymity.[40]

Williams is not an alien or other worldly creature in the saleschild's world; brown bodies are part of the saleschild's given world. The saleschild's perception of Williams's body—brown, round-faced, kinky-haired, together with the cultural implements, the clothes Williams is wearing—sums up to a type of body associated with undesirability, a type of body associated with the likelihood of committing theft.[41] Through the horizon of the given world, the saleschild perceives Williams as a general type. Husserl explains that *all* perceptions anticipate future perceptions on the basis of types. He writes that "every real thing whatsoever has . . . its general 'a priori,' . . . a type."[42] Alfred Schutz's work elaborates on this aspect of Husserl's work. The saleschild's perception of Williams demonstrates what Schutz designates as "they-orientation." "They-orientation" marks perception of remote and anonymous contemporaries. They-orientation contrasts with "we-orientation," which marks perception of intimate acquaintances.[43] While Husserl views all perception as typified, according to Schutz, perception via types occurs only when one is they-oriented.[44] Schutz's analysis appears more probable. Intimate acquaintances, one's friends, family, and lovers, usually defy types. When one is they-oriented toward the other, one perceives the other as a type; one sees an anonymous being. Being they-oriented, "the synthesis of recognition does not apprehend the unique person as [s]he exists within [her] living present. Instead it pictures [her] as always the same and homogenous, leaving out of account all the changes and rough edges that go along with individuality."[45] Hence, although the saleschild and Williams share the given world, and intersubjectivity is possible, the saleschild perceives Williams as a type because the saleschild is they-oriented toward her.

This framework is limited since Williams's features are anonymous to the extent that the saleschild sees her as a black woman, but her features are not so anonymous that the saleschild sees her as a woman or as a human being. Although the saleschild perceives her as a certain undesirable type, the saleschild could have perceived her as a desirable type, among a broader and more tolerable type, such as among women who enjoy shopping. Even if the saleschild is they-oriented toward Williams, the saleschild could have been they-oriented toward Williams by casting her into the shopping frenzied female type. Why does the saleschild cast Williams into one type and not another?

Schutz offers one explanation for the they-orientation and the selection of types. He advances the notion that individuals hold a specific field of interests, or a system of relevances. One determines one's system of relevances "by the fact that [one is] not equally interested in all the strata of the world within [one's] reach. The selective function of interest organizes the world . . . in strata of major and minor relevance."[46] Schutz's system of relevances indicates that one hierarchizes one's interests. One's interests determine that which one seeks to understand. When the saleschild perceives Williams as the undesirable black woman type, the saleschild exhibits a glimpse of his stratum of relevance. The saleschild positions Williams and racial consciousness outside his "stratum of relevance, which requires explicit knowledge."[47] He is not interested in Williams as a particular person, or what is more important, he is not interested in awareness of race questions. With the notion of stratums of relevances, Schutz accounts for the various "zones of blind belief and ignorance" held by different individuals.[48] Perhaps black women, class, or racial consciousness do not lie within the saleschild's range of interests.

Schutz's analysis provides one possible reason for the saleschild's selective anonymity and system of relevances. He argues that systems of relevances are institutionally derived and sanctioned. Schutz writes that "[t]he order of domains of relevances prevailing in a particular social group is itself an element of the relative natural conception of the world taken for granted. . . . In each group the order of these domains has its particular history. It is an element of socially approved and socially derived knowledge and frequently is institutionalized."[49] Of course, theorists of race and gender have already vehemently voiced the institutionalization of discrimination. Race theorists Michael Omi and Howard Winant have written on the institutionalization of discrimination that discrimination occurs on two different strata, structural/institutional and prejudicial/discriminatory.[50] Similarly, the institutionalization Schutz describes does not refer only to the formal laws within a society but also to the sedimented beliefs of our society. The saleschild does not solely derive his selective anonymity.

In a five-second interaction, the saleschild's they-orientation is not at issue. In a five-second interaction, the saleschild cannot know the particular person who is Williams. The institutionalization of systems of relevances explains why the saleschild casts Williams as the type to commit theft and not the type to love shopping. The saleschild surmises a conclusion based solely on the visible features of Williams's body, and the racialized meaning of her body plays a more prominent role than other stereotypes about women. The saleschild's understanding and prejudice of brown bodies triggers "a raison d'être for a thing which guides the flow of phenomena without being explicitly laid down in any one of them."[51] The saleschild's personal previous experiences with brown faces alone could not lead to such a quick decision. The saleschild is, after all, a seventeen-year-old boy. How much direct contact with brown faces could the saleschild have experienced? Rather, the sediment of ideas, the operative intentionality, and the horizon of the given world about brown bodies prevailing in our society nurtures the saleschild's perception. The saleschild no longer resynthesizes, rethinks the meaning of brown faces. The institutionalized system of relevances conditions the saleschild's understanding of brown bodies and leads him to prominently position the color of her skin in his system of relevances.

Phenomenology and the notion of the horizon helpfully illuminate this particular encounter, but Merleau-Ponty's phenomenological system has been criticized for depicting as natural the racist and sexist beliefs held in our society. Linda Martín Alcoff explains that critics charge phenomenology of taking "subjectivity and subjective experience as cause and foundation when in reality they are mere epiphenomenon and effect. Phenomenology is sometimes portrayed as developing metaphysical accounts of experience outside of culture and history."[52] In a separate article, Alcoff again explains the existence of "a fear that phenomenological description will naturalize or fetishize racial experiences."[53] The problem lies in Merleau-Ponty's portrayal of the horizon as inevitably arising from the world. As an inevitable occurrence, Merleau-Ponty fails to really depict the members of society as involved in influencing or negotiating the horizon. Our horizon, which includes a history of women's secondary status and a history of racism and colonialism, appears simply unavoidable. Merleau-Ponty's portrayal of the horizon depicts such a history as teleological developments of the world, as unavoidable historical evolutions. Feminists and race theorists contest precisely this implication of the horizon. They highlight the role of dominating cultures, the negotiations—including wars—and the social constructedness of human beings that have led to our present cultural and social environment.

Interestingly, in spite of such difficulties, Merleau-Ponty's notion of the horizon has been useful for feminists and race theorists. Gail Weiss evokes the horizon to elaborate the immediateness—so immediate as to be mistaken as inherent—of affiliations of specific bodies with certain negative associations. Merleau-Ponty's phenomenology productively highlights the immediateness of the affiliations because he emphasizes embodiment over consciousness with his notion of an embodied subjectivity. Referring to the works of Frantz Fanon, Weiss explains that members of minority communities may feel they possess inferior corporeal schemas, and this feeling of inferiority resides on the level of embodiment. Weiss writes that "the invisible social processes at work in the construction of a racially-coded corporeal schema . . . [are] always already operative, and for those societally designated as 'racial minorities,' the internalization of this racial epidermal schema . . . results in a (psychophysical) inferiority complex."[54] Similarly, Alcoff refers to the givenness of the horizon to explain the confusion of the cause and effect of racism. She writes that "the process by which human bodies are differentiated and categorized by type is a process preceded by racism, rather than one that causes and thus 'explains' racism as a natural result."[55] The notion of the horizon provides a conceptual framework for understanding the depth of the racial associations we make during our perceptions of our own and others' embodiment. Both Weiss and Alcoff utilize the idea of the horizon to illuminate the workings of racism and sexism embedded into our social cultural beliefs, well aware of the dangers involved.

While the notion of the horizon is apparently both useful and problematic for feminists and race theorists, the relevant issue for the present purpose is not the question of how racism and sexism got sedimented into the horizon but whether Merleau-Ponty's depiction of the horizon acknowledges the functioning of racism and sexism. The present question centers on whether he accounts for a struggle between diverging perceptions in their separate claims to more accurately represent the world.

Williams Understands the Horizon

Let me interrupt my phenomenological reading of this event, to elaborate Williams's own description of such events. What I find fascinating about her book, *The Alchemy of Race and Rights*, is that even without Merleau-Ponty's phenomenological language, Williams seems to be "doing phenomenology." Her words evoke phenomenology's concepts and ideas. Much in her book demonstrates the functions of the horizon. Williams shows acute awareness of how much the meanings in our society have an impact on what the members of society perceive about her embodiment and so prominently influence her experiences in the United States. She comprehends "that a part of ourselves is beyond the control of pure physical will and resides in the sanctuary of those around us; a fundamental part of ourselves and of our dignity depends on the uncontrollable, powerful, external observers who make up a society."[56]

It is important to note that living in our society with its horizon of meanings, its givens in the world, means not only that white bodies accept these meanings but that black bodies internalize the prevailing meanings as well. The notion of the horizon depicts how all members of society, including people of color, accept the association of certain bodies with negative meanings, even if, in the case of people of color, the negative associations define the self. Feminist theorist Annette Kuhn states that women identify with men; and Williams explains that people of color learn to see themselves through white people's eyes. She writes, "[T]he cultural domination of blacks by whites means that the black self is placed at a distance even from itself. . . . So blacks in a white society are conditioned from infancy to see in themselves only what others, who despise them, see."[57] Coherent with Weiss, Williams explains that the internalization of prevailing meanings does not simply occur on the level of consciousness, but on the very corporeal schemas of black bodies. One of the most striking consequences under these circumstances is the very real possibility that black people may forego economic opportunity because such economic advancement may also signify further loss of the self. Williams writes, "I think many people of color still find it extremely difficult to admit, much less prove, our desire to be included in alien and hostile organizations and institutions, even where those institutions also represent economic opportunity."[58]

Under these circumstances, Williams exhibits an understanding that the meanings in the horizon result from struggles over whose perceptions come to be accepted and hence sedimented into the horizon and whose perceptions are not accepted and ultimately rejected from the horizon. Williams pointedly muses, "There is great power in being able to see the world as one will and then to have that vision enacted."[59] Merleau-Ponty recognizes that perception has a relationship with power, that perception does not occur passively, and that the horizon must have arisen from struggles. But he does not address the ramifications of the racism and the sexism sedimented into his conceptualization of the horizon.[60] Merleau-Ponty takes a Nietzschean or Hegelian stance about the inevitableness of such struggles and does not concern himself with its implications to the people who lose the contestations over correct or true perception.

Williams does not take such a laissez faire attitude perhaps because she recognizes that the horizon includes meanings about her subjectivity/embodiment that clearly do not benefit her. Unlike Merleau-Ponty, I suspect Williams cannot sit back, calm in the idea that the contestations in meanings in the horizon will eventually and inevitably resolve themselves. She does not have the luxury of accepting a resolution on the basis of its inevitability. Rather, Williams urges that the black self cannot accept such prevailing meanings, explaining, "In such an environment, relinquishing the power of individual ethical judgment to a collective ideal risks psychic violence, an obliteration of the self through domination by an all-powerful other. . . . What links child abuse, the mistreatment of women, and racism is the massive external intrusion into [the] psyche that dominating powers impose to keep the self from ever fully seeing itself."[61] Clearly, passively accepting prevailing meanings in the horizon is not an option for all subjects.

This seemingly small moment when the saleschild and Williams confront each other with her ringing of the doorbell illustrates a pivotal moment of questioning and contesting or accepting and sedimenting a social meaning about her embodiment/subjectivity even deeper into the horizon. In this moment, in affirming the saleschild or Williams's perception of the situation, we decide on true and reasonable perception.

The Judiciousness of the Saleschild's Decisions

The decision to affirm the saleschild's surmisal or to affirm Williams's frustration depicts a contestation of meaning in the horizon. The majority of society has chosen to empathize with the saleschild's decision. Williams conveys that "even civil-rights organizations backed down eventually in the face of arguments that the buzzer system is a 'necessary evil.' "[62] Merleau-Ponty's analysis helps us to understand why; after all, the saleschild inhabits our world, with the givenness and the institutionalized systems of relevances of our culture and society. In relaying the "understandability" of the saleschild's behavior, Williams admits "[t]hat some blacks might agree" to the judiciousness of the saleschild's decision.[63] Merleau-Ponty's analysis, with the help of Schutz, highlights why members of our society might consider the saleschild's decision as judicious, sensible, and reasonable. Merleau-Ponty's work sheds light on why racist beliefs can be a part of the acceptable, the sensible, and the logical beliefs in our society. Connecting brown faces with undesirability and suspecting black female bodies of criminal inclinations represents an acceptable reaction given the horizon of our world.

Racist analysis has focused historically on egregious acts of power and overt signs of racism by white supremacists, such as the Nazis or the Ku Klux Klan. Focusing on such extreme acts of racism diverts attention away from the lived experience of racism and too easily relaxes the anxieties and responsibilities of the rest of us. For although we can perhaps conclude that our society does not condone egregious signs of racism, the small, seemingly forgivable, judicious, sensible, and understandable acts of racism that persist in our social horizon serve as the index of the tenacity of racist attitudes in our world. Because of our willingness to forgive the seemingly inconsequential, the seemingly reasonable signs of racism, racism continuously eludes us. Racism may be insidious not simply because it is a conscious, isolated exercise of power but because it is sedimented, pervasive, and reasonable.[64]

The acceptance of the judiciousness of the saleschild's decision leaves Williams with the descriptions of overreacting, being too sensitive, and acting unreasonably. Pondering moments in which society questions her sanity and encourages her to question her sanity fill her book: "What was most interesting to me in this experience was how the blind application of principles of neutrality . . . acted . . . to make me look crazy";[65] "[M]y story became one of extreme paranoia";[66] or in referring to herself, "You should know that this is one of those mornings when I refuse to compose myself properly . . . trying to decide if she is stupid or crazy."[67] We as a society fail to acknowledge that Williams is correct to be upset; instead, we support the saleschild's decision and relegate Williams to madness. At this moment, we create a particular meaning in the horizon. Merleau-Ponty's analysis too facilely passes over the plight of those who lose in the struggle for meanings in the horizon, but Williams's work points to where phenomenology could benefit from increased attention.

So should we absolve the saleschild of all responsibility? Merleau-Ponty's work suggests the answer—no. Drawing from Heidegger, Merleau-Ponty presents a rather complicated notion of agency and freedom. Freedom cannot be separated from the given world. He writes, "My freedom, the fundamental power which I enjoy of being the subject of all my experiences, is not distinct from my insertion into the world."[68] But as much as our freedom is integrally linked to the given world, the world does not constitute us; we also constitute the world.

As a subject, the saleschild does not simply bend to the whims of our culture. Every interaction with another provides an opportunity to affirm or to deny a shared cultural belief. The saleschild's action illustrates the "resistance offered by passivity."[69] Our willingness to accept the judiciousness of the saleschild's decision illustrates that we resist fighting racism through passivity. The saleschild resists an opportunity to deny a shared racist belief by passively accepting the racist, yet sensible belief. As Merleau-Ponty argues in regards to sedimented knowledge, "this acquired knowledge is not an inert mass in the depths of our consciousness . . . what is acquired is truly acquired only if it is taken up again in a fresh momentum of thought."[70] And as Husserl maintains, although one perceives by drawing on types, every act of perception is an opportunity to forge new types.[71]

After all this emphasis on the functioning of the horizon, Merleau-Ponty still ultimately leaves the individual alone in resisting the horizon. The notion of the horizon depicts the spatial, temporal, social, cultural, and historical meanings; as such it belies individual acts of manipulation. Individual subjects can hardly influence or change the horizon. Phenomenological notions such as the horizon helpfully explain the depth of the embeddedness of racist meanings, but for Merleau-Ponty to point only to individual acts of resistance to counter the meanings in the horizon seems limited indeed, if not futile. This depicts the limits of phenomenological analysis, and it epitomizes the reasons why racism is so pervasive and persistent.

The Primacy of Visibility over Communication and toward a Conclusion

This particular interaction between Williams and the saleschild, an interaction based solely on the visible, forecloses other possibilities of affecting the saleschild's decision. I specifically chose this interaction precisely because it depends solely on a visual surmisal and so highlights the pivotal role of the visible differences of the body in daily personal interactions. However, Merleau-Ponty, in accordance with the dominant trend in present day philosophy, emphasizes the importance of communication, of language, for influencing the child's use of his options to affirm or to deny prevalent social beliefs.[72] Merleau-Ponty believes in the ability to create a reciprocal relationship with the means of language. I cannot help but wonder if communication may be overvalued. My suspicion stems from the number of occasions in which one must quickly form a decision based solely on visible features. The frequency of these occasions far outnumbers occasions for fully communicating with the stranger, the other. Perhaps because communication is not an option in this interaction, full perception of the particular person who is Williams does not occur. It is precisely in these interactions that a phenomenological analysis can be of great assistance.

Notes

1. Patricia Williams, *The Alchemy of Race and Rights* (Cambridge: Harvard University Press, 1991), 44–45.

2. I limit myself primarily to the phenomenological concepts in this text for considerations of length and because the concepts from the *Phenomenology of Perception* suffice for the ideas I want to convey. In some ways, for the present analysis, I prefer the notions of embodiment and the horizon over the notion of the visible and the invisible and the chiasm. For my attempts at doing phenomenology with the phenomenological concepts from Merleau-Ponty's later works, see "The Meaning of Visible Differences of the Body," *American Philosophical Association Newsletter on the Status of Asian/Asian Americans* 2, no. 2 (Spring 2003): 34–37.

3. Maurice Merleau-Ponty, *Phenomenology of Perception*, tr. Colin Smith (London: Routledge and Kegan Paul, 1962), 360.

4. Merleau-Ponty, *Phenomenology*, 57.

5. Ronald Bruzina, *Logos and Eidos* (Paris: Mouton, 1970), 53.

6. M. C. Dillon, *Merleau-Ponty's Ontology* (Evanston: Northwestern University Press, 1988), 59–60.

7. *Ibid.*, 67–68. See also Merleau-Ponty, *Phenomenology*, 302.

8. Maurice Merleau-Ponty, *The Visible and the Invisible*, tr. Alphonso Lingis (Evanston: Northwestern University Press, 1968), 205.

9. Merleau-Ponty, *Phenomenology*, 71. See also *Visible*, 100.

10. Merleau-Ponty, *Phenomenology*, xvii–xviii, 84, 137, 451.

11. Ibid., 130.

12. Ibid., *Visible*, 237.

13. See Francoise Dastur, "World, Flesh, Vision," in *Chiasms: Merleau-Ponty's Notion of Flesh*, ed. Fred Evans and Leonard Lawlor (Albany: State University of New York Press, 2000), 38.

14. Merleau-Ponty, *Visible*, 253.

15. This is especially evident in the *fundierung* model.

16. Merleau-Ponty, *Phenomenology*, 347.

17. Ibid., 353.

18. Ibid., 56.

19. Corporeal schema describes the experience of the body as "neither purely subject (in which case it would be invisible to him) nor purely object (in which case it could not serve his primitive intentions); it is rather the ground of a style of interacting with the environment." Dillon, *Merleau-Ponty's Ontology*, 122.

20. Dillon, *Merleau-Ponty's Ontology,* 124.

21. Ibid., 123.

22. Merleau-Ponty, *Phenomenology,* 100.

23. Ibid., 387.

24. Ibid., xviii.

25. Merleau-Ponty describes operative intentionality: "[T]he life of consciousness—cognitive life, the life of desire or perceptual life—is subtended by an 'intentional arc' which projects round about us our past, our future, our human setting, our physical, ideological and moral situation, or rather which results in our being situated in all these respects" (*Phenomenology* 136).

26. Merleau-Ponty eventually relies less and less upon the notion of intentionality, both act and operative. Intentionality evokes too much of an affinity with consciousness, and Merleau-Ponty aspires to understand the body in both its materiality and cognitive capacity. The notion of operative intentionality—Husserl's recognition of an influence functioning in the world—Merleau-Ponty continues to explore in other forms; for he appreciates the idea of a guiding influence that arises from the world.

27. Merleau-Ponty, *Phenomenology,* 142. He cites from Grünbaum, *Aphasie und Motorik* 397–98.

28. Merleau-Ponty, *Phenomenology,* 110.

29. Dillon, *Merleau-Ponty's Ontology,* 136–37.

30. Ibid., 147.

31. Merleau-Ponty, *Phenomenology,* 111. See also Dillon, *Merleau-Ponty's Ontology,* 136–37.

32. Lawrence Hass, "Sense and Alterity: Rereading Merleau-Ponty's Reversibility Thesis," in *Merleau-Ponty, Interiority and Exteriority, Psychic Life and the World,* ed. Dorothea Olkowski and James Morley (Albany: State University of New York Press, 1999), 94.

33. Merleau-Ponty, *Phenomenology,* 353.

34. Ibid., 350–51.

35. Ibid., 348.

36. Ibid., 137.

37. Merleau-Ponty, *Visible,* 99–100.

38. Ibid., 57.

39. Ibid., *Visible,* 77.

40. Merleau-Ponty, *Phenomenology,* 215.

41. I cannot help wondering what clothes she was wearing.

42. Edmund Husserl, *Experience and Judgment,* tr. James. S. Churchill and Karl Ameriks (Evanston, IL: Northwestern University Press, 1973), 36.

43. Sartre and de Beauvoir have also advanced similar analyses.

44. Alfred Schutz, *On Phenomenology and Social Relations* (Chicago: University of Chicago Press, 1970), 227.

45. Ibid., 226.

46. Ibid., 100.

47. Ibid., 92.

48. Ibid., 100.

49. Ibid., 115.

50. See Michael Omi and Howard Winant, *Racial Formation in the Unites States from the 1960s to the 1990s* (New York: Routledge, 1994).

51. Merleau-Ponty, *Phenomenology,* 50.

52. Linda Martín Alcoff, "Merleau-Ponty and Feminist Theory on Experience," in *Chiasms: Merleau-Ponty's Notion of Flesh,* ed. Fred Evans and Leonard Lawlor (Albany: State University of New York Press, 2000), 252.

53. Linda Martín Alcoff, "Toward a Phenomenology of Racial Embodiment," *Journal of Radical Philosophy* 95 (May/June 1999): 18.

54. Gail Weiss, *Body Images: Embodiment as Intercorporeality,* (New York: Routledge, 1999), 27–28.

55. Alcoff, "Toward," 18.

56. Williams, *The Alchemy of Race and Rights,* 73.

57. Ibid., 62. See Annette Kuhn, "The Body and Cinema: Some Problems for Feminism," *Writing on the Body: Female Embodiment and Feminist Theory,* ed. Katie Conboy, Nadia Medina, and Sarah Stanbury (New York: Columbia University Press, 1997).

58. Williams, *The Alchemy of Race and Rights,* 118. She continues, "What the middle-class, propertied, upwardly mobile black striver must do, to accommodate a race-neutral world view, is to become an invisible black, a phantom black, by avoiding the label 'black' " (119).

59. Williams, *The Alchemy of Race and Rights,* 38.

60. Merleau-Ponty only demonstrates awareness of the existence of racism and sexism in his article, "The Child's Relations with Others," *The Primacy of Perception,* ed. James M. Edie, tr. William Cobb (Evanston, IL: Northwestern University Press, 1964).

61. Williams, *The Alchemy of Race and Rights,* 63.

62. Ibid., 44.

63. Ibid., 46.

64. For further explorations of a lived sense of race, see E. S. Lee, "Towards a Lived Understanding of Race and Sex," *Philosophy Today* (SPEP Supplement 2005): 82–88.

65. Williams, *The Alchemy of Race and Rights,* 48.

66. Ibid.

67. Ibid., 4. See also pages 78, 98, 119–20, 143, 182, 183, 184, 204, 207–08, 221, 228–29. (Thank you Aram Hernandez for researching all these references.)

68. Merleau-Ponty, *Phenomenology,* 358.

69. Ibid., 61.

70. Ibid., 130.

71. Husserl, *Experience and Judgment,* 37.

72. Merleau-Ponty, *Phenomenology,* 354.

11

Black American Sexuality and the Repressive Hypothesis

Reading Patricia Hill Collins with Michel Foucault

Camisha Russell

> Like all Americans, black Americans live in a sexually repressive culture. And we have made all manner of compromise regarding our sexuality in order to live here. We have expended much energy trying to debunk the racist mythology which says our sexuality is depraved. Unfortunately, many of us have overcompensated and assimilated the Puritan value that sex is for procreation, occurs only between men and women, and is only valid within the confines of heterosexual marriage. And, of course, like everyone else in America who is ambivalent in these respects, black folk have to live with the contradictions of this limited sexual system by repressing or closeting any other sexual/erotic urges, feelings, or desires.
>
> —Cheryl Clarke, "The Failure to Transform: Homophobia in the Black Community"

In the first chapter of *Black Sexual Politics*, Patricia Hill Collins briefly entertains the question of whether or not America is a "sexually repressive society."[1] She takes up the argument in response to the above statement from Cheryl Clarke's 1983 discussion of homophobia in the black community. The purpose of Clarke's discussion is to urge black Americans who are involved in struggles against white hegemony to avoid inadvertently adopting certain damaging attitudes toward sexuality (like homophobia) that are, in fact, part of the very white hegemonic culture they wish to fight. For Collins, however, the question becomes: "How can American culture be 'sexually repressive' when sexuality seems to be everywhere?"[2] After reviewing several examples of the hypervisibility of black sexuality in American popular culture, Collins seeks to refine our understanding of "repressive" as it applies to America and to black Americans, concluding that "Cheryl Clarke's observation that African Americans live in a sexually repressive culture speaks less to the prominence of representations of Black sexuality within an increasingly powerful mass media than to the *function* of these images in helping to construct a 'limited sexual system.' "[3]

Yet in *The History of Sexuality, Vol. I* (published seven years before Clarke's piece), Michel Foucault went to great lengths to argue *against* an understanding of the recent history of his European society as sexually repressive. In that work, he characterizes the "repressive hypothesis" as follows: "Nothing that was not ordered in terms of generation and transfigured by it could expect sanction or protection. Nor did it merit a hearing. It would be driven out, denied, and reduced to silence. Not only did it not exist, it had no right to exist and would be made to disappear upon its least manifestation—whether in acts or in words."[4] In other words, the "repressive hypothesis" is the belief that social forces attempt to silence or prohibit all expressions of sexuality outside the marital, reproductive context. Thus Clarke's argument that Puritan values prevail in American sexual culture, and that those values proscribe the free expression of sexual desires, clearly serves as one example of this hypothesis.

When Foucault notes how much we, in fact, speak about sex, however, he sees the need for much more than a simple reassessment of what we might actually mean by "repression." Performing a genealogy of sexuality and discourse on sex, Foucault seeks to address three serious doubts about the "repressive hypothesis":

> [1] Is sexual repression truly an established historical fact? . . . [2] Do the workings of power, and in particular those mechanisms that are brought into play in societies such as ours, really belong primarily to the category of repression? Are prohibition, censorship, and denial truly the forms through which power is exercised in a general way, if not in every society, most certainly in our own? . . . [3] Did the critical discourse that addresses itself to repression come to act as a roadblock to a power mechanism that had operated unchallenged up to that point, or is it not in fact part of the same historical network as the thing it denounces (and doubtless misrepresents) by calling it "repression"?[5]

Ultimately, Foucault argues that an understanding of society and its history as sexually repressive serves to mask the productive nature of contemporary power and the true mechanisms of its operation within contemporary society. Furthermore, he feels the model of repression casts ostensible efforts to increase the visibility of sexuality in society as rebellious and progressive forms of resistance when, on his account, they are actually necessary components of the hegemonic power system.

Indeed, though Collins does not make explicit reference to Foucault's views on the relationship between sexuality and productive power, much of her analysis in *Black Sexual Politics* points to a more complicated understanding of the role of black sexual visibility in maintaining racial hierarchies than the simple idea of repression implies. It is well beyond the scope of this chapter to attempt a Foucauldian genealogy of black sexuality in America. Though much of the work that Collins presents could contribute to such a project, I am more concerned here with pointing to the possibility of a genealogical approach than with carrying one out. Thus, in the first part of this chapter, I will look at the examples Foucault uses to build his argument against the repressive hypothesis and compare those examples to certain similar examples found in Collins' description of the structure of what she calls the "new racism."[6] In the second part of the chapter, I will discuss why Foucault believes the repressive hypothesis needs to be abandoned and ask how a similar renunciation of Clarke's repressive hypothesis might strengthen Collins' analysis of the "new racism." Finally, in the third part of the paper, I will discuss possible reasons for Collins' resistance to or rejection of a Foucauldian analysis, including the relative absence of discussions of race in *The History of Sexuality* and Collins' wish to argue for a new sort of erotic power that would offer an alternative to hegemonic power structures. Ultimately, however, I conclude that Collins' analyses have *already* implicitly exceeded the limits of the repressive model and that, while she may choose not to adopt a wholesale Foucauldian perspective, an explicit turn to a more Foucauldian, productive model of power would nevertheless offer her present arguments linking black sexuality to the "new racism" greater explanatory force.

Manifold Mechanisms

"Sex was driven out of hiding and constrained to lead a discursive existence. From the singular imperialism that compels everyone to transform their sexuality into a perpetual discourse, to the manifold mechanisms which, in the area of economy, pedagogy, medicine, and justice, incite, extract, distribute, and institutionalize the sexual discourse, an immense verbosity is what our civilization has required and organized."[7] Foucault begins his attack on the repressive hypothesis by bringing to light and characterizing some key examples of the "manifold mechanisms" that produce and maintain sexual discourse in society, giving it power. I will begin here by pointing to some similarities between those mechanisms and the operations of the "new racism" discussed by Collins. In particular, I will consider the role of confession in sexuality, the emergence of the "population" as a "problem," and Foucault's *figures* in relation to Collins' *controlling images*.

Confession

For Foucault, one of the primary ways that sex is "put into discourse" is through the mechanism of confession, which he describes as "one of the main rituals we rely on for the production of truth."[8] According to Foucault, it is widely believed that through confession we uncover and reveal the truth of ourselves. Thus one is compelled to tell all. Foucault states that "one confesses one's crimes, one's sins, one's thoughts and desires, one's illnesses and troubles; one goes about telling, with the greatest precision, whatever is most difficult to tell."[9] It is important that in doing so, one does not feel oneself controlled but rather liberated. Yet one does not confess to oneself. Rather, it is "a ritual that unfolds within a power relationship, for one does not confess without the presence (or virtual presence) of a partner who is not simply the interlocutor but the authority who requires the confession, prescribes and appreciates it, and intervenes in order to judge, punish, forgive, console and reconcile."[10] When these confessions focus themselves around sex and sexuality, says Foucault, "two processes emerge, one always conditioning the other: we demand that sex speak the truth (but, since it is the secret and is oblivious to its own nature, we reserve for ourselves the function of telling the truth of its truth, revealed and deciphered at last), and we demand that it tells us our truth, or rather, the deeply buried truth of that truth about ourselves which we think we possess in our immediate consciousness."[11] Thus confession is a means of making sex speak the hidden truth of ourselves, but this truth is always conditioned by the person who hears, interprets, and judges the confession. Yet the practice of confession is not sustained merely by some sort of institutional imperative or intellectual desire to pursue the truth for truth's sake. Rather, there is a specific source of pleasure that has been created through the ritual of confession, not only in hearing a confession, but in giving it, in making oneself and one's sexuality the subject of attention: "pleasure in the truth of pleasure, the pleasure of knowing the truth, of discovering and exposing it, the fascination of seeing it and telling it, of captivating and capturing others by it, of confiding it in secret, of luring it out in the open—the specific pleasure of the true discourse on pleasure."[12]

Let us then consider in this context Collins' discussion of contemporary television talk shows, which she sees as one example of the hypervisibility of black sexuality that might make one doubt the sexually repressive nature of American society. Collins characterizes such shows as providing "one important public medium for gaining sexual information" but as at the same time fostering "the commodification of sexuality" by "[s]tressing sexually explicit conversations that titillate rather than instruct."[13] She then criticizes the shows for the highly racialized scripts of their morality plays and their reinforcement of "longstanding societal beliefs about Black sexuality."[14] Paternity testing is a major theme on certain talk shows, portraying black and/or lower class women as too sexually promiscuous to be certain of their children's "baby daddies" and black and/or lower class men as too sexually and morally irresponsible to voluntarily claim paternity.

The talk show example is a well-placed insight but could be further developed in light of Foucault's observations about confession. For example, we can explore the role of the talk show in the field of black sexuality by considering its confessional nature—the fact that the people appearing on the shows appear voluntarily (though certainly not without compensation) to speak the "truth" of their lives? All the elements of confession discussed above seem present in the talk shows Collins describes. There is a known ritual in which all parties—host, guest, and audience—knowingly participate; there is a specific form of pleasure experienced on the part of each of these parties—the guests in particular gaining (along with their monetary compensation) their "five minutes of fame"; there is "truth" sought and revealed with the consent of, yet almost in spite of, the guests—not only in the form of the paternity test results, but in the affirmation of the degeneracy of black sexuality; and there is an authority who hears, interprets, and judges the confessions made. On this last point, Collins is instructive:

> Despite similarities that link all three shows, they do offer different scripts for solving the problems of these sexual spectacles. Part of the appeal of *The Montel Williams Show* lies in his role in this family drama—Williams plays the part of the caring yet stern Black patriarch who provides the fatherly discipline that so many of his guests seemingly lack. In contrast, Mr. Povich presents himself as a kindly White father, showing concern for his emotional albeit abnormal guests. Mr. Springer is merely a ringmaster—he doesn't get near his guests, preferring instead to watch the cursing and chair throwing from a safe distance. Discipline them, listen to them, or dismiss them—all three solutions apply to working-class and poor guests.[15]

Thus, each particular interpretation gives structure to the confessions and shapes the "truth" that is "revealed" about those making the confessions.

Population

A second conceptual mechanism Foucault identifies in the discourse on sexuality consists in a shift affected in the target of government intervention. "Governments perceived that they were not dealing simply with subjects, or even with a 'people,' but with a 'population,' with its specific phenomena and its peculiar variables," he writes, and this "emergence of 'population' as an economic and political problem" centered around matters of sex, thus, "it was necessary to analyze the birthrate, the age of marriage, the legitimate and illegitimate births, the precocity and frequency of sexual relations, the ways of making them fertile or sterile, the effects of unmarried life or of the prohibitions, the impact of contraceptive practices."[16] In other words, the identification of a new type of target for intervention conceived of primarily in statistical terms both made possible and justified new forms of intervention on the part not only of governments, but of doctors, educators, and other social institutions.

Returning to Collins and the American context, we might look for signs of an emerging problematizing of blacks, not merely as a group of people thought to share a set of (primarily negative) characteristics, but *as a statistically conceived and analyzed population* in the Foucauldian sense. One sign of this problematizing can be seen in the Moynihan report, which lies at the roots of what Collins calls "black gender ideology." According to Collins, "scientific discourse, mass media, and public policy all depict African Americans as either less able and/or willing to achieve dominant gender ideology. Instead, the images of Black masculinity and Black femininity in contemporary mass media suggest that a reversed and therefore deviant gender ideology hinders African American advancement. The message is simple—African American communities are populated by men who are 'too weak' and by women who are 'too strong.' "[17] In an important footnote, Collins briefly traces the history of this problematic of black gender norms, identifying it in the work of both W. E. B. Du Bois and E. Franklin Frazier, who considered deficient gender ideology among African Americans a factor in, but not the primary cause of, African American poverty and political powerlessness. Crucially, however, the problematic "was transformed yet again and moved into public policy forums in 1965 with the publication of the Moynihan report, *The Negro Family: The Case for National Action*." This, Collins asserts, "marked the beginnings of the modern debate on Black gender ideology."[18]

The Moynihan report identified the so-called "roots" of the "problem" in the Negro population as slavery, the Reconstruction, urbanization, unemployment, poverty, and the wage system; as its official title—*The Negro Family: The Case for National Action*—indicates, however, the "problem" *itself* was seen as manifest *within* "the Negro American family" and was to be demonstrated through statistics. As the section headings in the second chapter of the report declare: "Nearly a Quarter of Urban Negro Marriages Are Dissolved," "Nearly One-Quarter of Negro Births Are Now Illegitimate," "Almost One-Fourth of Negro Families Are Headed by Females," and "The Breakdown of the Negro Family Has Led to a Startling Increase in Welfare Dependency."[19] The chapter is full of tables, charts, and graphs cataloguing statistics regarding absentee husbands, illegitimacy ratios, "types" of family, family size, and "broken" homes in the Negro community, along with rates of unemployment. These are used to explain another set of tables, charts, and graphs concerning education attainment, school enrollment, IQ scores, juvenile delinquency, and drug use.[20] The Negro Family is portrayed as a "Tangle of Pathology"[21] with the tendency toward matriarchy as the lead concern.

The controversy that erupted surrounding the report notwithstanding, its appearance seems clearly to mark the emergence of the "Negro problem" as a problem of the Negro *population* in the Foucauldian sense—that is, understood in terms of collections of data and statistics about sexuality and the family, which are thought to call for particular forms of government intervention. The black gender ideology that holds that "Black men's and women's failure to achieve normal complementary gender roles adequately explains joblessness, poor school performance, poverty, poor housing, and other social problems"[22] justifies not only the placing of blame at the level of black families and communities but also state interventions at that same level.[23] "Problems" of black sexuality come to be viewed and treated as problems of the black population.

Figures and Images

Foucault sees a third mechanism organizing sexuality in the emergence of certain figures that correspond to certain strategies in the organization of sex. These figures—the hysterical woman, the masturbating child, the Malthusian couple, and the perverse adult on Foucault's account—served as "privileged objects of knowledge, which were also targets and anchorage points for the ventures of knowledge."[24] Foucault argues that rather than seeing the construction of such figures as part of a struggle against sexuality or even as part of an effort to gain control of or regulate it, "in actual fact, what was involved, rather, was the very production of sexuality. Sexuality must not be thought of as a kind of natural given which power tries to hold in check, or as an obscure domain which knowledge tries gradually to uncover. It is the name that can be given to a historical construct."[25] The appearance of these figures, then, suggests that power is not exclusively or primarily restrictive, repressive, or limiting but rather creative, constructive, and productive. This new form of control operates through the creation and proliferation of medically or socially pathological types. When individuals are classified according to these types, though they are certainly subject to control, their sexuality is not limited in the sense of some preexisting reality that is then repressed. The truth of sexuality is not *revealed* or *observed* in these figures but actually *made*.

For her part, Collins is very interested in the role of what she calls the "controlling images" of black sexuality. She argues that an assortment of gender- and class-specific, sexually inflected images of black people disseminated and perpetuated by the American mass media serve both to offer plausible explanations for the racial and socioeconomic status quo and to act as its justification. The images must be class specific both because black people now occupy multiple economic classes in the United States and in order to work within the color-blind ideology promoted after desegregation. Their gender-specificity works with and reinforces the notion that black people hold deviant gender roles, as described above, while the sexual inflection lends a biological necessity to the images while playing upon long-held white fear of black sexuality. Thus, for example, portraying working-class black women as "bitches" or "bad black mothers" justifies "the new social relations of hyper-ghettoization, unfinished racial desegregation, and efforts to shrink the social welfare state;"[26] while "representations of Black ladies, modern mammies, and educated Black bitches help justify the continued workplace discrimination targeted toward many middle-class African American women."[27] For working-class black men, there are images such as the bad boy athlete, the hustler, and the pimp that link their problems to excess physicality, inherent promiscuity, and a predatory nature and that imply that, for the safety of society, poor black men must be controlled and contained. By contrast, middle-class black men are portrayed as sissies or sidekicks and seem to be required to give up all pretense of their own (sexual) power in order to achieve professional and economic success, as seen in the depiction of the character of Heathcliff Huxtable on *The Cosby Show*.[28]

It is in this discussion of controlling images that Collins' own analysis comes closest to Foucault's. To reiterate, Foucault argues that the figures that appear in the discourse on sexuality and claim to represent *discovered* truths about sexuality are better understood as *manufactured* "truths" about sexuality that serve to create sexuality itself. Similarly, Collins does not believe that the mass media images described above simply report on black life and sexuality in America nor that they are mere effects of racism. Rather, she specifically argues that such images "help justify and *shape* the new racism of desegregated, color-blind America."[29] The productive nature of the images and their relationship to the racist exercise of power is clearly evoked, here, though we will ask later how far Collins actually takes this analysis.

Biopower and the "New Racism"

In *Black Sexual Politics*, Collins is concerned with what she calls the "new racism," which she sees as emerging from an increasingly global economy, a decrease in the power of local, regional, and national governments in favor of transnational systems, and the proliferation of mass media. According to Collins, the new racism "reflects the juxtaposition of old and new, in some cases a continuation of long-standing practices of racial rule and, in other cases, the development of something original."[30] She traces the specific and specifically gendered practices of racial oppression from chattel slavery to labor exploitation in rural Southern agriculture to urban industrialization and the ghettoization of black populations, arguing that these three racial formations "may have peaked during specific periods of African American history, but now they overlap, draw strength from one another, and continue to contribute to the new racism."[31] Furthermore, in contrast to overt forms of racial domination like chattel slavery or Jim Crow laws, Collins notes, "one important dimension of the new racism is to cover over the harm done to victims and mute their protest."[32] Thus, under the new racism, oppression operates differently (as Collins explains using terminology that seems to come to her from Foucault via the work of Ann Laura Stoler): "Contemporary forms of oppression do not routinely force people to submit. Instead they manufacture consent for domination so that we lose our ability to question and thus collude in our own subordination. . . . Within the United States oppression now takes a new form, one where society itself is saturated with the relations of warfare against selected members of society itself."[33] This new operation of oppression under the new racism puts forward a public face of color blindness and meritocracy, while using the controlling images discussed above to explain how blacks (through their own inadequacies) have failed to achieve social and economic equality.

Already in the examples from the first part of this chapter we saw some of the mechanisms of this new racism (operating through discourses on black sexuality), which I compared to mechanisms Foucault cites in building his case against the "repressive hypothesis." These examples and comparisons suggest that the power exerted around contemporary sexuality (whether European or black American) may not be fully or even best described under our ordinary understanding of repression. What remains to be seen, however, is whether or not simply complicating and refining our understanding of repression as Collins does in response to Clarke provides a sufficient response to this issue. To understand why Foucault rejects such an approach, we need to look further into the notion of power that he attributes to the "repressive hypothesis" and the alternative notion for which he argues.

For Foucault, the "thematics of repression" (as well as the opposing psychoanalytic theory that the law is *constitutive* of desire) rely fundamentally on a conception of power he calls the "juridico-discursive."[34] He identifies five principle features of this power:

> *The negative relation.* It never establishes any connection between power and sex that is not negative: rejection, exclusion, refusal, blockage, concealment, or mask. . . . Its effects take the general form of limit and lack.

> *The insistence of the rule.* Power is essentially what dictates the law to sex. . . .
>
> *The cycle of prohibition:* thou shalt not go near, thou shalt not touch, though shalt not consume, though shalt not experience pleasure, thou shalt not speak, thou shalt not show thyself; ultimately though shalt not exist, except in darkness and secrecy. To deal with sex, power employs nothing more than the law of prohibition. . . .
>
> *The logic of censorship.* This interdiction is thought to take three forms: affirming that such a thing is not permitted, preventing it from being said, denying that it exists. . . . The logic of power exerted on sex is the paradoxical logic of a law that might be expressed as an injunction of nonexistence, nonmanifestation, and silence.
>
> *The uniformity of the apparatus.* Power over sex is exercised in the same way at all levels. . . . It operates according to the simple and endlessly reproduced mechanisms of law, taboo, and censorship: from state to family, from prince to father, from the tribunal to the small change of everyday punishments, from the agencies of social domination to the structures that constitute the subject himself, one finds a general form of power varying in scale alone.[35]

What this analysis of the features of juridco-discursive power reveals is that although we act toward this power as if it is pervasive and experience ourselves as involved in important forms of difficult resistance, the figure of power we imagine as our enemy is, in fact, a straw man. Our impoverished picture is one of a power that is "poor in resources, sparing of its methods, monotonous in the tactics it utilizes, incapable of invention, and seemingly doomed always to repeat itself," a power for which "all the modes of domination, submission, and subjugation are ultimately reduced to an effect of obedience."[36]

Through this picture, the truth of power—the strength and multiplicity of its resources—is hidden and this, according to Foucault, is a tactical necessity not only for power itself but for those on whom it operates. He argues that "power is tolerable only on condition that it mask a substantial part of itself. Its success is proportional to its ability to hide its own mechanisms. . . . Not only because power imposes secrecy on those whom it dominates, but because it is perhaps just as indispensable to the latter: would they accept it if they did not see it as a mere limit placed on their desire, leaving a measure of freedom—however slight—intact?"[37] Thus we who see ourselves as *under* power in our conception of the power system are invested in that conception precisely because it allows us to see ourselves as essentially free or at least struggling toward freedom. It even offers us specific methods for engaging in that struggle.

According to Foucault, "What sustains our eagerness to speak of sex in terms of repression is doubtless this opportunity to speak out against the powers that be, to utter truths and promise bliss, to link together enlightenment, liberation, and manifold pleasures; to pronounce a discourse that combines the fervor of knowledge, the determination to change the laws, and the longing for the garden of earthly delights."[38] A more complicated understanding of the nature of power would require a more complicated understanding of resistance, and this fact acts in favor of power, making the complicated understanding unappealing.

Foucault does not argue that juridico-discursive power was never in operation. It is, rather, an old form of power best understood in terms of the sovereign or monarch who was said to have the "power of life and death," which amounted to the "right to *take* life or *let* live."[39] What Foucault sees, however, is a shift in the operation of power beginning in the eighteenth century, after which, while many forms of juridico-discursive power persisted, they were gradually penetrated by new mechanisms that could not be reduced to the negative, repressive model. The operation of these new methods "is not ensured by right but by technique, not by law but by normalization, not by punishment but by control," and such methods "are employed on all levels and in forms that go beyond the state and its apparatus."[40] This new power can be conceived of in terms of "a power to *foster* life or *disallow* it to the point of death"[41] and is observed concretely in modern times in two basic forms: (1) an *anatomo-politics of the human body* in which bodies are disciplined, optimized, made both useful and docile, and integrated into systems of control; and (2) a *biopolitics of the population* in which the biological functions of bodies are subject to intervention and regulation in terms of birthrate, mortality, level of health, life expectancy, and longevity.[42] It is this shift from juridico-discursive power to "biopower" that I would argue we read in Collins' arguments regarding the "new racism," even though Collins herself does not theorize the shift in terms of productive power and thus, in sticking with a model of repression and limitation, does not fully explain.

Foucault tells us that his picture of power is not that of "a group of institutions and mechanisms that ensure the subservience of the citizens of a given state" nor that of "a mode of subjugation which, in contrast to violence, has the form of the rule" (think of the brute force that characterized chattel slavery in contrast with the legalized segregation of the Jim Crow South). Nor is the picture of power that of "a general system of domination exerted by one group over another, a system whose effects, through successive derivations, pervade the entire social body" (think of models of socially, politically and economically institutionalized racism).[43] Instead, Foucault argues:

> Power must be understood in the first instance as the multiplicity of force relations immanent in the sphere in which they operate

> and which constitute their own organization; as the process which, through ceaseless struggles and confrontations, transforms, strengthens, or reverses them; as the support which these force relations find in one another, thus forming a chain or system, or on the contrary, the disjunctions and contradictions which isolate them from one another; and lastly, as the strategies in which they take effect, whose general design or institutional crystallization is embodied in the state apparatus, in the formulation of the law, in the various social hegemonies.[44]

In other words, what *appear* publicly to be the most obvious and, thus, most fundamental forms of power—the state, the law, and social hegemonies—are actually terminal forms produced and sustained by more complex and dispersed forms of power that are multiple and hidden from view. Discourses of sexuality serve as loci of these operations of power; power is immanent in sexuality and sexual relations; and this power plays a directly productive role. It is not the case that power over sexuality is simply exerted from the top and resisted at the grass roots. Power is produced in various relations at the bottom, and resistances occur within and are a part of the manifestation of that power that emerges at the top (and is then mistaken for power itself).

Placed in this context, Foucault goes on to offer four hypotheses about the deployment of sexuality: "[1] sexuality is tied to recent devices of power; [2] it has been expanding at an increasing rate since the seventeenth century; [3] the arrangement that has sustained it is not governed by reproduction; [4] it has been linked from the outset with an intensification of the body—with its exploitation as an object of knowledge and an element in relations of power."[45] We thus see how, on Foucault's account, discourses of sexuality serve to create, reinforce, and disguise the multiple operations of a new form of power. We can compare this insight to the three interrelated meanings Collins gives to sexuality in the introduction of her book:

> [1] Sexuality can be viewed as an entity that is manipulated within each distinctive system of race, class, and gender oppression, for example, the importance of rape to patriarchy, child prostitution to contemporary global sex work, or lynching to racial subordination. [2] Sexuality also can be seen as a site of intersectionality, a specific constellation of social practices that demonstrate how oppressions converge. For example, not only did the institutionalized rape of enslaved Black women support racial domination, it potentially produced children who would profit slave-owners, and it reinforced a gender regime. [3] Sexuality also can be analyzed as heterosexism,

> a freestanding system of oppression similar to racism, sexism, and class oppression, which shares similar goals and social practices.[46]

What we see when we compare these two descriptions—and indeed when we compare the two schemata as wholes—is that both Foucault and Collins recognize the importance of sexuality to the operation of power and the complexity of that operation. Countless fruitful similarities can be drawn between the two analyses. At the same time, in Collins' repetition of "oppression" above we see echoes of "repression" (or "sexually repressive society") that she has not renounced. These terms necessarily imply something real, true, genuine, or free in sexuality that is being denied, limited, or proscribed. Thus, in spite of the work Collins does to show us how power manufactures both consent and ostensible resistance—for example, by describing how singers like Jennifer Lopez and Destiny's Child draw on stereotypes about black sexuality for their success—she falls short of explaining why such stars should not use *their* sexuality as *they* see fit. Though she clearly recognizes it to be the case, her theoretical framework cannot fully explain how the very notion of sexuality with which people operate—that sexuality that they see and experience as *their own*—is a production of power. She tells us that our sexuality and pleasures are *limited* or *shaped* but stops short of telling us clearly that they are *produced.* To say that black sexuality is proscribed is to posit its preexistence or underlying truth prior to or outside of discourse.

Racism and Resistance

Thus it appears that Collins' analysis of the "new racism" would be enhanced by the abandonment of the "repressive hypothesis." The explicit adoption of an expanded notion of power and its operations in the discourse of sexuality as *productive* would both emphasize and support Collins' focus on the historically constructed and shifting nature of black sexuality, particularly as given to or forced upon black Americans by racist social structures. At this point, however, I would like to put forward and discuss two reasons for which the Foucauldian approach, as represented by *The History of Sexuality, Vol. I*, may not appear to be an appropriate resource for Collins' project. The first concerns Foucault's conception of racism and the second his thoughts on resistance.[47]

The role of race and racism in *The History of Sexuality* is difficult to pin down. In *Race and the Education of Desire*, Ann Stoler argues that: "In short, racism is not the *subject* of *The History of Sexuality.* Instead, it analyzes how a discourse of sexuality articulates and eventually incorporates a racist logic. This is the book's end-product. Racisms are not what Foucault analyzed; he looked rather to the ways in which a prior technology of sexuality provided a cultural susceptibility and discursive field for them."[48] In other words, race is more of a subtext of the work than an explicit theme of the text itself. Furthermore, according to Stoler, in the context of his larger project "the principle form of state racism which concerned Foucault was that of the Nazi state and its 'Final Solution,' " and thus "the focus is on the internal dynamics of European states and their disciplinary biopolitical strategies."[49] What then are we to make of racism and racialized sexual discourses like those in the United States, which are not, arguably, part of an explicitly genocidal project?

As we explore this question in terms of Foucault's notions of sexuality and power, one reservation that might emerge concerns the sense that, once the mechanisms of power have been dispersed and are seen as operating from the bottom up rather than the top down, we lose something essential in the idea of racism: the conviction that it operates against specific groups of people while producing benefits for other groups of people. If power is everywhere, and everyone's sexuality is being produced and controlled, how do we explain how certain groups seem to wield a lot of power while others seem to be perpetually disempowered? This question may appear particularly troubling in light of Foucault's argument that "[i]f one writes the history of sexuality in terms of repression, relating this repression to the utilization of labor capacity, one must suppose that sexual controls were the more intense and meticulous as they were directed at the poorer classes," whereas, on his reading, "the most rigorous techniques were formed and, more particularly, applied first, with the greatest intensity, in the economically privileged and politically dominant classes."[50] On Foucault's account, then, the primary concern in the development of technologies of sex "was not repression of the sex of the classes to be exploited, but rather the body, vigor, longevity, progenitor, and descent of the classes that 'ruled.' "[51] Such technologies were only secondarily subsequently employed as "an indispensable instrument of political control and economic regulation for the subjugation of the urban proletariat."[52]

Of course, Foucault is speaking here of class rather than race. Nevertheless, if we attempt to apply this analysis to Collins' project, racist portrayals of black sexuality risk appearing as a sort of "happy" accident whereby the powerful in the United States stumbled upon a way to control blacks using the same techniques with which they had been controlling themselves. Indeed, there appears to be a similarity between the form of this argument and Clarke's (cited at the beginning of this chapter), according to which black people must resist pursuing a sexual politics tied up with systems of domination and avoid being swept up in the negative repressive sexual system practiced by white people on themselves. On a certain reading of these arguments, racism in sexual politics may appear almost inadvertent.

Stoler, however, looking to read colonial discourses with *The History of Sexuality*, suggests another way to interpret Foucault's insistence that technologies of sex were first used by the bourgeois on themselves then applied to the context of racialized sexual discourses. Stoler suggests that the production of abnormal sexualities of racialized others was crucial to the task of producing, defining, and delimiting bourgeois sexuality itself. In other words, the bourgeois do not create their own sexuality and then demonstrate that racialized others do not measure up. Rather the discourse of bourgeois sexuality develops itself in conjunction with and in relation to racialized discourses of abnormal sexuality.[53] Though not a theme that Foucault addresses, such a theory seems very much in line with his productive conception of power. If we argue that the same mechanism is in operation in the United States and that black (deviant) sexuality operates as a constitutive other for white middle-class (normal) sexuality, we get at least three important results. First, we see that the productive notion of power still has greater explanatory weight than the merely repressive notion. Second, we see that discourses on black sexuality will be necessarily different than (though intimately connected with) discourses on white, middle-class sexuality and that the former will have specific disempowering effects while the latter will confer some benefits.[54] Finally, we see that the conformity to hegemonic sexual politics that Clarke urges blacks not to pursue will not truly be an option for all black people, in any case, since the continued perception of their "deviance" will be required for the constant reinscription of the norm.

A second possible concern about adopting a Foucauldian approach centers on the question of resistance. For Foucault, the supposed possibility of a clear and easy form of resistance to power is one of the primary reasons that we prefer to conceive of power in a limited, strictly repressive way. After all, if sexuality is simply repressed, one engages in resistance merely by speaking of or exercising it. Foucault does not, however, deny the possibility of resistance to his richer form of power. In fact, on his account, resistance is *necessary* to power. "Where there is power, there is resistance," he writes, "and yet, or rather consequently, this resistance is never in a position of exteriority in relation to power." Thus, a multiplicity of points of resistance are present throughout the power network, and they "play the role of adversary, target, support, or handle in power relations."[55] Their relationship to power is not one of simple opposition. Given that Collins is specifically concerned with formulating viable approaches for resistance to the forms of black sexual politics she opposes, Foucault's view may appear fatalistic, as if all attempts at resistance are futile and only serve the purposes of power.

Yet Foucault himself resists such an interpretation of his view. He insists that to say that "one is always 'inside' power, there is no 'escaping' it, there is no absolute outside where it is concerned, because one is subject to the law in any case" would be to "misunderstand the strictly relational character of power relationships."[56] To say that, by definition, resistances "can only exist in the strategic field of power relationships," argues Foucault, "does not mean that they are only a reaction or rebound, forming with respect to the basic domination an underside that is in the end always passive, doomed to perpetual defeat."[57] For Foucault, it is subscribing to the juridico-discursive notion of power and its effects on desire that carries *both* the risk of a facile conception of resistance ("if power is seen as having only an external hold on desire") *and* the contradictory risk of seeing no place whatsoever for resistance ("if [power] is constitutive of desire itself").[58] Thus the response called for would seem to be not the wholesale rejection of resistance but rather the careful consideration of various forms of resistance and their relationships to the structures and productions of power.[59]

Collins, I would argue, is already responding in this way. Early in *Black Sexual Politics* she offers a critical discussion of "the distinctive sexualized spectacles" performed by Sarah Bartmann (the "Hottentot Venus"), Josephine Baker, Destiny's Child, and Jennifer Lopez, arguing that such spectacles "invoke sexual meanings that give shape to racism, sexism, class exploitation, and heterosexism," while also providing certain benefits to the women who perform them, thus marking "the contradictions of Western perceptions of African bodies and of Black women's agency concerning the use of their bodies."[60] Collins does not deny the importance of the "agency" demonstrated by these women, but she does recognize that such "resistance" to racist/sexist disempowerment must be seen in light of the way it also serves to reinforce the mechanisms of that very disempowerment.[61] Similarly, Collins argues that rebellion should not be construed as a simple matter of breaking the rules as opposed to following them. "Rebellion can occur among people who seemingly follow the rules," she writes. "For heterosexual African American men, *choosing to love and commit to a heterosexual relationship with a Black woman is a rebellious act.*"[62] This is so not because such men are pursuing a politics of respectability but because in loving and committing to black women they are resisting depictions of themselves as hustlers, bad boys, and criminals, while at the same timing embracing women that society has demonized. By contrast, marrying interracially definitely *breaks* a rule, but, as Collins points out "such relationships may not be inherently progressive."[63] "Whether they appear to be following the rules or breaking them, Black love relationships of all types can uphold hierarchies of race, class, gender, and sexuality. Because hierarchy becomes intertwined with love and sexual expression, this is when oppression is more effective. But rebelling not simply against the rules *but against what the rules are designed to do* creates space for a very different set of individual relationships, and a more progressive Black sexual politics."[64] Here, then, Collins has explicitly recognized that resistance is not a simple question but one that can only be grappled with by understanding the wider context of the power within which it is situated and the relational nature of the two forces.

Furthermore, as we also saw in the above example concerning black women's sexualized performances, Collins does not favor resistances that attempt uncritically to take "control" of sexualities in the very form in which power produced them. Rather, she urges black men and women to "rescue and redefine sexuality as a source of power rooted in spirituality, expressiveness, and love" in order to "craft new understandings of Black masculinity and Black femininity needed for a progressive Black sexual politics."[65] She takes inspiration here from Audre Lorde's essay "Uses of the Erotic: The Erotic as Power," in which the erotic is defined as "the deep feelings within each of us in search of love, affirmation, recognition, and a spiritual and/or physical connection to one another," and must thus be reclaimed as "a domain of exploration, pleasure, and human agency" in order to foster individual empowerment.[66]The erotic on this definition stands in contrast to the sexuality described above, which, through mechanisms such as confession, interventions on the level of "population," and controlling images/figures, is both produced by and essential to the operation of power.[67] To say that what Collins and Lorde want to claim as the erotic must be understood as a concept very different from what Foucault understands as sexuality is not to claim (as Foucault would no doubt be quick to reject) that the former, as resistance, does not still exist within rather than outside of a network of power relations. Naturally, as an oppositional concept, our understanding of the erotic will necessarily, at least in part, be defined in contradistinction to more commonly held understandings of sexuality. Nevertheless, I would argue that the attempt to adopt and maintain Lorde's notion of the erotic as an alternative to current scripts for black sexuality would constitute an example of the more complicated form of resistance for which Foucault seems to call and, thus, that Collins' understanding of resistance is far from a naïve one. Nor, I contend, is it an understanding of resistance that relies on a limited view of power as strictly or primarily repressive, in spite of Collins' early invoking of the "repressive hypothesis."

These questions regarding Foucault's views on racism and resistance in *The History of Sexuality* are neither simple nor insignificant; any attempt to incorporate a Foucauldian perspective into Collins' analyses (or vice versa) must take them seriously. I hope to have shown, however, that such questions do not pose an insurmountable obstacle to such incorporation. What can be called a Foucauldian "approach" is by no means incompatible with Collins' project in *Black Sexual Politics*. In fact, as I attempted to show in the first parts of this chapter, there is already a great deal of similarity between Collins' account of the development of the "new racism" and Foucault's genealogy of sexuality, and a more Foucauldian, productive model of power would seem to offer Collins' arguments for the role of black sexual politics in the "new racism" even greater explanatory force.

Ultimately, however, Collins chooses not to make that move. Not only does she choose not to explicitly reject the "repressive hypothesis," but she actually foregrounds it by making (a modified version of) Clarke's claim central to her opening chapter. By way of conclusion, then, I would like to return to Clarke's essay to interrogate the role of the "repressive hypothesis" in her analysis. Clarke's target is homophobia in the black community and her contention is that those in black liberation movements who spurn "the assimilationist goals of the politically conservative black bourgeoisie" have failed to question "the value of heterosexual and male superiority" and have thus crucially failed to transform themselves, continuing instead to uphold parts of the very hegemonic system they seek to destroy.[68] This call for a questioning of dominant notions of sexuality is, of course, very much in keeping with Collins' approach to resistance described above. Furthermore, an understanding of America as a sexually repressive society is particularly compelling in the context of discussions of heterosexism and homophobia. Thus Clarke asserts: "The expression of homophobic sentiments, the threatening political postures assumed by black radicals and progressives of the nationalist/communist ilk, and the seeming lack of any willingness [to] understand the politics of gay and lesbian liberation collude with the dominant white male culture to repress not only gay men and lesbians, but also to repress a natural part of all human beings, namely the bisexual potential in us all."[69] Thus, repression seems to speak to something important about the experience of gays and lesbians in American society, especially that of gays and lesbians of color. This language of the repressing of something "natural," however, once again underestimates power and denies its productive mechanisms, calling for the relatively straightforward solution of forcing black leaders to recognize this "natural" fact so that they will be logically compelled to alter their homophobic attitudes. A more complex analysis, however, would look at the coconstitutive relationships among heterosexuality, homosexuality, black sexual politics, and white middle-class sexuality and would ask how those various constructions serve the (racist) purposes of hegemonic power systems. This latter approach need not deny the lived experience of gays and lesbians of color as "repressed"[70] but offers an understanding of power networks essential to more complex and effective forms of resistance—as did Stoler's insight regarding the need for a racialized other in the construction of white European middle-class sexuality. While keeping in mind the good reasons members of certain groups have to feel their sexuality has been limited or repressed, I believe we can expand our notion of power in Collins' analyses beyond the model of repression and, in so doing, deepen our understanding of the relationship between sexuality and the "new racism." Indeed, it would seem that Collins herself has long since exceeded the limits of her own repressive model.

Notes

1. Patricia Hill Collins, *Black Sexual Politics* (New York: Routledge, 2005), 35.

2. Ibid., 36.

3. Cheryl Clarke, "The Failure to Transform: Homophobia in the Black Community," in *Home Girls: A Black Feminist Anthology*, ed. Barbara Smith (New York: Kitchen Table, 1983), 43; original emphasis.

4. Michel Foucault, *The History of Sexuality, Vol. I: An Introduction*, trans. Robert Hurley (New York: Vintage Books, 1990), 4; *Histoire de la sexualité 1: La volonté de savoir* (Paris: Éditions Gallimard, 1976), 10.While this chapter focuses on Foucault's "repressive hypothesis" as laid out in *The History of Sexuality*, the analysis begun here could also be productively extended by incorporating parts of Foucault's later lectures at the Collège de France, for example, his genealogy of race and racism in *Society Must Be Defended*, his work on population in *Security, Territory, Population*, and his taxonomies of pathological types in *Abnormal*.

5. Foucault, *History of Sexuality*, 10; *Histoire de la sexualité*, 18.

6. Collins, *Black Sexual Politics*, 54–55.

7. Foucault, *History of Sexuality*, 33; *Histoire de la sexualité*, 45–46.

8. Foucault, *History of Sexuality*, 58; *Histoire de la sexualité*, 78.

9. Foucault, *History of Sexuality*, 59; *Histoire de la sexualité*, 79.

10. Foucault, *History of Sexuality*, 61–62; *Histoire de la sexualité*, 82–83.

11. Foucault, *History of Sexuality*, 69; *Histoire de la sexualité*, 93.

12. Foucault, *History of Sexuality*, 71; *Histoire de la sexualité*, 95.

13. Collins, *Black Sexual Politics*, 39.

14. Ibid., 40.

15. Ibid., 41.

16. Foucault, *History of Sexuality*, 25–26; *Histoire de la sexualité*, 36.

17. Collins, *Black Sexual Politics*, 182.

18. Ibid., 332.

19. Lee Rainwater and William L. Yancy, *The Moynihan Report and the Politics of Controversy* (Cambridge: MIT Press, 1967), 45. "Table of Contents" from reprinted text of *The Negro Family: The Case for National Action*.

20. Rainwater and Yancy, *Moynihan Report*, 51–60. Chapter 2 of the reprinted text of *The Negro Family: The Case for National Action*.

21. Rainwater and Yancy, *Moynihan Report*, 45. "Tangle of Pathology" is the title of chapter 4 of the report.

22. Collins, *Black Sexual Politics*, 183.

23. A clear example of such state intervention would be various restrictions and limitations placed on the reproductive freedom of women on welfare. As Dorothy Roberts writes in *Killing the Black Body*, "welfare has taken on a new social role: it is no longer seen as charity but as a means of modifying poor people's behavior. Chief among the pathologies to be curtailed by new regulations is the birthrate of welfare mothers—mothers who are perceived to be Black" (202). According to Roberts, "Policies that discourage women on welfare from having children are justified by a set of myths about the connections between family structure, welfare, race, and poverty. These myths hold

that the promise of benefits induces childbirth, that welfare dependency causes poverty, and that marriage can solve the problem of children's poverty" (217). On Foucault's account, myths of this sort are myths of a "population," not of a "people."

24. Foucault, *History of Sexuality*, 105; *Histoire de la sexualité*, 139.

25. Foucault, *History of Sexuality*, 105; *Histoire de la sexualité*, 139.

26. Collins, *Black Sexual Politics*, 137.

27. Ibid., 146.

28. Ibid., 129.

29. Ibid., 147; my emphasis.

30. Ibid., 54–55.

31. Ibid., 84.

32. Ibid., 12.

33. Ibid., 50–51. On pages 223–24, Collins attributes to Foucault the conception of oppression as "normalized war within *one* society." Her footnote to this comment (18, p. 336) indicates that it comes from Stoler's analysis in *Race and the Education of Desire* (1995).

34. Foucault, *History of Sexuality*, 82; *Histoire de la sexualité*, 110.

35. Foucault, *History of Sexuality*, 83–85; *Histoire de la sexualité*, 110–12.

36. Foucault, *History of Sexuality*, 85; *Histoire de la sexualité*, 112–13.

37. Foucault, *History of Sexuality*, 86; *Histoire de la sexualité*, 113–14.

38. Foucault, *History of Sexuality*, 7; *Histoire de la sexualité*, 14.

39. Foucault, *History of Sexuality*, 136; *Histoire de la sexualité*, 178.

40. Foucault, *History of Sexuality*, 89; *Histoire de la sexualité*, 118.

41. Foucault, *History of Sexuality*, 138; *Histoire de la sexualité*, 181.

42. Foucault, *History of Sexuality*, 139; *Histoire de la sexualité*, 183.

43. Foucault, *History of Sexuality*, 92; *Histoire de la sexualité*, 121.

44. Foucault, *History of Sexuality*, 92–93; *Histoire de la sexualité*, 121–22.

45. Foucault, *History of Sexuality*, 107; *Histoire de la sexualité*, 141.

46. Collins, *Black Sexual Politics*, 11–12.

47. These criticisms resemble, but are not based upon, what Paul Patton indentifies as the two themes to which criticism of Foucault constantly returns: "[F]irst, his descriptive analyses of power provide us with no criteria for judgment, no basis upon which to condemn some regimes of power as oppressive or to applaud others as involving progress in human freedom. . . . Second, critics complain that he offers no alternative ideal, no conception either of human being or of human society freed from the bonds of power." Patton challenges the legitimacy of such criticisms. Paul Patton, "Foucault's Subject of Power," in *The Later Foucault*, ed. Jeremy Moss (London: Sage, 1998), 64.

48. Ann Laura Stoler, *Race and the Education of Desire: Foucault's* History of Sexuality *and the Colonial Order of Things* (Durham: Duke University Press, 1995), 22.

49. Stoler, *Education of Desire*, 28–29.

50. Foucault, *History of Sexuality*, 120; *Histoire de la sexualité*, 158–59.

51. Foucault, *History of Sexuality*, 123; *Histoire de la sexualité*, 162.

52. Foucault, *History of Sexuality*, 122; *Histoire de la sexualité*, 161.

53. This is also a point that Collins recognizes. See *Black Sexual Politics*, 30.

54. According to Patton, later clarifications on Foucault's part regarding his notion of power, as in "The ethic of care for the self as a practice of freedom" (in *The Final Foucault*, ed. James Bernauer and David Rasmussen [Cambridge: MIT Press, 1988],

1–20), reveal that Foucault did have an understanding of domination as a specific form of power, identifying it with "stable and asymmetrical systems of power relations" while making it clear that "such systems are secondary results, achieved within or imposed upon a primary field of relations between subjects of power." Patton, "Foucault's Subject of Power," 68.

55. Foucault, *History of Sexuality*, 95; *Histoire de la sexualité*, 125–26.

56. Foucault, *History of Sexuality*, 95; *Histoire de la sexualité*, 126.

57. Foucault, *History of Sexuality*, 96; *Histoire de la sexualité*, 126.

58. Foucault, *History of Sexuality*, 83; *Histoire de la sexualité*, 109.

59. That the call for such a response represents Foucault's considered view is supported by several later statements. For example, in "The Subject of Power" he writes: "In any case, to live in society is to live in such a way that action upon other actions is possible—and in fact ongoing. A society without power relations can only be an abstraction. Which, be it said in passing, makes all the more politically necessary the analysis of power relations in a given society, their historical formation, the source of their strength or fragility, *the conditions which are necessary to transform some or to abolish others*." Michel Foucault, "Afterword: The Subject and Power," in *Michel Foucault, Beyond Structuralism and Hermeneutics*, by Hubert L. Dreyfus and Paul Rainbow (Chicago: University of Chicago Press, 1982), 222–23; my emphasis. Likewise, he writes in "Clarification on the Question of Power": "It is absolutely true that when I write a book I refuse to take a prophetic stance, that is, the one of saying to people: here is what you must do—and also: this is good and this is not. I say to them: roughly speaking, it seems to me that things have gone this way; *but I describe those things in such a way that the possible paths of attack are delineated*." Michel Foucault, "Clarifications on the Question of Power," in *Foucault Live (Interviews 1966–84)*, ed. Sylvère Lotringe, trans. John Johnston (New York: Semiotex(e), 1989), 109–01; my emphasis.

60. Collins, *Black Sexual Politics*, 27–28. In these same pages, Collins does distinguish Bartmann from the rest of the list, arguing that: "Bartmann may not have been aware of the power of the sexual stereotypes that were created in her image, but women of African descent who followed most certainly were." At the same time, however, Collins is loathe to deny Bartmann all agency, pointing out: "What Bartmann lost by being displayed as a 'freak' is far clearer to us through our modern sensibilities than what she might have gained for herself and her family."

61. For those who would balk at the use of the word "agency" in any discussion claiming to take place within a Foucauldian framework, consider the following from Patton: "While [Foucault's] language [on power during the 1970s] appeared to dehumanize the social field entirely, abstracting from any notion of human agents or agency, Foucault nevertheless sought to address the kinds of historical phenomena which would ordinarily be regarded as the effects of human agency by means of an impersonal, non-subjectivist language of strategy and tactics. . . . Later discussions such as "The Subject of Power" appear to revert to a more familiar language of human agency: power relations are said to arise whenever there is action upon the actions of others. In other words, power relations are conceived here not simply in terms of the interaction of impersonal or inhuman forces, but in terms of action upon the action of "free" agents. However, "free" means no more than being able to act in a variety of ways." Agency, then, is not anathema to Foucault's notion of power, but rather the essential precondition of it in its very multiplicity. Patton, "Foucault's Subject of Power," 66.

62. Collins, *Black Sexual Politics*, 250.

63. Ibid., 250.

64. Ibid., 251; my emphasis.

65. Ibid., 51. Note here the similarity between Lorde's proposal and a movement identified and described favorably by Foucault in "The End of the Monarchy of Sex": "A movement is taking shape today which seems to me to be reversing the trend of 'always more sex,' of 'always more truth in sex,' a trend which has doomed us for centuries: it's a matter, I don't say of rediscovering, but rather of fabricating other forms of pleasure, of relationships, coexistences, attachments, loves, intensities." Michel Foucault, "The End of the Monarchy of Sex," in *Foucault Live (Interviews 1966–84)*, ed. Sylvère Lotringe, tr. John Johnston (New York: Semiotex(e), 1989), 144.

66. The contrast here between "sexuality" as described by Collins and Foucault and the "erotic" as put forward by Lorde is not the same as the contrast drawn by Foucault in *The History of Sexuality* between *ars erotica* and *scientia sexualis*. The former is a contrast between a locus of power and a strategy of resistance. The latter is a contrast between, on the one hand, an "Eastern" pleasure "understood as a practice and accumulated as experience" and "evaluated in terms of its intensity, its specific qualities, its duration, its reverberations in the body and soul," knowledge of which is used "in order to shape it as though from within and amplify its effects," and, on the other hand, our "Western" set of classifications and "procedures for telling the truth of sex which are geared to a form of knowledge-power." Foucault, *History of Sexuality*, 57–58.

67. Collins, *Black Sexual Politics*, 52.

68. Clarke, "Failure to Transform," 198.

69. Ibid., 207.

70. Indeed, the belief that Foucault's approach entails such a denial is belied by a close reading of *The History of Sexuality*, as, for example, where Foucault writes: "We have not only witnessed a visible explosion of unorthodox sexualities; but—and this is the important point—a deployment quite different from the law, *even if it is locally dependent on procedures of prohibition*, has ensured, through a network of interconnecting mechanisms, the proliferation of specific pleasures and the multiplication of disparate sexualities" (49, my emphasis). In later statements, Foucault offers even more explicit acknowledgment of local experiences of repression, as in "The End of the Monarchy of Sex," where he not only acknowledges that "numerous strict prohibitions exist" even if only as part of "an economic complex where they might mingle with incitements, manifestations and valorizations" (138) but also clarifies that "[i]t's not a question of denying sexual misery, but it's also not a question of explaining it negatively by repression. The whole problem is to understand which are the positive mechanisms that, producing sexuality in such or such a fashion, result in misery" (141). Thus there is no reason to hold that a Foucauldian account cannot allow for the lived experience Clarke wishes to describe.

Bibliography

Clarke, Cheryl. "The Failure to Transform: Homophobia in the Black Community." In *Home Girls: A Black Feminist Anthology*, edited by Barbara Smith, 197–208. New York: Kitchen Table, 1983.

———. "Lesbianism: An Act of Resistance." In *This Bridge Called My Back: Writings by Radical Women of Color*, edited by Cherrie Moraga and Gloria Anzaldua. Watertown, MA: Persephone, 1981. Reprinted in *Words of Fire: An Anthology of African-American Feminist Thought*, edited by Beverly Guy-Sheftall, 242–51. New York: New, 1995.

Collins, Patricia Hill. *Black Feminist Thought: Knowledge, Consciousness, and the Politics of Empowerment*. Boston: Unwin Hyman, 1990.

———. *Black Sexual Politics: African Americans, Gender, and the New Racism*. New York: Routledge, 2005.

———. *Fighting words: Black Women and the Search for Justice*. Minneapolis: University of Minnesota Press, 1998.

Foucault, Michel. *Abnormal: Lectures at the Collège de France, 1974–75*. Edited by Valerio Marchetti and Antonella Salomoni; translated by Graham Burchell. New York: Picador, 2003.

———. "Afterword: The Subject and Power." In *Michel Foucault, beyond structuralism and hermeneutics*, by Hubert L. Dreyfus and Paul Rainbow, 208–26. Chicago: University of Chicago Press, 1982.

———. *Les Anormaux: cours au Collège de France, 1974–1975*. Edited by Valerio Marchetti and Antonella Salomoni. Paris: Éditions Gallimard, 1999.

———. "The Ethic of Care for the Self as a Practice of Freedom." In *The Final Foucault*, edited by James Bernauer and David Rasmussen, 1–20. Cambridge: MIT Press, 1988.

———. *Foucault Live (Interviews 1966–84)*. Edited by Sylvère Lotringe; translated by John Johnston. New York: Semiotex(e), 1989.

———. *Histoire de la sexualité 1: La volonté de savoir*. Paris: Éditions Gallimard, 1976.

———. *The History of Sexuality, Vol. I: An Introduction*. Translated by Robert Hurley. New York: Vintage Books, 1990.

———.*Il faut défendre la société: cours au Collège de France, 1975–1976*. Edited by Mauro Bertani and Alessandro Fontana. Paris: Éditions Gallimard, 1997.

———. *Sécurité, Territoire, Population: cours au Collège de France, 1977–1978*. Edited by Michel Senellart. Paris: Éditions Gallimard, 2004.

———. *Security, Territory, Population: Lectures at the Collège de France, 1977–78*. Edited by Michel Senellart; translated by Graham Burchell. New York: Palgrave Macmillan, 2007.

———. *Society Must Be Defended: Lectures at the Collège de France, 1975–76*. Edited by Mauro Bertani and Alessandro Fontana; translated by David Macey. New York: Picador, 2003.

Lorde, Audre. "Uses of the Erotic: The Erotic as Power." In *Sister Outsider: Essays and Speeches*, 53–59. Freedom, CA: Crossing, 1984.

Patton, Paul. "Foucault's Subject of Power." In *The Later Foucault*, edited by Jeremy Moss, 64–77. London: Sage, 1998.

Rainwater, Lee, and William L. Yancy. *The Moynihan Report and the Politics of Controversy*. Cambridge: MIT Press, 1967.

Roberts, Dorothy. *Killing the Black Body: Race, Reproduction, and the Meaning of Liberty*. New York: Vintage Books, 1997.

Stoler, Ann Laura. *Race and the Education of Desire: Foucault's History of Sexuality and the Colonial Order of Things*. Durham: Duke University Press, 1995.

12

Calling All Sisters

Continental Philosophy and Black Feminist Thinkers

Kathy Glass

> Is there any way to make a case about "women in general" that doesn't in fact represent the situation of one group of women only?
>
> —Elizabeth V. Spelman, 1988, 79

Continental philosophers and black activists-intellectuals have historically engaged in feminist politics, yet their writings are marked by cultural, economic, and racial[1] difference. Given these distinctions, to what extent do the continental and black theoretical traditions converge? Is it feasible or desirable to theorize a cross-cultural, transracial sisterhood? Focusing on the writings of Simone de Beauvoir, Hélène Cixous, Audre Lorde, and bell hooks, this chapter argues that, while continental efforts to theorize women's experiences have frequently duplicated patriarchal patterns of racist exclusion and/or tokenistic incorporation, it is possible—and indeed necessary—to theorize sisterhood across the boundaries of race, class, and sexuality to affect radical social transformation. Yet hooks's scholarship reminds us that *Feminism Is for Everybody.*[2] I therefore draw on the writings of Cornel West, who is committed to race and gender equality, to analyze the tension between male- and female-gendered voices within a feminist context.

The first section of this chapter will explore continental philosophers' and black feminists' efforts to wrest away "woman" from the patriarchal order, to redefine the term for themselves. It then examines the contours of sisterhood and community posited by each tradition, with particular attention to the manner in which black feminists elaborate upon and complicate continental philosophy.

I start with Simone de Beauvoir's *Second Sex* ([1949) 1993) and build on critiques of her study, which puts black women under erasure while emphasizing the structural oppression hindering white, European, middle-class women. Although her book is addressed specifically to a French, rather than American, audience, Beauvoir makes multiple references to the conditions of racism and sexism endemic in the United States in the 1940s. Remarkably progressive in her observation that both racist and sexist practices reinscribe white male power, she fails to theorize a space for black women, of any economic background, in her study.

Continental philosopher Hélène Cixous also engages racial dynamics in her attempt to liberate women from patriarchal forces. Her feminist tract, "The Laugh of Medusa" ([1975) 2001), urges those of her sex to engage in "feminine writing," a liberating body-centered female practice meant to release women's repressed creative power and transform "phallogocentric" structures. While she acknowledges that "there is . . . no general woman, no one typical woman,"[3] she nonetheless lapses into essentialism via racially charged figurative language. In claiming Africa, for women in general, as the site of darkness, danger, and femininity, she merely reinforces romantic and problematic assumptions about the continent. Thus, her appropriation of "blackness" furthers the goals of women in general but has ambivalent implications for black women.

Unlike the continental philosophers discussed above, black feminists Audre Lorde and bell hooks argue that explicitly engaging women's diversity is essential to the feminist movement. In redefining dominant constructions of womanhood, they add to the category "woman" those of age, orientation, class, and, the social category of race. Rather than ignore material differences among women, Lorde argues that such distinctions must be "seen as a fund of necessary polarities between which our creativity can spark like a dialectic."[4] In her view, cross-racial community will become possible only when women learn how to "make common cause with those others identified as outside the structures in order to define and seek a world in which we can all flourish."[5] Unlike Lorde, hooks' approach to politics is postmodern; but the latter's stance on community is consistent with Lorde's in that she too concludes that women "can be sisters united by shared interests and beliefs, united in our appreciation for diversity" and "in our struggle to end sexist oppression."[6]

The final section of this chapter engages the writings of West; in solidarity with feminist concerns, his voice enables an analysis of the dialogic relation between race and gender politics. While the discourses of continental philosophers and black feminists under discussion have historically diverged on the issue of white supremacy, the theoretical models offered by Lorde, hooks, and West engage the blind spots embedded in the continental tradition. Their interrogations of whiteness, patriarchy, and exploitation make possible the emergence of an oppositional antiracist feminist politics likely to ensure meaningful and lasting change.

[E)racing Black Women in *The Second Sex*

Feminist critics have long noted the problematic elements of Beauvoir's *Second Sex*; and I shall later recount some of these critiques. But Beauvoir's key supposition that women and racialized minorities experience oppression in similar—yet distinct—ways has progressive implications that remain relevant to twenty-first-century cultural activists. This relational approach to analysis, crucial to the project of creating cross-racial alliances between women, enables the insight that "no group ever sets itself up as the One without at once setting up the Other over against itself;[7] just as woman "assume[s) the status of the Other" to man,[8] Jews "are 'different' for the anti-Semite, [and) Negroes are 'inferior' for American racists."[9] Drawing on Hegel's theory of oppositional consciousness, Beauvoir provides a bird's eye view of oppressive systems. This characterization of power is useful because it undermines assumptions that individual acts of kindness eradicate discrimination. While respectful interpersonal relations are essential to the improvement of society, she further stresses how broad structures of oppression operate, highlighting potential sites of social transformation.

Beauvoir further makes note of the "deep similarities between the situation of woman and that of the Negro" because "[i)n both cases the former masters lavish more or less sincere eulogies, either on the virtues of 'the good Negro' with his dormant, childish, merry soul . . . or on the merits of the woman who is 'truly feminine'—that is, frivolous, infantile, irresponsible—the submissive woman."[10] In each case, the master emerges as the privileged opposite of the binary configuration: mature, rational, responsible—and therefore dominant over both subordinate groups. But as her critics note, Beauvoir fails to satisfactorily explore the diversity of subjectivities within the categories "Negro," "woman," and "man."[11] She, in effect, neglects to examine how white male supremacy harnesses the forces of racism and sexism to subordinate women and men who are black. She virtually ignores the distinctions that would later find expression in Kimberle Crenshaw's "Mapping the Margins: Intersectionality, Identity Politics, and Violence against Women of Color" (1995), which complicates facile understandings of identity, allowing for rigorous analyses of racist and sexist practices.

Such limitations aside, Beauvoir's broad strokes help to expose how patriarchy and racism can operate in similar ways to increase white male power. Arguably, she builds a case, intentionally or not, for the construction of a cross-cultural, Gramscian "historic bloc"[12] that could disrupt the commonsense assumptions underpinning unjust sociopolitical relations, potentially bringing together disparately situated subjects. Locating common ground in the midst of diverse interests, no matter how contingent or provisional, could conceivably create conditions for shifting coalitions and strategic collaboration across communities.

Not only does Beauvoir's study open onto coalitional possibility, but it also resonates with postmodern antisexist and antiracist projects that reject racial and gendered essences. Anticipating essentialists' late-twentieth-century objections to the poststructuralist interrogation of stable identities, Beauvoir undermines the validity of essences but fully engages the existential reality of oppressed persons. Citing empirical evidence, Beauvoir writes: "The biological and social sciences no longer admit the existence of unchangeably fixed entities that determine given characteristics, such as those ascribed to woman, the Jew, or the Negro";[13] but subjects in these categories still live as embodied beings in the material realm. While "the eternal feminine, the black soul, [and) the Jewish character"[14] are mere constructions, they are nevertheless accepted as "essences," to which dominant groups appeal to justify differential sociopolitical treatment. Women, then, still contend with sexism, Jews with anti-Semitism, and blacks with racism. Simone de Beauvoir's suspicion of fixed identities and engagement with the lived conditions of the oppressed, resonates with hooks's endorsement of postmodern tools that may serve to "dismantle the master's house."[15] According to hooks, "[w]hen black folks critique essentialism, we are empowered to recognize multiple experiences of black identity that are the lived conditions which make diverse cultural productions possible."[16] In conjunction with hooks's "postmodern blackness,"[17] a "postmodern whiteness" might further serve to disrupt binary, hierarchal thinking, enabling the formation of political coalitions to enact social transformation. I borrow and expand David Witzling's "postmodern whiteness," which performs an important "cultural critique" that is "central to the sensibility of postmodern whiteness."[18] Specifically, Witzling suggests that "[t]o reposition whiteness, as hooks and others demand, the white critic must recognize his or her own implication in a racist social system."[19] Such recognition is an important step in the process of social change. Illustrating this practice, Jeffrey Paris' "Interrogating Whiteness" analyzes a dialogue between bell hooks and Cornel West, yet at the same time he reflects on his own whiteness. Paris's essay explores the hooks-West interaction, in particular, because their *Breaking Bread* demonstrates the process whereby productive dialogue occurs between individuals who are willing to have their identities "fractured and rebuilt, disrupted and progressively re-imagined in the context of strategic resistance and social change."[20] Reflecting the fragmented nature of dialogue, and the complexity of the self,[21] Paris produces a fractured text, one section of which reads:

> For I can engage these Black bodies safely, from a distance of (mere?) words and marks, Black marks on White background (the White which is never questioned, never attributed its own difference). Am I hereby making further use of my privilege, simultaneously consuming their bodies and making them present by putting them on my text/table . . . ? I hope not, for I hope that I am interrogating myself, putting my own subjectivity in-process and thus on-trial, to disclose and to resituate my own identity. . . . See my Whiteness that sits behind the mask of Black letters. Look at the spaces that are already full of content, of matter, of flesh.[22]

In problematizing power relations, Paris makes visible the uneven terrain of racialized identity. Rather than engaging hooks' and West's dialogue as a neutral, transcendent being, Paris marks his whiteness and gives it flesh, acknowledging its historical privilege. This self-reflective, critical whiteness, aware of its own presence, which makes possible honest engagement with the "other," is what Beauvoir's *Second Sex* lacks.

For all its strengths, Beauvoir's study fails to fully explore the racism integral to white women's historical reluctance to align themselves politically with black women. She, indeed, concedes that, if "they [women) are white, their allegiance is to white men, not to Negro women,"[23] but Beauvoir stops short of interrogating the whiteness that has made possible white women's lack of empathy for their black counterparts. The resignation implicit in her observation suggests that racism necessarily functions as an inevitable obstacle to the collaboration between black and white women. Needless to say, replacing this fatalism with an active inquiry into the nature and consequences of whiteness is an essential step in the formation of a cross-racial community of feminists. As Paris writes in his engagement with *Breaking Bread*, "White men cannot dialogue until they are self-identified as White and understand the social/political privileges which provide buffers against the endangered subjectivity of publicly marginalized persons, such as women, people of color, les/bi/gays, and disabled persons."[24] As we shall see, hooks urges white women to engage in a similar process whereby they acknowledge their own whiteness, that which "assumes the authority to marginalize other identities, discourses, narratives, perspectives, and voices."[25]) Failing to contest the "absolute *presence*" of whiteness,[26] which keeps intact the "binary relationship of self-Other," merely reinforces the boundary between "black" and "white," rendering ineffective the effort to engage in meaningful cross-cultural interaction. The honest assessment of whiteness as a sociohistorical force must therefore precede the formation of inclusive community.

From a very different standpoint, however, Beauvoir tries to account for white women's loyalty to patriarchal arrangements. Specifically, she explains that "woman may fail to lay claim to the status of subject because she lacks definite resources, because she feels the necessary bond that ties her to man regardless of reciprocity, and because she is often very well pleased with her role as the *Other.*"[27] Unfortunately, the nature of this "necessary bond," which secured white women's allegiance to their mates, remains vague. Shedding light on the dynamics of *racial* bonding, hooks writes of contemporary white women who bond on the basis of identity politics: "The "whiteness" that bonds them together is a racial identity that is directly related to the experience of nonwhite people as "other" and as a "threat." When I speak to white women about racial bonding, they often deny it exists."[28] Even as white women challenge the "male metanarrative voice,"[29] their denial of white supremacy's presence prevents them from fully recognizing their situatedness in racialized structures, and complicity with whiteness, which undermines the formation of cross-racial female solidarity.

Giving further evidence of white women's fear-based investment in the status quo, Beauvoir notes that, during the Civil War, "no Southerners were more passionate in upholding slavery than the women."[30] This is partly because, "[i)f she belongs to the privileged elite that benefits from the established social order, she wants it to be unshakable and she is notably uncompromising in this desire."[31] The nature of the "benefits" that women accrue on account of whiteness, however, is unnamed. Instead, Beauvoir portrays them as victims. Men are more open to change, she explains, because a man "knows that he can develop different institutions, another ethic, a new legal code; aware of his ability to transcend what is, he regards history as a becoming."[32] Since "woman takes no part in history, she fails to understand its necessities; she is suspiciously doubtful of the future and wants to arrest the flow of time."[33] Put another way: in their immanence, women are ineffective and ignorant victims of their status. They are victims, in Beauvoir's characterization, of white male power. Not understanding themselves as historical agents, they therefore put their faith in masculine laws to which they blindly cling.[34]

But we must complicate facile representations, as racial supremacy yielded white women power over nineteenth-century blacks of both sexes. Illuminating this power is Mrs. Flint, who "uses cruelty toward slaves to establish authority over them" in *Incidents in the Life of a Slave Girl.*[35] Although she suffered the indignity of her philandering husband's abusive sexual relations with his slaves, Mrs. Flint enjoyed the authority and power of whiteness, which she, and others like her, exercised relentlessly over their slaves. If women indeed, as Beauvoir recommends, "renounce all the advantages conferred upon them by the alliance with the superior caste,"[36] they would necessarily have to name and renounce the "invisible weightless knapsack of special provisions" bestowed by whiteness in the process.[37]

Feminist critics have frequently lamented that Beauvoir ultimately posits the experiences of primarily white, middle-class European women as metonymic for the condition of women in general.[38] Endeavoring to clarify her terminology, Beauvoir writes: "When I use the words *woman* or *feminine* I evidently refer to no archetype, no changeless essence whatever. . . . It is not our concern here to proclaim eternal verities, but rather to describe the common basis that underlies every individual feminine existence."[39] Despite this caveat, the signifier "woman" remains tightly bound, more often than not, to the signified "white woman." While there are indeed references to black women and their subordinate condition relative to that of the white population in America, Beauvoir marginalizes black women in her protofeminist exploration. Scholars have long speculated as to why Beauvoir, who clearly knew of such diversity, failed to engage it in this particular work.[40] While intentionality continues to confound, Beauvoir's book impacted decisively on the politics of white American feminists, who gained access to the English translation of *The Second Sex* in 1953; as the record shows, mainstream feminist writings reproduced Beauvoir's oversights throughout the 1960s.

While *The Second Sex* does not stress difference within the category "woman," Cixous's "Laugh of Medusa" proclaims multiplicity. Refusing to tightly bind the signifier "woman" to a designated signified, she notes that "there is, at this time, no general woman, no one typical woman."[41] And, intriguingly, she posits "Cixous"—the textual persona—as "universal woman subject who must bring women to their senses and to their meaning in history."[42] This ahistorical gesture, which positions a race- and classless woman in a utopian, liberating role, effectively masks white supremacist structures, which combine racism with the burden of sexism borne by women of color. It further renders invisible the struggles of the impoverished and the aged.

Ignoring these particularities, Cixous admonishes women to "Write!"—to engage in "*ecriture feminine,*" a type of feminine writing that rethinks the speech/writing binary and is "characterized by the explicitly female body parts that [have) been repressed by traditional discourse and [are) being ex-pressed by the woman writer."[43] Banking on the essentialist assumption that when woman dares to "write [her) self,"[44] the "immense resources of the unconscious [will) spring forth," Cixous invites her to unleash these creative powers. In her view, "writing is precisely *the very possibility of change*, the space that can serve as a springboard for subversive thought, the precursory movement of a transformation of social and cultural structures."[45] While Cixous does not write to cultivate feminist community *per se*, she does endeavor to "challenge. . . . literary tradition, cultural practices, and dominant ideological forms" that have restricted women historically.[46] While Cixous refrains from specifying the nature of this transformation and avoids advocating prescriptive solutions to social injustice, she does offer the reader a vision of hope for change. Rather than constructing "woman" as victim, she asserts: "Now, I-woman am going to blow up the Law: an explosion henceforth possible and ineluctable; let it be done, right now, *in* language."[47] Affirming the possibility of "shatter[ing) the framework of institutions," and "blow[ing) up the law,"[48] "The Laugh of Medusa" figures women as resilient agents of social transformation capable of mounting a powerful challenge to patriarchal forces. But her resounding manifesto inevitably begs the question: must we theorize women's oppression to disrupt it? Without specifying the nature and degree of women's differentiated oppression, is it possible to eradicate it?

Rather than naming the differences among women, she curiously notes that women, "the repressed of culture, our lovely mouths gagged with pollen . . . we are black and we are beautiful."[49] Eliminating social markers altogether, Cixous herds all women into an undifferentiated mass aligned with blackness. Addressing the "repressed," Cixous invokes the black pride slogan—"black is beautiful"—thereby linking the sexual oppression of women in particular to the struggle of blacks in general. She further notifies women that "because you are Africa, you are black. Your continent is dark. Dark is dangerous."[50] To valorize the feminine, that mysterious abyss that Freud notoriously associated with the female sex, Cixous embraces and celebrates the continent figured as the site of women's creative powers. By appropriating Africa, Cixous not only redeploys Freud's assumption that the "Dark Continent" best describes the inscrutability of women, but she further invokes racialized representations of Africa—and by extension, peoples of African descent—as chaotic and unruly. In claiming for women a racialized "darkness," that which has been denigrated, dismissed, and marginalized, Cixous simultaneously reinforces conventional African imagery, which justified nineteenth-century colonialist and imperialist projects. As hooks observes in *Yearnings: Race, Gender, and Cultural Politics*, postmodern theory becomes problematic when it "appropriates[s) the experience of 'Otherness' to enhance the discourse or to be radically chic."[51] While activists should work to combine their struggles, and unite their platforms, they do a disservice to the cause of justice when they cannibalize the other.[52] More helpful than racial appropriation is the practice of cross-cultural collaboration theorized by Angela Davis in her interview with Lisa Lowe. In brief, Davis's "women of color formation" consists of female activists from diverse backgrounds who suffer different degrees of oppression[53] and yet coalesce around the shared desire for sociopolitical change. Davis describes the potential of such a formation as "exciting" because it bases its identity "on politics rather than the politics on identity."[54] While this model shows how women of color have successfully negotiated a "provisional identity" behind which to unite, it contains lessons for women—of all backgrounds—who wish to unite for political ends. Instead of exploiting difference, as Cixous seems to do, Davis demonstrates the cooperative process whereby women of distinct backgrounds, differentially oppressed, work to respect diversity *and* cultivate solidarity.

The "impractically ideal" aspects of Cixous's project,[55] which consists of visionary theory, strongly contrast with the pragmatism coursing through Lorde's materially grounded "Master's Tools Will Never Dismantle the Master's House," which asserts: "It is a particular academic arrogance to assume any discussion of feminist theory without examining our many differences,"[56] Making her comments at the Second Sex Conference, also attended by Cixous in 1979,[57] Lorde laments that only two black female panelists have been invited to attend. They were not only contacted "at the last hour,"[58] but they were further relegated to the one panel at the conference where "the input of Black feminists and lesbians [was) represented."[59] Identifying the exclusionary and tokenistic practices of the conference organizers as patriarchal tools intended to "divide and conquer" along the lines of difference,[60] Lorde challenges her listeners, from an identity-centered perspective, to engage the material realities of women who are poor, black, third world, and lesbian.[61] Instead of denying difference, she urges women to acknowledge it and to permit this knowledge to transform "white american feminist theory" and praxis.[62] In Lorde's view, ignoring distinctions merely enables the status quo, allowing white privilege to flourish unchecked. Rather than positing white women's lived realities as the norm from which othered women necessarily diverge, she urges white women to face the realities of color, class, age, and orientation within the category "woman" and learn how these distinctions produce "difference in [their) oppressions."[63] In so doing, women better position themselves to challenge white supremacist patriarchal norms. But change and seeking "new ways of being in the world" not only require an alternative approach to reading difference; engaging the other without and the other within are also central to Lorde's progressive praxis.[64] She thus advises her audience that "Racism and homophobia are real conditions of all our lives in this place and time. I urge each one of us here to reach down into that deep place of knowledge inside herself and touch that terror and loathing of any difference that lives there. See whose face it wears."[65] Transformation, then, requires an examination of not only what's "out there," but also of what's "in here." Indeed, she wants white feminists to engage in honest dialogue with—and allow feminist theory to be transformed by—"[p)oor women and women of Color."[66] But also key is the interrogation of one's own bigotry. To what extent have we—as women of all backgrounds—internalized sexist and bigoted assumptions? How do these assumptions prevent women from reaching out to the so-called other, whoever she may be? Urging women to be self-reflexive, vulnerable, and willing to change, Lorde challenges them to consider their own implication within the system and the extent to which women, of all colors, perpetuate racist and sexist ideologies.

hooks further emphasizes the importance of fearless reflection and dialogue as central to liberation and the formation of female community. In "Sisterhood: Political Solidarity between Women," she critiques "[t)he vision of sisterhood evoked by women's liberationists" in the 1960s, as it "was based on the idea of common oppression." This view is flawed, as we have seen, since "[w)omen are divided by sexist attitudes, racism, class privilege, and a host of other prejudices."[67] Particularly interested in creating an inclusive model of feminist community, hooks urges women to confront and eliminate these divisions,[68] because "[a)bandoning the idea of sisterhood as an expression of political solidarity weakens and diminishes the feminist movement."[69] More visionary than Beauvoir, who rhetorically accepted white women's "allegiance" to men of their caste,[70] hooks invests in the possibility of forging new alliances. Rather than shying away from difference, hooks asserts that "[s)olidarity strengthens resistance struggle."[71]

bell hooks also urges women to avoid another pitfall of 1960s activism: bonding primarily as "victims" of male power.[72] While it is necessary to engage the reality of discrimination, defining one's self primarily as victim can be "psychologically demoralizing," and counterproductive for women whose "survival depends on continued exercise of whatever personal powers they possess."[73] How, then, might women cultivate solidarity in the midst of difference?

Like Lorde, hooks argues that women must "acknowledge and confront the enemy within."[74] Self-reflection being critical to the process of change, hooks asserts: "Before we can resist male domination we must break our attachment to sexism; we must work to transform female consciousness."[75] In practical terms, this requires that women purge themselves of "sexist socialization."[76] While sexism, as expressed between men and women, is easily recognizable as "male domination,"[77] hooks foregrounds the "male-supremacist values" that express themselves between women. In particular, "male-supremacist values are expressed through suspicious, defensive, and competitive behavior. It is sexism that leads women to feel threatened by one another without cause. . . . Acceptance of sexist ideology is indicated when women teach that there are only two possible behavior patterns: dominance or submissiveness."[78] In effect, hooks calls for a transformation of values within the feminist movement. Exchanging values of competition, fear, and division for collaboration, love, and compassion is central to the large goal of cultivating solidarity. This means accepting, fully engaging, and allowing oneself to be informed by the lived experiences of all women, straight and gay, black and brown, red and yellow. In sum, forgoing binary thinking and zero-sum relationship models in favor of more complicated and equalitarian formations is required, as they build trust and acceptance between women from diverse backgrounds.

Attacking sexism, however, in isolation from racism would be problematic, since the latter "is so interconnected with sexist oppression."[79] But challenges to racism contribute to the development of female solidarity only when they manifest themselves in meaningful ways. In hooks' view,

> [w)e will know white feminists have made a political commitment to eliminating racism when they help change the direction of the feminist movement, when they work to unlearn racist socialization prior to assuming positions of leadership or shaping theory or making contact with women of color so that they will not perpetuate and maintain racial oppression or, unconsciously or consciously, abuse and hurt nonwhite women. These are the truly radical gestures that create a foundation for the experience of political solidarity between white women and women of color.[80]

Merely inviting women of color into white feminist spaces is a superficial gesture, as hooks rightly notes.[81] True antiracist change, however, requires sustained effort on all sides. Not only does hooks urge white women to do the inner work discussed above, which includes challenging white supremacy and "the perpetuation of a white race,"[82] but she also challenges women of color to divest themselves of sexism and "internalized racism," which can pit them against themselves[83] and each other. Women of color must be careful to root out traces of self-hate that can accumulate in their psyches, given the oppression they face. And interethnic differences might be fruitfully understood as opportunities for learning *about* and learning *from* one another,[84] rather than cause for separation. Combining this inner work with concrete antiracist acts means that white feminists, and those of color, must share the task of formulating feminist theory and praxis. Dividing along the lines of difference weakens women as a whole, but as Davis's "women of color formation" shows, an inclusive stance toward diversity enables the emergence of strength through solidarity.

Women alone, however, cannot eradicate sexism and racism. Feminist calls for solidarity must be answered by women and male allies alike. In her dialogue with black scholar and intellectual Cornel West in *Breaking Bread,* hooks speaks directly to strategies for addressing "sexism in Black life."[85] West, historicizing the problem of patriarchy in black communities, notes that

> "[u)nfortunately, in North American society, one of the major means by which Black men are empowered is to have power over Black women . . . The question is how do we sever Black male notions of empowerment from requiring the active subordination of Black women? . . . how do we make the majority of Black men disinvest from a definition of power which requires subordination of Black women? We have to have reflections on Black male agency that are healthy and empowering in a substantive way."[86]

Just as hooks invites women, black and white, to interrogate their own bigotry and fear, West urges black men to do the same.

West not only encourages black men in general to engage in transformative reflection, but he further models that self-reflexivity for the reader. Identifying himself as a product of patriarchal culture, he notes that "[i]t's a tough issue because it seems to me every man, including myself, is thoroughly shaped by patriarchal values which means that our values, no matter how feminist we proclaim ourselves to be, are inevitably tainted all the way through."[87] He further notes: "I grew up in traditional Black patriarchal culture and there is no doubt that I'm going to take a great many unconscious, but present, patriarchal complicities to the grave because it is so deeply ensconced in how I look at the world. Therefore, very much like alcoholism, drug addiction, or racism, patriarchy is a disease and we are in perennial recovery and relapse. So you have to get up every morning and struggle against it."[88] Identifying change as an ongoing process requiring daily work, West invites men—black and white—to be vigilant about their own participation in the patriarchal and racist structures in which they are steeped. Moreover, he challenges men to marry antipatriarchal thinking with progressive praxis; while a critique of "the patriarchal family" is indeed productive,[89] also required is the creation of alternative relational models. In particular, he suggests: "We need organizations that exemplify to people on an everyday basis what can be done in terms of new families, new churches, de-patriarchalized churches. What would a Black church look like without patriarchy? What would a Black family look like?"[90] In short, West calls for imaginative alternatives to structures that increase the power of men, at the expense of women. Although he focuses primarily on the transformation of black patriarchal relations, West's proposals provide a model for white men who also wish to interrogate their own complicity with structures of domination.

Several years following her dialogue with West, hooks asserted in *The Will to Change* that "[m)en need feminist thinking."[91] Not only is patriarchy detrimental to women, as we have seen, but it also harms men because the patriarchal "system has denied males access to full emotional well-being."[92] They are taught "a form of emotional stoicism" according to which "they are more manly if they do not feel, but if by chance they should feel and the feelings hurt, the manly response is to stuff them down, to forget about them, to hope they go away."[93] Such indoctrination produces "emotional numbness"[94] yet allows for the free expression of male anger.[95] At work here are the "patriarchal gender roles," which teach boys to dominate females and "enjoy killing."[96] Clearly, these sexist teachings undermine, rather than enhance, men's ability to develop healthy relationships with themselves and others.

Intervening in these norms, hooks calls for men to embrace a "[v]isionary feminism" which "is rooted in the love of male and female being, refusing to privilege one over the other."[97] Since "[t]he soul of feminist politics is the commitment to ending patriarchal domination of women and men, girls and boys,"[98] progressive feminism provides a useful framework within which to envision equitable alternatives to exploitative power relations. While the desired outcomes may not manifest themselves as quickly as one would hope, hooks rightly stresses that "the commitment to the process of change and convergence. . . . opens up the possibility of love, renewal, and reconciliation."[99] Committing to this process requires vulnerability and a willingness grow; it demands openness and the strength to eradicate structures that no longer serve us. Such a commitment—to justice, self-reflection, communion, and change—will indeed make possible the emergence of nonpatriarchal male-female relations. It will also create the conditions for cross-cultural, transracial sisterhood and solidarity.

Notes

1. I enclose "race" in quotations marks in order to underscore that it is not a biological essence, but rather socially constructed.
2. See bell hooks, *Feminism Is for Everyone* (2000).
3. (1975) 2001, 204.
4. (1979) 1984, 111.
5. (1979) 1984, 112.
6. 1997, 411.
7. (1949) 1993, xlv.
8. (1949) 1993, lix.
9. (1949) 1993, xlv–xlvi.
10. (1949) 1993, liii.
11. Simons 1979.
12. See Antonio Gramsci, *Selections from the Prison Notebooks* (1971). "Historic bloc" refers to a union of forces capable of challenging hegemonic structures.
13. (1949) 1993, xlii.
14. (1949) 1993, xlii.
15. See Audre Lorde, "The Master's Tools Will Never Dismantle the Master's House," in *Sister Outsider* (1984).
16. 1990, 29.
17. 1990, 29.
18. 2006, 410.
19. 2006, 410.
20. 1995, 74.
21. 1995, 74.
22. Orig. emphasis, 1995, 74–75.
23. (1949) 1993, xlviii.
24. 1995, 79.

25. Yancy 2002, 567.
26. 2002, 567.
27. (1949) 1993, l.
28. 1997, 404.
29. Yancy 2002, 578.
30. (1949) 1993, 632.
31. (1949) 1993, 632.
32. (1949) 1993, 632.
33. (1949) 1993, 632.
34. (1949) 1993, 631–32.
35. Spelman 1997, 361.
36. (1949) 1993, l.
37. McInstosh 1988, 291.
38. Simons, 1979.
39. Orig. emphasis, [1949) 1993, lx.
40. See Oyeronke Oyewumi (2000) and Elizabeth Spelman (1988).
41. (1975) 2001, 2040.
42. (1975) 2001, 2040.
43. 2001, 2037.
44. (1975) 2001, 2043.
45. Orig. emphasis, [1975) 2001, 2043.
46. Lindsay 1986, 47.
47. Orig. emphasis, [1975) 2001, 2050.
48. (1975) 2001, 2051.
49. (1975) 2001, 2042.
50. (1975) 2001, 2041.
51. 1997, 26.
52. For a discussion of "strategic essentialism," see Diana Fuss, *Essentially Speaking: Feminism, Nature, and Difference* (1989.
53. 1997, 317–18.
54. 1997, 318.
55. Lindsay 1986, 52.
56. (1979) 1984, 110.
57. See Lindsay 1986, 52.
58. (1979) 1984, 110.
59. 1979, 110.
60. (1979) 1984, 112.
61. (1979), 1984 110.
62. (1979) 1984, 112.
63. (1979) 1984, 112.
64. (1979) 1984, 111.
65. Orig. emphasis, [1979) 1984, 113.
66. (1979) 1984, 112.
67. 1997, 396.

68. 1997, 396.
69. 1997, 396.
70. xlviii (1949) 1993.
71. 1997, 396.
72. 1997, 397.
73. 1997, 397.
74. 1997, 398–99.
75. 1997, 398.
76. 1997, 398.
77. 1997, 399.
78. 1997, 399.
79. 1997, 402.
80. 1997, 404.
81. 1997, 403.
82. 1997, 402.
83. 1997, 404.
84. 1997, 404.
85. 1991, 106.
86. 1991, 107.
87. 1991, 124.
88. 1991, 125.
89. 1991, 109.
90. 1991, 109
91. 2004, 118.
92. 2004, 31.
93. 2004 5, 6.
94. 2004, 6.
95. 2004, 7.
96. 2004, 13, 11.
97. 2004, 123.
98. 2004, 123.
99. This comment arose in the context of hooks's discussion of black men and women, yet I extend it, as it seems applicable to men and women, generally (1991, 124).

Afterword

Philosophy and the Other of the Second Sex

George Yancy

> I stand before you as a member of an endangered species: as an African American woman in philosophy.
>
> —La Verne Shelton, "The Peculiar Position of a Woman of Color When World Fame Isn't Enough," in *Overcoming Racism and Sexism*

> It's not obvious to me that philosophy has *anything* special to offer Black women today.
>
> —Anita L. Allen, "Interview with Anita L. Allen," *African-American Philosophers*

Black feminist standpoint epistemology places emphasis upon the concrete experiential *here* of social reality, a *here* that is embodied and socially transversal. Theorizing from the perspective of a concrete experiential *here* underscores black feminists' valorization of critical subjectivity and a skeptical sensibility regarding epistemologies that often masquerade as "neutral" and "objective" while concealing ideological underpinnings. Within the context of black feminist thought, then, which is by no means monolithic, there is an emphasis placed upon the *lived* texture of experience and how that experience, and the knowledge production that comes out of that experience, is fundamentally shaped according to historical and cultural location. While continental philosophy constitutes a heterogeneous corpus in terms of methodological emphases, styles of argumentation and writing, and conclusions reached, I think that a central motif within continental philosophy is that we find ourselves thrown within the context of the world as given, as situational facticity. Continental philosophy stresses that it is from the *here* of our thrown-ness that we engage the world but always already against the backdrop of value-laden and historically mediated meaning. The ontology of the self is always already ahead of itself and implicated within preexisting complex engagements. Within continental philosophy, then, there is an emphasis placed upon historical context and mediated modes of knowing and being. Hence, given the aims of *Convergences: Black Feminism and Continental Philosophy*, it makes sense for me to begin from what appears to be an important point of conceptual family resemblance: emphasis upon the contingent, experiential, and contextual *here* of our contemporary factical-historical moment.

There has been much in the news at the time of this writing regarding the alleged racial profiling of Dr. Henry Louis Gates Jr. I will not run through the many publicized details regarding the incident with Sgt. James Crowley. And while I believe that the incident speaks to the significance of racism in America, I would like to shift attention to the case of Megan Williams.[1] The shift contests the power of selective media representation and how such representations are predicated upon problematic norms governing what is "newsworthy." While Williams's *lived* phenomenological and existential nightmare, which was caused by white racism, preceded Barack Obama's presidential election, there was a teachable moment of profound implications that ought to have been engaged prior to the Gates-Crowley controversy. However, the moment was missed, and the seriousness of Williams's situation seems to have been placed under erasure.

The reader may recall that in September 2007, six white adults held Megan Williams, a twenty-year-old black woman, prisoner in a trailer in West Virginia. Williams's captors raped her, poured hot water and hot wax on her body, forced her to drink out of the toilet and to eat feces (possibly dog, rat, and human), cut off and yanked out her hair, forced her to lick their toes, sodomized her with a wooden handle stick, taunted her with sexist and racist slurs ("slut," "bitch," and "nigger"), cut her ankle and stabbed her thigh, and forced her to perform oral sex on one of the white women. In fact, we are told that she was also forced to lick the anus of one of the white women. She then vomited and was forced to lick up her own vomit.[2] While the color line was literally present in Gates' home, Williams' pain and horror exceed linguistic instantiation and demonstrate how the color line bespeaks white racist perversion and bloodlust and replicates the history of whiteness as terror. As Williams was being tortured, she recounts that she was told, "This is what we do to niggers around here." The scene is one of spectacle. The activity of gazing upon the despised and violated black body—the marked "black nigger bitch"—as it is forced to eat feces and drink from a toilet, also functions as a site of white racist pleasure, masochism, and dominance. The horror of the situation does not speak to the vulnerability of so-called women qua women but speaks to the *specificity* of pain and suffering endured by a *poor Black woman*, who was also *mentally challenged*. It is here that one might speak of a "quadruple jeopardy."

The gaze that violated and objectified her body was not simply the theorized *male* gaze, that site of scopic sexual objectification with its circuits of desire and perversion. Rather, what is unique here is the operative hegemony of the *white female* gaze, and, as one might argue, the "ablest gaze." It was the white female gaze that also saw to it that it was not enough that Williams's black body was sexually violated but that it had to be reduced to an eater of feces and a drinker of urine, forced to mimic white (male and female) fantasies of the black body as animalistic and infrahuman, fixed as a "thing" of teratology, a monster, something freakish, abnormal, and capable of the most disgraceful acts.[3] Postcolonial theorist Gayatri Spivak asks, "Can the subaltern speak?" Megan Williams's voice was muted by those who *silenced* her through forcing her literally to eat shit and perform cunnilingus. And while pornography, as a site of specific male violence and visual mutilation, has been critiqued in terms of its pictorials of women in positions of sexual subservience, and how, through various sexual performances, women are both symbolically and literally forced to be silent, voiceless, bound, and gagged, the *white female gaze* as a site of pornographic violence in this case is in need of greater analysis and theorization.

So why recount Megan Williams's horror in a text that is about convergences between black feminism and continental philosophy? Williams's case is a clarion call for black feminists to stay the course as black women and women of color continue to suffer along multiple axes of denigration. Her situation is also an incitement to whites working within the continental tradition to nurture forms of critical self-reflexivity vis-à-vis their whiteness as a site of power and privilege. In the details of Williams's ordeal, one wonders whether philosophical discourse is adequate to the challenge of articulating the pain and suffering. Yet black feminist thought must continue to *voice* and fight against the horrors faced by women of color and strive to make sense of such experiences, even as discursive frames of reference may fall short, even as theory may falter. However, the horror of Williams's situation places important demands on continental philosophy's conceptual resources to engage the complex *lived* reality of race. For example, while white feminists within the continental tradition have critiqued phallogocentrism, concerns pertinent to black feminists and black women have not been given the attention that they seriously deserve. While convergences are important, as this text has clearly demonstrated, it is important that white continental feminists give as much philosophical attention to whiteness, its historical formation, axiological assumptions, and epistemic orders, as they have given to phallogocentrism. Because of the ontological expansionist tendencies of whiteness, it is also important that black feminists remain cognizant of and militate against the structural and willful ignorance of both white feminists working within the continental tradition and white continental feminists. Given the historical arrogance and myopia of white feminism, problems specific to women of color can be easily "whitewashed" and thereby lead to the centering of whiteness and the process of usurping black feminist critical discursive spaces, transforming and reconfiguring them into spaces of white control.

More to the point, analytic philosophers, given their preoccupation with conceptual analysis, would not see the importance of Williams's situation as a "proper" subject for philosophical analysis. After all, Williams's situation lacks conceptual precision and philosophical abstraction. Her situation mocks the hypothetical brains in a vat scenario. As a non-Cartesian *sum*,[4] her situation speaks to the muck and mire of history, subjectivity, agency, white racist interpellation, intersubjectivity, embodiment, and specificity of black women's *Erlebnis*. Post–World War II Germany and France are complex lived spaces and traditions of philosophical fruition/production that are nevertheless white. It is here that black feminist thought must militate against the possible *conceptual whiteness* of continental philosophy. I recall talking with a white male colleague after a lecture dealing broadly with deconstructive and postmodern approaches to the self. I was critical of what many have taken to be the obvious dismissal of certain problematic conceptions of the self that grew out of modernity. I raised the point that people of African descent have a different relationship to modernity and that this might impact how they think about questions of the self vis-à-vis modernity. His response was that black people ought to learn from us (read: whites) that concepts of the self grounded in modernity are simply philosophically useless. After all, or so he implied, whites have already gone down the philosophically fruitless road of modernity when it comes to conceptions of the self, so they (whites) can save us (blacks) the effort. Not only did he conflate importantly different historical trajectories that people of African descent have had in relationship to modernity, but there was also a sense of white hubris and paternalism.

In keeping with the epigraph by Anita Allen, black feminists must ask critically if philosophy (analytic *or* continental) has *anything* special to offer them. That philosophy does have something special to offer black women, more generally, must not be assumed *prima facie*, which I *don't* think this text does. To put this concretely, what does continental philosophy offer someone like Megan Williams? Can it make sense of the multiplicative sites of oppression that she had to endure? Black women are not simply the "second sex," but the "third sex," the other to the second sex—white women. It might be argued that black women have no other according to whom they might constitute themselves as the One. Contra this view, it might be argued that black "disabled" bodies are the other to black women's "normal" body constitution.

It might also be argued that black lesbian, bisexual, transgendered and queer bodies are the other to black heterosexual, heteronormative women. While I think that this is an important point to be explored, particularly in terms of the issue of multiplicative oppressions and multifarious identity construction, I would argue that within the white racist imaginary, black women, because they are black, are already in some sense deemed "disabled." Within this context, to be black *is* to be disabled. And given the white racist myth-making around the uninhibited, polymorphous nature of black women's sexual urges, it might be argued that Black women are always already nonheteronormative. On this score, it might be said that black women are in some sense sexually monstrous—quintessential "superfreaks."

In Beauviorian terms, white women set themselves up as the One while setting up black women as the other over against itself.[5] Providing an insightful existential analysis of the reduction of women, that is, white women, to their immanence, Simone de Beauvior writes that white men "propose to stabilize her [a white woman] as object and to doom her to immanence since her transcendence is to be overshadowed and forever transcended by another ego (*conscience*) which is essential and sovereign."[6] What is important here is that white women were able to retrieve, so to speak, their transcendence through the reduction of black women to their immanence, to a form of static and *essential* blackness. Indeed, Sarah Bartmann, the so-called Hottentot Venus, constituted the denigrated black other in terms of which French women's ego formation in the early nineteenth century took place. The arrogant perception of white women during second-wave feminism overlooked and denied important differences between themselves and women of color. On this score, white feminists assumed that their experiences constituted *the* epistemological and ontological grounds of knowledge production. While they critiqued patriarchal hegemony, they did not critique the ways in which whiteness reasserted their own imperialist hegemony over women of color. Concerning whiteness as constituting a form of solidarity, bell hooks argues that "unconsciously, [white women] felt close to one another because they shared racial identity. The 'whiteness' that bonds them together is a racial identity that is directly related to the experience of non-white people as 'other' and as a 'threat.' "[7]

In the case of Megan Williams, one might argue that there is a double silencing. She was literally silenced by her captors and then silenced by the media. Unlike Gates' situation, we were not bombarded daily with the particulars of Williams's experience of undeniable white racism. The teachable moment ought to have been that racism, in its most virulent form, continues to plague America and that black women's bodies suffer along multiple oppressive axes. Moreover, the teachable moment ought to have been that Williams's tragic narrative belies the rhetoric of a postrace America and that white men *and* white women are agents of racist oppression and racist myth-making vis-à-vis the black female body. If black feminism is to converge with continental philosophy productively, it is important that white women working within the continental tradition avoid resistance when it is pointed out that they are being complicit in supporting structural racism and that their habits of being continue to perpetuate whiteness as a site of privilege and power. Just as there are white male philosophers who do continental philosophy but are insensitive to the philosophical needs of white women, there are white women who do continental philosophy who are insensitive to the philosophical needs of black women.

If African American women in philosophy are members of an endangered species, perhaps it is because philosophy has indeed failed black women. After all, philosophy has been historically white and male. Its epistemic orders have been exclusionary toward white women and women of color, though, as argued, women of color were positioned and treated as the other of the second sex. *Convergences: Black Feminism and Continental Philosophy*, with its critical cadre of women from philosophy, rhetoric, ethics, and African American studies makes a daring and bold effort to communicate across disciplinary boundaries, to explore conceptual tensions, to explicate points of conceptual compatibility, to complicate received assumptions within the context of both continental philosophy and black feminism, and to demonstrate points of illumination through hybridic theorization. These are all extremely important sites of convergence. The text does not deploy continental philosophy to *justify* black feminist thought, a move that would not give due recognition to the independence of black feminist thought. There is a pragmatist sensibility and an interdisciplinary thrust throughout the text that sees the importance of deploying variegated philosophical conceptual tools that work toward the illumination and dismantlement of multiple sites of oppression.

Convergences: Black Feminism and Continental Philosophy functions as a call to engage in a critical conversation. The text is a dialogical convergence of multiple voices that refuse to elide differences but welcome possibilities of conceptual augmentation through philosophical *blending*. Moreover, the contributors to this text consist of a diverse group of women, including black, Asian, white, and Latina, who themselves constitute a site of convergence of differences. The editors of this important text are not canonical gatekeepers but feminist warriors, embodied women philosophers who refuse to replicate hegemonic centers and totalizing discourses. They refuse to deify philosophical categories, and they repudiate the notion that one can do philosophy from nowhere. At the very core of this important text is the question of the meaning of philosophy itself—its morphology, its aims, its embodiment, and its possibilities.

Notes

1. As this book project was nearing publication, reports surfaced that Megan Williams will recant her previous statements regarding her testimony that she was kidnapped, sexually assaulted, and tortured by six whites. As it stands, Bobby Ray Brewster, his mother, Frankie Lee, Danny Combs, George Messer, Karen Burton, and her daughter Alisha Burton were all charged with kidnapping. Karen Burton was given one ten-year sentence for violation of civil rights and two two- to ten-year sentences for assault. Frankie Brewster received ten to twenty-five years for second-degree sexual assault. They had both pleaded guilty in exchange for reduced sentences. Bobby Brewster pleaded guilty to second-degree sexual assault, conspiracy to commit kidnapping, and malicious assault. He was sentenced to thirteen to forty years in prison. Danny Combs will serve twenty years for conspiracy to commit kidnapping. He pleaded guilty to sexual assault, assault during the commission of a felony, and conspiracy to commit kidnapping or holding hostage. Alisha Burton and George Messer both pleaded guilty to assault and kidnapping and were sentenced to ten years each.

That Williams will apparently recant her earlier charges, saying that she lied because she was angry with one of the defendants with whom she had a relationship, is extremely baffling. I say this because all six of the accused pleaded guilty. Had they not pleaded guilty, one might understand Williams's change of heart. How do we make sense of the physical evidence used in the case and the confessions of all six in the light of Williams's claim that she lied? How can six individuals plead guilty for crimes that they did not do—indeed, horrible crimes? Surely, they could have said that Williams was fabricating the entire story given that she exaggerates and is apparently "mentally challenged." Could they have undergone processes of "collective harassment" or "collective bullying" to confess? Did they consciously exert an effort to get their stories right so that they would be certain to get lighter sentences? And what do we do with the physical evidence? Was it planted by Williams? Was the prosecutor in the case so disgusted by the presence of six *poor* whites that she wanted to see them imprisoned? Will the accused only now claim that they were pressured into pleading guilty? My sense is that Williams's new claim that she lied is deeply troubling, especially given the recent death of her adopted and supportive mother. The events that Williams initially said occurred are not inconsistent with the sheer degradation and dehumanization that racist whites have historically visited upon black female bodies. As of this writing, all six whites are in prison because of the evidence in the case and because of their confessions, not simply because of what Williams said. For details regarding sentencing and coverage of Williams's reversal of her earlier claims, see http://en.wikipedia.org/wiki/Megan_Williams_case; http://www.google.com/hostednews/ap/article/ALeqM5idqSRBiNk7vY4jU-JyXYVNvdVXDgD9BFKRV00.

2. See http://blackandmissing.blogspot.com/2007/10/update-interview-with-megan-williams.html.

3. Some of the material preceding this superscript was taken from my book, *Black Bodies, White Gazes: The Continuing Significance of Race* (Lanham, MD: Rowman and Littlefield, 2008), see especially the introduction.

4. See Charles W. Mills, *Blackness Visible: Essays on Philosophy and Race* (Ithaca: Cornell University Press, 1998), see especially chapter 1.

5. Simone de Beauvior, *The Second Sex,* tr. and ed. H. M. Parshley (New York: Vintage Books, 1952/1989), xxiii.

6. Ibid., xxxv.

7. bell hooks, *Feminist Theory: From Margin to Center* (Boston: South End, 1984), 55.

Contributor Notes

Tina Chanter (Ph.D. Stony Brook University) is currently professor of philosophy and the director of placement and recruitment at DePaul University. She is author of *Ethics of Eros: Irigaray's Re-writing of the Philosophers* (Routledge, 1995); *Time, Death and the Feminine: Levinas with Heidegger* (Stanford University Press, 2001); *Gender: Key Concepts in Philosophy* (Continuum, 2007); and *The Picture of Abjection: Film, Fetish, and the Nature of Difference* (Indiana University Press, 2007). She is editor of *Feminist Interpretations of Emmanuel Levinas* (Penn State University Press, 2001), coeditor of *Revolt, Affect, Collectivity: The Unstable Boundaries of Kristeva's Polis* (State University of New York Press, 2005), and coeditor of *Sarah Kofman's Corpus* (State University of New York Press, 2008). She is also editor of the Gender Theory series at the State University of New York Press. Her current book project is *The Political Legacies of Antigone.*

Maria del Guadalupe Davidson (Ph.D. Duquesne University) is assistant professor of African and African American studies at the University of Oklahoma. She is the author of *The Rhetoric of Race: Toward a Revolutionary Construction of Black Identity* (University of Valencia Press, 2006) and with George Yancy coeditor of the book *Critical Perspectives on bell hooks* (Routledge, 2009).

Kathryn T. Gines (Ph.D. The University of Memphis) is assistant professor of philosophy at Pennsylvania State University. Some of her publications include "Race Thinking and Racism in Hannah Arendt's The Origins of Totalitarianism," in *Hannah Arendt and the Uses of History: Imperialism, Nation, Race, and Genocide* (Berghahn Books, 2007); "The Ambiguity of Assimilation: Commentary on Eamonn Callan's, 'The Ethics of Assimilation,' " in *Symposia on Gender Race and Philosophy* 2, no. 2 (May 2006): 1–6; "Sex and Sexuality in Contemporary Hip-Hop" in *Hip Hop and Philosophy: Rhyme 2 Reason—a series in Pop Culture and Philosophy* (Open Court, 2005); and "Sartre and Fanon: Fifty Years Later" in *Sartre Studies International* 9, no. 2 (2003): 55–67. She has also published book reviews related to black feminism and continental philosophy including "Book Review: Anna Julia Cooper, Visionary Black Feminist: A Critical Introduction," by Vivan M. May (Routledge, 2007); *Black Women's Intellectual Traditions: Speaking Their Minds*, by Kristin Waters and Carol B. Conaway, eds., (University of Vermont Press, 2007); *Black Women in the Ivory Tower, 1850–1954: An Intellectual History*, by Stephanie Y. Evans (University Press of Florida, 2007); and *Daughter of the Revolution: The Major Nonfiction Works of Pauline E. Hopkins*, by Ira Dworkin,, ed. (Rutgers University Press, 2007) in *SIGNS* 34, no. 2 (2008); and "Sonia Kruks' *Retrieving Experience*: A Review" in *Sartre Studies International* 8, no. 2 (2002).

Kathy Glass (Ph.D. University of California at San Diego) is assistant professor of English at Duquesne University. Her areas of research include African American literature, black feminist critical theory, American literature, women's studies, American studies, and black studies. Her publications include *Courting Communities: Black Female Nationalism and "Syncre-Nationalism" in the Nineteenth-Century North* (Routledge, 2006) and "Tending to the Roots: Anna Julia Cooper's Sociopolitical Thought and Activism," *Meridians: Feminism, Race, Transnationalism* 6, no. 1 (2005)

Beverly Guy-Sheftall (Ph.D. Emory University) is the founding director of the Women's Research and Resource Center and the Anna Julia Cooper Professor of Women's Studies at Spelman College. She is also the president of the National Women's Studies Association. She has published a number of texts within African American and women's studies, which have been noted as seminal works by other scholars, including the first anthology on black women's literature, *Sturdy Black Bridges: Visions of Black Women in Literature* (Doubleday, 1980), which she coedited with Roseann P. Bell and Bettye Parker Smith; her dissertation, *Daughters of Sorrow: Attitudes toward Black Women, 1880-1920* (Carlson, 1991); *Words of Fire: An Anthology of African American Feminist Thought* (New Press, 1995); and an anthology she coedited with Rudolph Byrd entitled *Traps: African American Men on Gender and Sexuality* (Indiana University Press, 2001).Her most recent publication is a book coauthored with Johnnetta Betsch Cole, *Gender Talk: The Struggle for Women's Equality in African American Communities* (Random House, 2003). In 1983 she became founding coeditor of *Sage: A Scholarly Journal of Black Women*, which was devoted exclusively to the experiences of women of African descent.

Robin M. James (Ph.D. DePaul University) is an assistant professor in the philosophy department at the University of North Carolina Charlotte. Her current work focuses on the race-gender politics of contemporary popular music and critical-race feminist approaches to traditional philosophical aesthetics. She has published articles on topics such as white embodiment, aesthetic taste, and hipness; technology and black female sexuality in contemporary Hip-Hop and R&B; and Judith Butler's and Peaches's common feminist strategies. She is presently developing a project that pushes Jacques Ranciere's notion of politics as aesthetics to consider questions of gender, race, and musicology. Her band, Citation: Obsolete, makes posthuman soul music that, like her research, addresses the intersection of racial-sexual politics, digital technology, and aesthetic values.

Emily S. Lee (Ph.D. Stony Brook University) is currently assistant professor of philosophy at California State University, Fullerton. She is the author of "The Meaning of Visible Differences of the Body," *American Philosophical Association Newsletter on the Status of Asian/Asian Americans* 2, no. 2 (Spring 2003): 34–37, and "Towards a Lived Understanding of Race and Sex," *Philosophy Today* (SPEP Supplement 2005): 82–88. Her current work includes "Ambivalence and Phenomenological Ambiguity," *Philosophy Today*, forthcoming, and "The Meaning of Visible Differences of the Body," *Are All the Women Still White?* ed. Janell Hobson and Imee Kerlee (Routledge, forthcoming).

Anika Maaza Mann (Ph.D. University of Memphis) is assistant professor of philosophy at Morgan State University. She has published articles in the areas of race theory and modern philosophy, including "Contradictions of Racism: Locke, Slavery, and the Two Treatises," coauthored with Robert Bernasconi in *Race and Racism in Modern Philosophy* (2005). Her current research focuses upon the interstices between continental philosophy, African American philosophy, and feminist philosophy.

Donna-Dale L. Marcano (Ph.D. University of Memphis) is currently assistant professor of philosophy at Trinity College in Hartford, CT. She has published on Sartre and Race as well as the French feminist Julia Kristeva. She is currently working on developing black feminist thought from within the discipline of philosophy.

Diane Perpich (Ph.D. University of Chicago) is assistant professor of philosophy at Clemson University. Her research interests include contemporary continental philosophy, especially French philosophy and the work of Emmanuel Levinas, as well as feminism, gender, and sexuality, social and political thought, and ethics. She is the author of The Ethics of Emmanuel Levinas (Stanford University Press, 2008) and is at work on a book addressing the phenomenological contributions to European social and political thought. She is the coeditor of the *Journal of French Philosophy* and is also coediting and translating a collection of writings by the French social movement Ni Putes Ni Soumises. She teaches courses on gender and sexuality, philosophy and technologies of the body, social and political thought, and contemporary continental philosophy.

Aimee Carrillo Rowe (Ph.D. University of Washington, Seattle) is assistant professor of rhetoric at the University of Iowa. Her teaching and writing address the politics of representation and feminist alliances, third-world feminism, and whiteness and antiracism. Her book *Power Lines: On the Subject of Feminist Alliances* (Duke University Press, 2008), offers a coalitional theory of subjectivity as a bridge to difference-based alliances. Her writing appears primarily in interdisciplinary outlets such as *Hypatia* (Summer 2007), *Radical History Review* (Summer 2004), and *NWSA Journal* (Summer 2005).

Camisha Russell is a doctoral student in the philosophy department at Penn State University where she holds a Bunton-Waller Graduate Award. Her research and teaching interests include social-political philosophy, philosophy of race, African American philosophy, and feminist theory.

Traci C. West (Ph.D. Union Theological Seminary) is associate professor of ethics and African American studies at Drew University (Madison, NJ). She is the author of *Disruptive Christian Ethics: When Racism and Women's Lives Matter* (John Knox, 2006), *Wounds of the Spirit: Black Women, Violence, and Resistance Ethics* (New York University Press, 1999), and editor *of Our Family Values: Religion and Same-sex Marriage* (Praeger, 2006). She has also published many articles on violence against women, clergy ethics, racism, sexuality, and other justice issues in church and society. Her articles that are most relevant to the themes in this volume include "Is a Womanist a Black Feminist? Marking the Distinctions and Defying Them: A Black Feminist Response," in *Deeper Shades of Purple: Womanism in Religion and Society*, ed. Stacey M. Floyd-Thomas (New York University Press, 2006); "Mind, Body, Spirit: Sexism and the Role of Religious Intellectuals," in *The Crisis of the Negro Intellectual Reconsidered*, ed. Jerry G. Watts (Routledge, 2004); "Spirit-Colonizing Violations: Racism, Sexual Violence and Black American Women," in *Remembering Conquest: Feminist/Womanist Perspectives on Religion, Colonization and Sexual Violence*, ed. Nantawan Boonprasat Lewis and Marie Fortune (Haworth Pastoral Press, 1999).

George Yancy (Ph.D. Duquesne University) is associate professor of philosophy at Duquesne University. He has published in numerous scholarly journals, including *Philosophy & Social Criticism, The Journal of Speculative Philosophy*, and *African American Review*. He is the editor of eleven books and the author of *Black Bodies, White Gazes: The Continuing Significance of Race* (Rowman and

Littlefield, 2008), which received an honorable mention from the Gustavus Myers center for the Study of Bigotry and Human Rights. In 2008, Yancy was nominated for Duquesne University's Presidential Award for Faculty Excellence in Scholarship.

Index